ARCHAEOLOGY

THE BASICS
2ND EDITION

Clive Gamble

Routledge
Taylor & Francis Group

LONDON AND NEW YORK

First published 2008
by Routledge
2 Park Square, Milton Park, Abingdon, OX14 4RN

Simultaneously published in the USA and Canada
by Routledge
270 Madison Avenue, New York, NY 10016

Routledge is an imprint of the Taylor & Francis Group, an informa business

© 2008 Clive Gamble

Typeset in Aldus Roman and Scala Sans by
Taylor & Francis Books
Printed and bound in Great Britain by
Antony Rowe, Ltd, Chippenham, Wiltshire

British Library Cataloguing in Publication Data
A catalogue record for this book is available from the British Library

Library of Congress Cataloging in Publication Data
A catalog record for this book has been requested

ISBN13: 978-0-415-35974-0 (hbk)
ISBN13: 978-0-415-35975-7 (pbk)
ISBN13: 978-0-203-00770-9 (ebk)

CONTENTS

ILLUSTRATIONS

Figures

BOXES

TO THE READER

The book in your hand is not a textbook: it makes no attempt at comprehensive coverage, and it contains no exercises. Instead, it aims only to get you thinking about one of the most important and fascinating topics you could ever hope to encounter: archaeology, the investigation of the human past. Our created past surrounds us and it matters. Indeed, it is probably our most important legacy. I hope this short book will quickly persuade you of this and show you that nothing is more interesting, more stimulating or more rewarding than the study of archaeology.

My book is designed as a basic introduction to the subject. I have chosen eight aspects of archaeology and covered one in each chapter. Archaeologists do not always agree and I have set out some of the current debates as well as several of the major questions that archaeologists are tackling, whether as researchers, managers, curators, specialists or a combination of all of these aspects of the profession.

The reader I have in mind for this book is someone who has not yet entirely made up their mind about archaeology. This means they are not sure if they want to find out more; whether ley lines and the Bermuda Triangle are more interesting (believe me they're not!) than the everyday life of a medieval peasant or the evolutionary origins of humans. I have also written the book for those who are a few steps further on. You have been bitten by the archaeology 'bug' and want to know more. You may be reading archaeology for pleasure, studying it at university, taking it in conjunction with another subject or just intrigued by a website you have browsed or a museum or monument you have visited.

What this book is not about are the techniques of field archaeology. Many excellent books already exist on that subject and I would recommend Philip Barker (1982), Jane McIntosh (1999) and Kenneth Feder (2004). What I hope my book will do is kick-start your archaeological imagination so that the experience of handling and studying objects, fieldwalking and surveying landscapes and buildings, arranging exhibits and presenting the past to the wider world will become even more immediate and rewarding.

ACKNOWLEDGEMENTS; FIRST EDITION

Of the very many people who over the past 30 years have shaped my interest in archaeology I would like to single out the following, who not only made this project possible but also made it fun: Vicky Peters of Routledge for suggesting the idea and Polly Osborn and Julene Barnes for seeing it through to completion; Chris Gosden, Randy McGuire and Tim Darvill, who provided invaluable and insightful comments on the manuscript; Penny Copeland, who illustrated it so well; all my students, too numerous to mention, who can now really say they have heard it all before; and my friends and colleagues at the University of Southampton, particularly Justin Dix, Yvonne Marshall, David Peacock, Simon Keay, Thomas Dowson, Martin Millett, David Hinton, John Robb, Dave Wheatley, Elaine Morris, Stephanie Moser, Jon Adams, Tim Champion, John McNabb and James Steele, as well as those who have moved on elsewhere, Colin Renfrew, Arthur ApSimon, Brian Sparkes, Stephen Shennan, Peter Ucko, J. D. Hill and Julian Thomas. For financial support and research leave I should like to thank the University of Southampton. And finally an apology to Melissa Gamble and Tom Gamble, who finished their archaeological degrees before I finished this book, the past is always in front of you.

ACKNOWLEDGEMENTS; SECOND EDITION

This edition would never have been completed without the editorial assistance, demanding questions and organisational skills of Fiona Coward. I am very grateful for all her insights and advice. Penny Copeland drew the new figures with her customary skill, and Linda Mitchell did invaluable proofreading. The text benefited from the comments of three anonymous referees and those from Ken Feder were particularly useful. Michael Balter kindly read the sections on Çatalhöyük. Several of the changes in this edition have arisen from my involvement with the British Academy Centenary Project *From Lucy to language: the archaeology of the social brain*. I would like to thank my co-directors Robin Dunbar and John Gowlett as well as all the project members for providing such an inspiring context for reflecting on what archaeology can achieve. At Royal Holloway, Department of Geography, I have particularly benefited from discussions about the roles of archaeology and geography in the study of the past and the many stimulating seminars with landscape surgeons and Quaternary scientists. I should particularly like to thank Rob Kemp, Nick Branch, Danielle Schreve, Karen Till, David Lambert, Felix Driver, Phil Crang, David Gilbert, David Simon, Tara Woodyer, Matt Grove, Dora Moutsiou, Rebecca Sheldon and Hilary Geoghegan. This edition is dedicated to Martin Dalgleish and the Social Climbers of Nevis for many thought-provoking discussions on the Upper Round Road.

WHAT IS ARCHAEOLOGY?

THE ARCHAEOLOGICAL IMAGINATION

Archaeology is exciting. The excitement comes from using our archaeological imagination to go where we can never travel, to the past, and to think about time and objects in very different ways from those of our everyday experience to understand better who we are by knowing where we have come from.

Humans have always had an archaeological imagination. At one level it is that taken-for-granted ability to reconstruct in our daily lives what went on from the evidence left behind; footprints in the sand point to visitors, a room littered with glasses and bottles adds up to a party. At another level this imagination has been sharpened and refined into a professional discipline over the past 200 years, and this is the sense in which I will use the phrase throughout this book. We now routinely excavate, catalogue, measure, describe and analyse the objects and monuments of the past. These standard archaeological techniques are widely accepted and understood. They have even become metaphors to investigate our inner selves. Every time we 'dig into the sub-conscious' or 'peel back the layers of personality' we are imitating archaeologists. Most importantly, these methods have assisted archaeologists in developing a way of thinking about things long gone. This is the excitement of archaeology.

Discovering unplundered tombs is one thing, but the ability to explore our capacity to think well beyond everyday experience and to incorporate into our lives the activities and artefacts of former people is riches indeed.

MEMORY AND SOCIETY

Archaeology is one of the ways we remember. We do this not just by finding out about the things we have lost to decay, destruction and fading memories, but also by using archaeological discoveries to construct the past. This means that archaeology is a social activity involved in the creation of a memory that may be local, national or even global in scale and complexity, and it is this activity that leads to my definition of the subject.

Archaeology is the study of the past through material remains. It is about three things: objects, landscapes and what we make of them.

Objects are what archaeologists spend most of their time digging up, describing and ordering by the categories of time and space. This is where most of the excitement comes from, and however hard we analyse and try to explain it away the anticipated thrill of discovery still makes most archaeologists' hearts beat a little faster. *Landscapes* remind us that much of what archaeologists do involves space and distance. Space has at least equal weight to time because different objects are found in different places as much as at different times.

The geography of the past starts with our investigations into what goes on in our own backyard, the prehistory and history of a village or town as revealed by archaeological discoveries, supplemented where possible by written records. Such *local* archaeologies often provide a strong sense of place and identity for those living there. As a result, local museums, keeping houses and cultural centres, combined with local Archaeological and Historical Societies, have always been the backbone of collective local memories. At the next scale of the *region* we see the amalgamation of local memories into larger political identities. It is no accident that national museums and the creation of nation states went hand in hand in the nineteenth and twentieth centuries. And finally, there is a *global* scale. Here archaeologists reflect on universal processes, such as human origins and the rise of civilisation. Their aim is to better understand the concept of Humankind by studying the past. It is at these three scales – local, national and global – that the all-important third part of my definition above, 'and what we make of them', comes into play to give us the great variety of interpretations, and some fundamental disagreements, about what archaeology is and what it should be.

ENCOUNTERING ARCHAEOLOGY

Archaeologists are usually defined by what they do when out excavating. But digging and the subsequent analysis and reporting on what they find is only one of their activities. As the subject has grown and matured over the last 50 years so there has been a revolution in what archaeologists study, from Archaeogenetics to the Zatopecs. Today there is an archaeology of nearly everything.

As a result, the answer to 'what is archaeology?' is more complicated than you first thought. The subject seems bewildering in its diversity of interests and 'isms'. My partial roll-call of what archaeology is tells you only one thing: that archaeology can be whatever you want it to become. So, what was it that fired your archaeological imagination to find out what makes the subject tick beyond the everyday, the common sense and the familiar? Was it Lara Croft, or *Gladiator*? Dusk in Egypt's Valley of the Kings, or dawn at Petra in Jordan? A beep from your metal detector? The stones of Stonehenge, the mounds of Moundville or the Roman baths at Bath? Will you own up to an autographed poster of the *Time Team* on your bedroom wall? Was it a particular museum display or – what did it for me – an artist's reconstruction in a book of life as it once was.

And never belittle that tangible thrill of discovery, that initial contact with archaeological practice, when you first peeled back the layers with your trowel to reveal stone tools, potsherds, bones and walls and, if luck was with you, metal, bodies, art or even *gold* – although of course your trench supervisor took over at that point!

HOW DID ARCHAEOLOGY GET STARTED?

Archaeology is an activity that people become passionate about. It focuses our enthusiasm and generates excitement. From the outset an archaeologist develops a special relationship with objects, land-scapes and their interpretation.

These passions have changed over time, reflected in the histories of archaeology that have emerged from simply chronicling discoveries by eccentrics, to examine instead the wider social and political contexts that created the discipline (Trigger 1989). Perhaps the biggest influence began 200 years ago during the Enlightenment and continued with the rise of Science that began with this move-ment. The notion of Universal Mankind (what today we would call humankind) was one of the key concepts to emerge from these social and intellectual changes. The origins and development of 'Man' and 'Mankind' became a project for archaeologists to investi-gate (Thomas 2004: 53).

UNCOVERING RICHES

The seeds from which modern archaeology grew were planted by the British antiquarians Camden and Aubrey in the sixteenth and seventeenth centuries, just prior to industrialisation. In the eigh-teenth century, a growing fascination with the classical monuments of Greece and Italy fuelled treasure hunting in buried cities such as Pompeii and Herculaneum, and classical architecture, artefacts and literature provided an ancient authority to establish the new world order (Fagan 2001, 2004). But the process went further. The sand was first removed from monuments in Egypt in 1798 so they could be recorded, while the hard task of hacking the jungle from the ruins of Borobudur in Java began in the 1810s, and from the Mayan ruins in Central America in the 1840s. At the same time investigations began in the Mesopotamian cities of Nineveh and Nimrud.

The languages of these ancient civilisations needed deciphering. This was achieved for Egyptian hieroglyphs in the 1820s and for Babylonian and Assyrian cuneiform by 1857, and once deciphered, the lists of kings and pharaohs supplied a chronology for the wealth of discoveries that fleshed out civic and artistic achievements.

CHRISTIAN THOMSEN AND THE THREE-AGE SYSTEM

Much of this early work was text- rather than object-based, its focus historic rather than prehistoric. It is now widely recognised that a turning point came in 1819 when C. J. Thomsen classified the collections of the Museum of National Antiquities in Copenhagen in terms of a three-age, chronological model. Since he was dealing with prehistoric objects, his scheme stretched the archaeological imagination back to a time well before texts. Thomsen, of course, had no dates either from calendars or king lists to guide him, and his chronological scheme drew from two major sources. Technology provided the first, with his division of materials into successive Stone, Bronze and Iron Ages, and a technique known as seriation, though he would not have called it that, provided the second. Thomsen's seriation took the finds in each collection that the museums had acquired and looked at the changing proportions of items between them. This allowed him to establish which objects repeatedly co-occurred with which others as well as spotting any changes. These patterns among the artefact types confirmed the basic technological divisions. It is for this reason that his scheme has stood the test of time.

Thomsen's three-age model represents a fine example of empirical, inductive research, where a classification is built by observing patterns in the data. It is clear from his famous guidebook to the collections, published in 1836 and translated into English in 1848, that Thomsen attached great importance to the contexts and associations of finds in devising his scheme. In this respect a longstanding interest in coins may have given him the inspiration to see stylistic change in prehistoric artefacts over time. However, as Trigger (1989: 84) points out, Thomsen did not borrow a dating device from a subject such as geology but instead developed a new technique, seriation of types, that was appropriate for archaeological evidence. Furthermore, he never gave the impression of having been influenced by earlier philosophers who conjectured that society had progressed through stages en route to the present – an age of hunters, followed by farmers, and finally civilisation. If he had, then his scheme might be described as deductive, testing a hypothesis – the progressive nature of social change – with archaeological observations. Others did just that, notably Sir John Lubbock (1865), while E. B. Tylor (1865) and Lewis Henry Morgan (1877) built similar schemes by ranking the contemporary cultures of the world in ascending, and by inference ancestral, order.

HOW HAS ARCHAEOLOGY CHANGED?

To the founding fathers such as Thomsen or Lubbock the biggest changes since their day would be the application of science in archaeology. They would be amazed at our ability to derive a date from a bone, hearth or wooden building and so refine our understanding of the order in which things happened. The scale of excavation and the quantity of finds would also impress them and they would no doubt be satisfied that the terms they coined, such as 'Neolithic', and the sequence of Stone, Bronze and Iron Ages, had not only stood the test of time but were in many quarters still central to our understanding of the past. Basically, the methods that carved the continuum of the past into significant categories were worked out over 150 years ago.

But in the meantime archaeologists have not simply got better at doing stylistic analysis or logging their stratigraphic sections more precisely. Instead the discipline has been swept along by changing political, social and economic climates and their intellectual underpinnings. Consequently many of its present aspirations would be unrecognisable and unfathomable to those early pioneers.

ANTHROPOLOGICAL ARCHAEOLOGY

The big change has been the development in the past 50 years of an anthropological archaeology. This is a broad umbrella which shelters most of the approaches discussed in Chapter 2. Some of its keywords are science, theory, relevance, quantification and interpretation. Prior to its appearance the practice of archaeology was dominated by culture history approaches, which were started by Thomsen and fuelled by evolutionary thinking about society in the nineteenth century. These approaches emphasised progress, description, dating and ethnicity. Colin Renfrew (1982: 6) has rightly referred to a period of some 80 years from 1880 to 1960 before anthropological archaeology as the 'long sleep of archaeological theory'. Charles Orser (1999: 280 – 81) sums up where archaeology is today as a result of the big changes that have taken place since 1960 (Box 1).

This is what the archaeological imagination feeds on. Of course not everyone approves of the changes. Many archaeologists regard self-reflection as a sign of weakness. Still more find what Orser refers to as the 'basic stuff' of social relationships too vague. They prefer to deal in 'hard facts', while at the same time networking madly to raise funds, get their work noticed and be part of the professional archaeological community, as well as enjoying a life outside the subject. Precisely the 'basic stuff' that structured the past.

BOX 1 THE FOUR CHARACTERISTICS OF ARCHAEOLOGY TODAY.

- It is multiscalar. How can we go from the single potsherd to the civilisation of which it was a part (Chapter 4)? How do we match up the micro-scale, everyday activity of someone making a pot with the long-term macro-scale experience of the formation and collapse of the Mayan empire (Chapter 7)?
- It is mutualistic. As Orser explains, the basic stuff of human life in all times and places (Chapter 4) are the social relationships that people create and maintain. The best way to conceive of these is as networks (Chapter 6) that for all sorts of reasons overlap, shift and change and hence are mutually interrelated rather than independently associated.
- It is globally focused. Although you can dig only one site at a time, the aim must be to place it within a wider world. You need to look beyond the physical boundaries of your bit of data and see its wider significance (Chapter 6).
- It is reflexive. We have come to realise that archaeological data are not just curiosities but powerful knowledge for people alive today (Chapter 8). By reflecting on what they do, and why, archaeologists think about their research and the impact it can have on other people. The most striking examples lie in the impact on indigenous, First Nation peoples, for example Native North Americans and Australian Aborigines, who until recently had no voice in the investigation and interpretation of their past. The return of cultural property under US Federal Law (Native American Graves Protection and Repatriation Act 1990) is an example of how their cultural rights are now recognised.

(Orser 1999)

TWO BASIC CONCEPTS

Accepting the sort of archaeology that Orser describes leads to some important conclusions. As my earlier definition made clear, archaeology is what we make it, not what was made for us. The past needs us to interpret it. Without our concepts and ideas it has no significance. With them it takes on many different meanings and so contributes to modern life. This may at first seem rather confusing. Surely, you might say, the past is just about finding and describing objects. If so then why do archaeologists disagree, and why, as we shall see in Chapter 2, are there so many different theories? I will come back to these questions throughout this book. But to begin with we need to be very clear about two basic concepts – facts and essence – in order to appreciate where the fundamental disagreements lie.

FACTS AND STORIES

Facts, or observations of data, are never simple. Neither are they neutral or value free. Facts are theory-laden, they come with baggage. They cannot be read objectively but arrive ready interpreted owing to such factors as the history of the subject and the way they have been incorporated into our stories about the past. As a result, the archaeologist does not so much breathe life into facts by, say, placing pots in a battleship curve to investigate the changing proportions of different types over time (Figure 3.5), or analysing animal bones as evidence of how a prehistoric butcher made decisions. Rather, his or her interpretation is already driven by theory, however implicit and unrecognised.

Facts only become meaningful when they are contained within stories. Rather than striving for a single narrative, which some archaeologists still favour, the current trend is towards a variety of stories about the past. That variety is driven by different assumptions and theories about what the past is and how the evidence is best interpreted. Now you may feel unhappy with the idea of many pasts. You may feel that your archaeological imagination requires certainty rather than a myriad of alternatives. Wouldn't life be easier with just one version of the Neolithic or the Roman Empire? Something we could all agree on. But unless you plan to lead a very sheltered archaeological life this won't happen. Archaeologists are now very attentive to the process by which our knowledge of the past is created. This is what it means to be questioning and reflexive (Box 1), and the price that is paid is the loss of some of the old certainties about how we thought the past worked.

ESSENCE AND ESSENTIALISM

How can you spot a theory-laden fact? Easily. Just ask yourself what essences or properties you believe are involved. Consider the biological essentialism found in so many representations of the past in books, magazines and museum dioramas that depict men as hunting and making spears while women gather plant foods and scrape hides (Gifford-Gonzalez 1993; Moser 1998). Such essentialism is a very common approach to classification, and is particularly strong in archaeology. What happens is that things become defined by the properties, or essences, they were expected to have in the first place. If this happens then there will only be one version of the past.

HOW ARCHAEOLOGY HAS CHANGED

There is no better way to illustrate these basic concepts and the changes the subject has undergone than to see archaeologists in action. It is a feature of the subject that we return to famous sites not only to acquire new and more precise data but to re-interpret them for our generation. As a result there are often as many layers of different interpretations for a monument such as Stonehenge as there are stratigraphic levels within the site itself. These different campaigns of fieldwork, not to mention re-interpretations from the published evidence, serve as marker posts for the development of the subject.

CASE STUDY 1: CHANGING ANGLO-SAXONS

The developments in archaeology over the past 50 years, from culture history to anthropological archaeology, are well illustrated by the three successive major investigations of the Anglo-Saxon ship-burial site of Sutton Hoo in the county of Suffolk, eastern England (Carver 1998). The various campaigns, and in particular the first, uncovered fabulous objects that pointed to the burial of a king; a good example of an ideal type whose essence was inherent in the rich accoutrements.

THE SPIRIT OF PLACE

The cemetery with its mounds and earlier prehistoric settlements had been hacked into by grave robbers in the seventeenth century and by antiquarians in the nineteenth century. All we know about them are the holes they left. Our knowledge of what they missed begins when Mrs Edith Pretty, a practising spiritualist, decided in 1938 to hire a local, self-taught archaeologist, Basil Brown, to find out what was in the mounds on her land at Sutton Hoo. Brown dug trenches through several of the mounds and in 1939 returned to the largest. Here he uncovered with great skill the trace of an Anglo-Saxon longship which had been dragged up on to dry land to act as a giant coffin 1300 years ago.

Long before the invention of 24/7 broadcasting, news of such a spectacular find spread quickly along the very small archaeological grapevine. The powers-that-be intervened. In the interests of national importance the authorities, represented by the British Museum and the Government's Office of Works, replaced Brown and his advisors at the local museum. They gave the plum job of digging the burial chamber within the ship to a Cambridge archaeologist, Charles Phillips. He in turn brought in Stuart Piggott and W. F. Grimes, who later became professors at Edinburgh and London universities respectively.

The spectacular array of 263 objects, including silver bowls from Constantinople, exquisitely crafted gold buckles, royal insignia, a lyre and the occupant's sword and helmet, were uncovered in only 17 days during the summer that England declared war on Germany. As Martin Carver describes it:

> It had been one of those magical excavations that few are given to experience: when every day brings a new discovery, and each find discovered reveals the glimmer of the next. Moments of disciplined restraint and stiff upper lip, while photography and drawing are undertaken, are followed by gasps of excitement and jubilant chatter, taking stock and racking the imagination for every eventuality before the tense commitment of raising the object from the ground.
>
> (1998: 16)

Then, in what is still the greatest act of individual generosity in respect of excavated treasure, Mrs Pretty gave the entire collection, worth millions, to the British nation for nothing, not even an honorary title.

SUTTON HOO SCIENCE AND SCHOLARSHIP

The second campaign, between 1965 and 1971, was slower. Led by Dr Rupert Bruce-Mitford from the British Museum, it was meticulous, scientific and very scholarly. The two watchwords in 1939 had been recovery and recording. In Bruce-Mitford's reinvestigations they became authenticity and accuracy. The ship was redug and the remaining, corroded artefacts reassessed and reassembled. Brown's spoil tips were sieved for anything that might have been missed. Parallels to the artefacts were hunted down and everything recorded in three massive volumes completed in 1983. Here was the State reporting on one of its assets.

Science-based archaeology played a key role in the second phase and made it possible to realise the goals of accuracy and authenticity. For example, a little bronze stag had originally been thought to come from the top of the helmet. But when the composition of the alloys in the stag, the helmet and the metal surrounding a great whetstone were analysed, the match showed that it should be reunited with this last object. That is how you can now see it on display in the British Museum, where it is known as the King's 'sceptre'.

SUTTON HOO IN A MANAGERIAL AGE

How much more remained to be discovered? The third and latest investigations, between 1983 and 1992, employed new scientific advances in prospection and excavation techniques, but most importantly the archaeologists now changed the questions. The Sutton Hoo landscape, with its evidence for multi-period occupation, rather than the mounds alone became the prime focus.

These campaigns were led by Martin Carver, whose research proposal was selected in open competition by the national management committee responsible for the site. It was the first British archaeological project to have a published and publicly scrutinised project design. The questions it framed drew on information from an 'evaluation' and 'strategy' phase that was carried out before any digging began (Carver 1998: 176). How different to 1938 when it had been curiosity, perhaps tinged by spiritualism, that motivated research, and even 1965 when plans were very much kept in-house and played close to the chest. Carver's investigations were part of wider changes as British archaeologists accepted that if their discipline was to grow, then it had to adopt professional standards. The watchwords in this third phase were management and accountability.

The project design set out to place Sutton Hoo in its archaeological context. Carver's investigations tackled the question at a variety of analytical scales and with a battery of techniques. Non-destructive methods such as ground-penetrating radar and geophysical survey were used to find out about the site. Greater time-depth was achieved by sampling the prehistoric settlement. More of the cemetery was excavated to better judge the status and position of the original finds within the wider society of which Sutton Hoo was a part. Graves, with much less in them, now took months rather than a fortnight to dig and record. As a result, bodies were found as traces in the sand. The surrounding region was systematically studied through The Kingdom of East Anglia survey. The pattern of land use and settlement was reconstructed to answer the question why such wealth should have been found in what today is regarded as a rural backwater. And in order to meet the accountability criteria, Carver set out to interest the public in the work and explain it to them. After all, the public had benefited from Mrs Pretty's generosity and it was in their name that the site had been placed under State protection through existing Ancient Monument legislation. Television coverage, impractical in 1939, meant that 13 million people watched the excavations in the 1980s, compared with perhaps a hundred who visited the original dig.

SUTTON HOO AS A HERITAGE ISSUE

Ironically, science provided the means both to aid and to destroy archaeology: the latest investigations at Sutton Hoo were partly prompted by the threat of treasure-hunters using metal detectors. Mrs Pretty's selflessness was matched by others' greed for treasure, and such venality has extended in many directions. At the close of the project, the Nation, in the shape of the appropriate government agency, was invited to buy the site but valued it at only £3000. A plea for private sponsorship failed. Eventually The National Trust stepped in and with £3.6 million from the Heritage Lottery Fund the site was secured.

We should not be surprised. At the same time archaeologists had discovered in London the remains of the Rose theatre, where all of Christopher Marlowe's plays opened and where Shakespeare's *Titus Andronicus* was first performed in 1592. A site of unquestionable national significance, the Rose now lies wrapped in clingfilm and covered by sand in the basement of the office block that stands there (Wainwright 1989). Preserved for the future, yes, but hardly accessible to the present. The State likes its heirlooms but will not fork out the financial compensation that is involved in stopping a city office block from being built.

The successive campaigns at Sutton Hoo provide in microcosm an illustration of the change from an amateur to a professional discipline. At the same time the conceptual framework has shifted from an exclusively culture history approach to consider the wider issues raised under the umbrella of anthropological archaeology (Chapter 2). The process was repeated in every country over the past 60 years, a shift that also involved the increasing use of science to validate claims and an awareness of contemporary issues.

'Who owns the past?' is a big question that all archaeologists now face. Flashpoints such as the Rose theatre are extreme examples which polarise the various views and raise critical questions about professional ethics. Do you, as an archaeologist, side with the heritage lobby and the famous actors who claimed the site must be saved and displayed, or with the developer who was guided by planning legislation and arrived at a solution, preservation in situ, with the proper authorities? Should the past halt progress, even if it is just another office-block? Would the arguments have been different if a hospital had been planned for that location?

At Sutton Hoo the move from individual ownership to protection by a national heritage organisation also involved controversy. Some archaeologists questioned whether the 1980s excavations were appropriate. Now they are divided over how to develop the site as a tourist and educational attraction, as proposed by the saviours of the site, The National Trust, ('Tourist centre "would destroy Saxon site"', the *Guardian*, 11 October 1999).

The lesson to take away is that archaeologists do not just dig things up. Our campaigns also create the symbols that people use to contest fundamental issues of concern in the modern world (Chapter 8).

CASE STUDY 2: TANGLING WITH AGRICULTURAL ORIGINS

For many years the high, treeless plateau of Anatolia was a blank on the prehistoric map of Turkey. British archaeologist James Mellaart changed that just before nightfall on a cold November day in 1958 when he visited the huge habitation mound at Çatalhöyük near the town of Konya. He quickly realised from the pottery and stone tools on the surface that this was a vast Neolithic site. He returned in 1961 with permits, a dozen archaeologists and local workmen to do the digging. In four breathless seasons he established that Çatalhöyük had been created in 1000 years by repeatedly building houses, one on top of the other.

The rate of accumulation at Çatalhöyük is impressive. Today the mound stands 17.5 metres proud of the plain it sits on with possibly another 4 metres of archaeological deposits below the present ground surface. This means that on average the mound was growing at more than 2 centimetres a year. In time it also came to cover 13 hectares in a high density mosaic of flat roofed, square and rectangular houses that were home to some 8000 people. Çatalhöyük was a well-organised Neolithic town occupied between 9400 and 8400 years ago, reminiscent of the pueblos of Arizona and New Mexico where entry to rooms was also by ladders from the roof.

A FORK IN THE ROAD

Çatalhöyük translates as 'mound at the forked road' which is an appropriate local name for the impact Mellaart's excavations would have. The Neolithic period had been described by its great champion Gordon Childe (1942) as taking place in the 'grey night of remote prehistory'. Mellaart, however, had found its technicolour dawn. Above all Çatalhöyük is known for its vivid art and sculpture. The mud-brick rooms may be small but they have figurative and patterned wall paintings and clay-modelled animal skulls, particularly bulls with large horns. These were painted in bright, earth colours and even within these dimly lit rooms must have had a dramatic impact.

Many of the rooms had human skeletons buried in the floors while elsewhere terracotta figurines of fecund females, that Mellaart dubbed goddesses, were found. This vibrant culture, rich in human and animal symbolism (Box 2) led him to conclude that Çatalhöyük was a matriarchal society based on the worship of female fertility. For Mellaart (1967: 221) Çatalhöyük represented a spectacular development in human civilisation. What he had uncovered showed the creative power of the Neolithic revolution founded on efficiently organised food production and conservation.

BOX 2 HOW ÇATALHÖYÜK CHANGED THE WORLD.

According to its first excavator, James Mellaart (1967: 11), the site is remarkable for its:

- wall paintings and plaster reliefs;
- sculptures in stone and clay;
- advanced technology in the crafts of weaving, woodwork, metallurgy and obsidian (volcanic glass);
- numerous sanctuaries testifying to an advanced religion complete with symbolism and mythology;
- buildings indicating the birth of architecture and conscious planning;
- advanced practices in agriculture and stockbreeding;
- numerous imports and a flourishing trade in raw materials.

The second fork in Çatalhöyük's road relates to the issues of where farming originated and what it led to. The age and unexpected sophistication of Çatalhöyük suggested that Anatolia might be the place where the early experiments in domestication took place. The region was always recognised as part of a much wider bio-zone in the Middle East where the key domesticates of wheat and barley occurred in their natural state, but until Çatalhöyük it had lacked any evidence for Neolithic occupation. Indeed, the oldest evidence for domestication is still to be found elsewhere in the region. But the size and complexity of Çatalhöyük indicates that the Neolithic people of Anatolia were the first to know what to do with these changes in food production: become an urban power.

From such a location farmers, organised according to new religious principles, could go east towards the major rivers of the Tigris and Euphrates, where the earliest civilisations would emerge. Much later they headed west into Europe.

The Neolithic revolution, as proposed by Childe, changed the world through farming and put it on its course to the present. If that was the case then Çatalhöyük provided the archaeological evidence for when and where this tipping point occurred in human history.

HIATUS AND CHANGE

Mellaart's last digging season was in 1965. Although he wanted to continue there were problems with conserving the delicate sculptures and other fragile finds, including textiles and wooden artefacts. The science of conservation needed time to catch up. There was also his controversial involvement, that led to the loss of his excavation permit, with a mysterious Bronze Age treasure from northern Turkey.

What followed was a hiatus; a term used to describe a gap in an archaeological sequence when nothing happened because people abandoned the site for a time. The hiatus in digging at Çatalhöyük lasted almost 30 years, more than enough time for a new generation of archaeologists to be trained. During this time Çatalhöyük was not forgotten and in fact acquired iconic status within the Goddess Movement of the 1970s. This movement coincided with the rise of feminist critiques of institutions and power that were biased towards the male. Inspired by archaeologist Marija Gimbutas (2001), Çatalhöyük provided an example of an original religion that was focused on female imagery and, following Mellaart, a matriarchal structure.

Work resumed in 1993 with an international team led by Ian Hodder. There was however some continuity. Childe had taught Mellaart and in turn Hodder had attended Mellaart's lectures. But there the similarity ends. In that 30 years archaeology had changed in scale, funding and purpose. For example, Çatalhöyük would now be investigated by over 100 archaeologists that in Michael Balter's (2005: 4) opinion, 'represents the greatest concentration of scientific firepower ever focussed on an archaeological dig'. While Mellaart was interested in filling in the map of prehistory, the new Çatalhöyük dig has a Mission Statement (Box 3) that addresses issues of science, heritage and the visitor experience. The multi-million dollar funding needed to achieve these aims now comes from many sources: industrial sponsors and private corporations as well as research foundations and councils.

BOX 3 THE MISSION STATEMENT OF THE ÇATALHÖYÜK PROJECT.

The full text can be found at http://www.catalhoyuk.com/mission.html

Çatalhöyük is an example of the important Anatolian contribution to the development of early societies. A site of this importance for Turkish and global heritage needs careful conservation and presentation to the public. It poses problems of conservation of mud brick and wall plaster, and problems of site management which have a wider applicability to many sites in the Eastern Mediterranean. . . .

The aims of the current international project at Çatalhöyük involve full-scale modern archaeological excavation and conservation, and promotion of the site for visitor access. . . . The work aims at extensive uncovering of new areas of the site and the recovery, conservation and presentation of paintings and sculpture. The work is planned to continue over 25 years.

The ultimate aim is to provide the Turkish Ministry of Culture and Tourism with a well planned heritage site. . . . By providing a range of visitor experiences the full heritage potential of the site can begin to be exploited.

The main research direction is to place the paintings and symbolism within a full environmental, economic and social context. Central questions concern the origins of the site and its early development, social and economic organisation and variation within the community, the reasons for the adoption and intensification of agriculture, the social context for the early use of pottery, temporal trends in the life of the community, trade and relations with other sites in the region.

MANY VOICES

As conceived by Hodder (1999), his long-term project at Çatalhöyük is an exploration of how the archaeological process of discovery and interpretation can evolve. Understanding the past comes from engaging with archaeological practice. It is important, as the dig's official biographer puts it (Balter 2005: 4), to understand the community of archaeologists 'with its own unique blend of friendships, rivalries, traditions, and rituals' if we are to understand the Neolithic community they are investigating. How is this done?

By allowing many voices a say in interpretation rather than just leaving it to the Director to state the significance of the site. You can see the results in the diaries of staff and their daily Blogs on the project's website (http://www.catalhoyuk.com/) and in its monographs (Hodder 2000). The outpouring of their private thoughts nicely matches the claustrophobic privacy of Çatalhöyük's mud-brick architecture and the secrets it contained.

CHANGING THE SYMBOLS

Çatalhöyük is dominated by symbols and these have been the focus of attention for Mellaart, Gimbutas and Hodder. But the move has been from seeing them as simple representations of religion and ritual to a broader investigation of how we engage with the material world. Consequently, are the wall-paintings and figurines a way of exploring the minds of prehistoric people; a Neolithic Blog perhaps? They were certainly regularly updated, as Hodder's precise contextual excavations, backed up by detailed scientific analysis, have shown. As a result, it is now known that the walls of the houses were replastered annually. The art and its symbols were transient rather than permanent. The delete key was always being pressed but the Blog remained there as successive, hidden layers. Furthermore, the average life of a house at Çatalhöyük ranged between 40 and 120 years. So between two to six generations saw the annual transformation and the rooms became a material metaphor for the addition and renewal of both individual and social memories. The rooms, as Hodder argues, were also the spaces for their lives to become entangled with material culture in complex ways. These were the places where they answered questions such as how to protect people and things from misfortune, how to keep while giving, and how to deal with the implications of living with the dead, since they were buried under the floor.

With these questions the significance of Çatalhöyük changes. Where once it stood at the fork in the road that led from the Neolithic economy to the present world, now its rich data point to another path that asks why we came to think the way we do. The first fork understands the drive to domestication and farming as purposeful since what followed – urban life, civilisation and eventually the modern world – was beneficial. The second fork, as put by Hodder (1990a), sees agriculture and sedentism as unintended consequences of a symbolic world that had always existed, but which was now made material in ways that invited novel connections to be made.

At least two interpretations of the archaeological record are therefore on offer at Çatalhöyük. This was not the case at Sutton Hoo where adding detail rather than investigating the interpretive process was paramount. My two examples of how archaeology has changed differ most when it comes to their target audiences. Outside of Northwest Europe Sutton Hoo has little impact. Art history aside it is one example among hundreds of how political power was organised and displayed before the modern nation state. It is however an excellent example of archaeology at those local and regional scales I described at the beginning of the chapter. Çatalhöyük also covers these scales but at the same time its findings address the global issue of how we use the past to understand our changing humanity. Both studies show that the archaeological imagination never stands still.

FOLLOWING UP

Luckily many excellent textbooks now exist to guide your footsteps as you discover what archaeology is about. These include: Robert Preucel and Ian Hodder (1996), Christopher Gosden (1999) and Matthew Johnson (1999a) on archaeological and anthropological theory; Julian Thomas (1996) on the archaeological imagination; Robert Wenke (1990), David Hurst Thomas (1998) and Kevin Greene (2002) on aims, methods, theories and techniques; Colin Renfrew and Paul Bahn (1991, 2005) on just about every topic; and finally the doyen of archaeological writers Brian Fagan (1996, 1997, 1999). Suitably guided we can now turn our attention away from the question 'What is archaeology?' to consider 'How many archaeologies are there?'

2

HOW MANY ARCHAEOLOGIES ARE THERE?

The past would be very boring if we all agreed about it. And archaeology would not last very long if we also thought we could work out a final answer to questions such as how we became human. The opportunity for fresh discoveries and new techniques means that the picture will always change. But even so many archaeologists believe there is one true past. It is not new data that concerns them but rather their deeply held convictions about the concepts we should use to provide the theoretical framework for interpreting the evidence.

There are many types of archaeology but I like to boil them down to two: culture history and anthropological archaeology. These represent two alternative paradigms or ways of doing archaeology. A paradigm is a set of beliefs and assumptions about how the world, in this case archaeological enquiry, works and should be investigated in order to gain knowledge. There are also disagreements, some of them serious, within each camp that can also be regarded as paradigmatic (Johnson 1999a). The arguments, like all messy divorces, are about custody of the offspring or the future of our archaeological imagination. A very selected list of the important players is given in Box 4.

BOX 4 KEY FIGURES IN THE MAJOR APPROACHES.

Culture history: almost all archaeologists at some time in their careers, from the great founding fathers such as Oscar Montelius, William Henry Holmes, Arthur Evans, Leonard Woolley, Abbé Breuil, Alfred Kidder, Albert van Giffen and Mortimer Wheeler to this year's crop of graduate students.

Anthropological archaeology: fewer in number at a global scale than the culture historians. Under such a broad umbrella (Figure 2.1) the following groupings can be found. For each of these I have listed some of the leading exponents with the caveat that this may reflect only a part of their career.

- Culture process: Lewis Binford, Colin Renfrew and Kent Flannery
- Feminist: Margaret Conkey, Joan Gero, Janet Spector, Lynn Meskell
- Marxist: Gordon Childe, Bruce Trigger, Randy McGuire
- Interpretive: Ian Hodder, Chris Tilley, Michael Shanks, Julian Thomas
- Neo-Darwinian: Rob Boyd, Robert Dunnell, Stephen Shennan

WHAT EXPLAINS THESE PATTERNS?

In practice it is often difficult to separate the approaches, and during their careers people have switched allegiance, which is only to be expected. However, one way to highlight the differences in approach depends on whether a rational or relational perspective to interpretation is taken (Box 5). A rational approach looks for cause and effect, testing a hypothesis and seeking explanation in terms of the ways in which things were organised and functioned. The patterns of the past are therefore part of that universal project, the study of Mankind (or these days, humankind), that began 250 years ago in the Enlightenment.

By contrast a relational approach attributes a different significance to the same patterns in the archaeology. People did not make choices about what to eat, where to build a village or how to design a building on the basis of pure rationality or efficiency. Such decisions were also influenced by the webs of relationships that were forged between other people, objects and landscapes. Rather than universal desires and needs – what we understand for example as economic behaviour driven by notions of supply, cost and margins – a relational view emphasises local interpretations of the world as people build their social lives with the resources to hand.

BOX 5 INTERPRETING THE PATTERNS IN ARCHAEOLOGICAL DATA.

RATIONAL STANDPOINTS

- Culture history archaeology: sees the past as working in many ways like a simplified version of the present. 'It stands to reason' that identity has always been linked to badges such as flags and designer labels and that these have always motivated people to compete and succeed.
- Processual archaeology: sees the organisational system, whether it is a socio-cultural complex adapting to its environment or the components of the brain studied by cognitive archaeologists, as having a rational, universal logic to its operation.
- Neo-Darwinian archaeology: draws on the theory of natural selection and the cultural transmission of ideas, or memes, through a population.

RELATIONAL STANDPOINTS

- Feminist archaeology: the important categories of age (child, adult) and gender (male, female) are never just the result of biology but are always constructed by reference to social relations.
- Interpretive archaeology: people are constructed from ties not only with other people but also with the world of objects.
- Marxist approaches move more freely between the two standpoints, while Matthew Johnson (1999a) has pointed out that Marxist influence far outweighs the contribution of any individual Marxist practitioner.

CULTURE HISTORY

Culture history is the default setting for most archaeological enquiry. It has received a rough ride over the past 30 years, but even so Thomas (1995) estimates that in Britain the output of over half of university-based archaeologists still best fits this description, though the archaeologists concerned might not realise it. On a world scale culture history also seems to be what the majority of archaeologists think they are doing. For example, Paddayya (1995: 138), writing of Indian archaeologists, concludes that most of them are at best disinterested in theory and regard the discipline primarily as a fact-gathering enterprise. The French archaeologist Paul Courbin is vehemently anti-theoretical, stating that the goal is the establishment of facts and nothing more (1988: 112).

Such statements should not imply that culture history is entirely without any concepts or theories (see Taylor 1948), but rather that its practitioners emphasise the primacy of data, facts and classification. They are truly Thomsen's children. Allied with this focus on facts is the notion that an inductive approach (Box 16) is best suited to archaeological enquiry. Putting things in the right order, chronologically and geographically, is the most important goal for the culture historian. Hence a synthesis such as Gordon Childe's *The Dawn of European Civilisation* went through six editions between 1925 and 1957. This reflects the culture history view that new data, rather than new frameworks, are the most important aspect in the development of archaeology. A good framework allows the data to 'speak for themselves' and what they tell the 'listening' archaeologist is when change took place and from what direction it came. Very often any further interpretation is regarded as speculation and if it occurs it will only be found hidden away in the closing remarks rather than the body of the report.

CULTURE HISTORY: POINTS FOR AND AGAINST

Culture history has had many notable successes. Through the methods of stylistic analysis (Chapter 5), seriation and the principle of stratigraphy (Chapter 3) it has built up regional sequences in all parts of the world. These have been refined with the advent of absolute dating techniques such as radiocarbon dating (Chapter 3), so that the phases, horizons, periods and cultures of the past now usually have a temporal as well as a geographical measure. For example, using the technique of 'ceramic stratigraphy', Alfred Kidder (1924) was able to produce, one year before Gordon Childe's ground-breaking survey of European prehistory (1925), a detailed synthesis of Southwestern prehistory in the United States. The explanation of change was either *in situ* cultural development, where continuity could be traced among the potsherds, or a form of group diffusion from elsewhere if new pottery types with no antecedents appeared in the region.

Once available, such culture histories married prehistory to the coin- or text-dated classical and historic periods. Conceptually, the majority of archaeologists in all three periods have always agreed over issues of method if not explanation.

Culture history has also revealed broad patterns which have stood the test of time. We still use terms such as 'Neolithic' and 'Basket-maker' as shorthands to denote periods and phases, and broad agreement exists on their contents. It is also an adaptable approach that in some areas has continued to develop. The economic prehistory of Grahame Clark (1952) built on the earlier work of Worsaae and Kidder and proposed new investigations and frameworks for investigation. Major works have continued to appear, including Stuart Piggott (1965) for Europe, Gordon Willey (1966) for North and Central America, Henry de Lumley (1976) for France, Peter Bellwood (1978) for the Pacific and Sigfried de Laet (1994) for the world. Finally, the hundred-plus books in the *Ancient Peoples and Places* series point to the synthetic achievements of culture history on a global scale.

But, as Lyman, O'Brien and Dunnell (1997) point out, what culture history has never developed is a convincing theory for either change or stability. Change is seen as an inherent property, an essence, of the system being studied. It depends upon common sense, expressed in simple language, to make this point. Change is attributed to migration, diffusion and innovation, since this is how modern societies apparently define what they are and how they became that way. In large measure this is a transfer of the colonial experience to the societies of the past. Culture history's approach to stability is a similar homespun tale, this time of 'if it ain't broke, don't fix it'.

ANTHROPOLOGICAL ARCHAEOLOGY

A new archaeology was required to overturn the stereotype of archaeologists as the stamp collectors of the past. This duly arrived in the 1960s but the newness of that first truly anthropological archaeology has to be put into context (Figure 2.1).

In the twentieth century there were at least three 'new' archaeologies (Box 6), all of them North American and all recognised at the time (Wylie 1993: 20).

Why the North American continent should be in a constant state of archaeological revolution can probably be explained by the four-field approach to anthropology that the ethnographer Franz Boas set in place at the beginning of the last century. These four fields, still available in many US teaching departments, are: linguistic, physical, social and archaeological anthropology. The pulls and pushes between these fields have always had repercussions, but these have not had much impact in Europe, where archaeology tends to be taught either separately or as an adjunct of history, with an emphasis on written sources as the way to understand the past (see Chapter 4, analogy).

BOX 6 NORTH AMERICA'S THREE 'NEW' ARCHAEOLOGIES OF THE TWENTIETH CENTURY. THE NEXT ONE IS NOW OVERDUE.

- 1910s – The stratigraphic revolution, inspired by work in the pueblos of the Southwestern United States.
- 1940s – Cultural ecology, which looked at the variety of human cultures and their adaptation to the environment. The importance of Native American ethnography was critical as a means of explanation.
- 1960s – Processual archaeology, which proposed a scientific methodology including hypothesis testing and a call for archaeology as anthropology.

PROCESSUAL ARCHAEOLOGY 1962–69

The third new archaeology (Box 6) is regarded as the big one. In print it began with a paper by Lewis Binford (1962), 'Archaeology as anthropology'. This short paper was concerned with process, how the various cultural systems that made up a society fitted together and worked. It dealt with the issues of adaptation and change in such systems by identifying three realms of behaviour – environmental, social and ideological – which could be inferred from artefacts and the contexts in which they were found. It stressed the importance of quantification and prediction to qualify archaeology as a scientific approach, and most importantly it drove explanation out from its hiding place behind common sense and tradition. Explication, putting assumptions down and challenging them, was a key objective. Ten years later, on the radio, Binford summed up as follows:

> The New Archaeology gives explicit recognition to the relationship between procedure or method and the kinds of questions we seek to

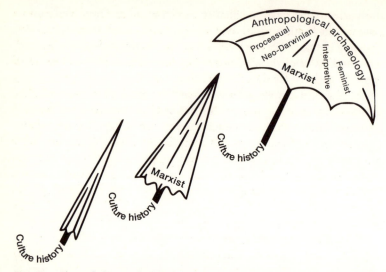

Figure 2.1 The unfurling umbrella of archaeological theory. When fully opened there
are many theoretical approaches to be found under anthropological
archaeology, only some of which are shown here. However, you are still
left holding the handle of the umbrella, the familiar culture history.

get answers to. It also says that we must give priority to the testing of
these general propositions in order to be able to make accurate statements about the past.

(Binford 1972b: 175)

Back in 1962 he supported his revolutionary programme with a
regional example. In the process he sought to expose such fuzzy
explanations for change as 'influence', 'stimuli' and the 'migration
of culture' that culture historians applied.

CULTURE PROCESS

The accent on process and the system was crucial. Unlike culture
history, where similarities and differences were explained by
peoples' shared cultural norms, processual archaeology, as the new
archaeology came to be known, explained variation in terms of how
people participated in culture to different degrees. Culture was our
principal means of adaptation. Moreover, it varied as the situation

demanded. It was not applied by a society or cultural system, as a by-rote solution to its survival and existence at all times and places. Instead, culture was presented as organisationally flexible. All aspects of it, from the design on pots to coping with environmental hazards, were under selection to adapt.

Processual archaeology then searched for the reasons why adaptive variation occurred. New archaeologists like Binford and Kent Flannery set great store by the philosophers of the scientific method who championed framing hypotheses and then testing them. What they were after were explanations that did not simply invoke the concept of culture to explain culture, a common criticism of culture history. Rather they were looking for cause, or as Flannery (1967) put it, looking for the system of organisation behind the Indian behind the artefact.

This search for cause also led the processual archaeologists to consider why cultural systems might not change. Stability was approached from the perspective of ecosystem analysis, with inputs, outputs and self-regulatory mechanisms that balanced the whole system in what was known as homeostasis. For analytical purposes the system could be broken down into component parts, or subsystems, such as craft specialisation, population, subsistence, trade and ritual (Figure 2.2). The interrelationships could then be examined, feedback between the various elements observed and outcomes predicted.

The edited volume *New Perspectives in Archaeology* (Binford and Binford 1968) sums up the hopes and achievements of the early years of processual archaeology. The advantages of a theoretical approach were summed up as follows:

> The practical limitations on our knowledge of the past are not inherent in the nature of the archaeological record; the limitations lie in our methodological naïveté, in our lack of development for principles determining the relevance of archaeological remains to propositions regarding processes and events of the past.
>
> (Binford and Binford 1968, in Binford 1972a: 96)

This led the British new archaeologist David Clarke to define archaeology pugnaciously as 'in essence . . . the discipline with the theory and practice for the recovery of unobservable hominid behaviour patterns from indirect traces in bad samples' (1979: 100).

Figure 2.2 Analysing an archaeological culture as a set of interrelated subsystems (after Clarke 1968: Figure 17). The five components of the internal system under study interact with each other and with the four components of the external environment: fauna, climate, geology and flora. The latter include another social system shown here by the circle Sn.

PROCESSUAL ARCHAEOLOGY: POINTS FOR

Trigger (1989: 2) made the important observation that Binford's lead suggested a more productive approach than culture history because he recognised two dialogues: one internal to the discipline as archaeologists developed methods for inferring past human behaviour from archaeological evidence, and an external one addressing general issues concerning change and the evolution of that behaviour. This dialogue marked the beginnings of a critical self-awareness of what archaeology is, and without processual archaeology it would not exist.

In order to get those two dialogues going simplicity and in some cases plain language had to be jettisoned as processual archaeology sought new ways to express things. I feel these were minor sacrifices to get the archaeological imagination working in new and more productive ways. But the gripes about jargon rumble on, rather like complaints about contemporary art. This just confirms David Clarke's view that 'each archaeology is of its time but since many deplore the time they will certainly be unhappy with its archaeology' (1979: 85).

BOX 7 MIDDLE-RANGE THEORY: A SET OF BRIDGING ARGUMENTS FROM THE PRESENT TO THE PAST.

Middle-range theory is more a set of methods than a theory. They are middle range because the issues addressed are not the big theoretical ones needed to explain why culture changes or how humans evolved. Neither are they the low-level issues such as the law of superposition (Chapter 3).

Instead, middle-range theory reminds us that we still do not know that much about the archaeological record. We need to know how it was formed, what survives, and why, and how we can go from inert observations in the present to the investigation of the once active processes that produced the record in the past. Only with a better understanding of the archaeological record, and how we go about reanimating it in the archaeological imagination, can we then return to the big questions with a better chance of getting an acceptable answer.

PROCESSUAL ARCHAEOLOGY: POINTS AGAINST

The major problem with processual archaeology lies in its insistence on a scientific approach that treats archaeology as akin to a repeatable experiment. In its early days it was strong on the discovery of laws of human behaviour, but it soon became apparent that the laws that were emerging were, in Flannery's phrase 'Mickey Mouse' laws (1973: 51). These dealt with small segments of behaviour in a rather obvious way; for example, 'as numbers of people increase on a site so too do the number of storage pits'. The general laws dealing with change have remained elusive.

Starting in the 1970s, the reaction to such criticism has been to investigate middle-range rather than general theory (Box 7). As we shall see in Chapter 3, middle-range theory seeks to bridge the interpretive gulf between the static, dead facts we dig up and the invisible but once dynamic behaviour that created the patterns in the data that we study. By concentrating on middle-range theory as a methodological issue we have learnt a great deal about butchering animals, making pots and chipping stone, thanks to experimental and ethnoarchaeological studies. We know more than we ever dreamt possible about what hyenas can do to a bone (Brain 1981). What is not clear is how these observations, that set out to understand how patterns in the archaeological record are made, can then be built into a larger scheme of understanding. Some stay at the level of materials analysis (Skibo, Walker and Nielsen 1995), while others such as Binford foray into bigger questions such as Neanderthal behaviour and the transition to agriculture. But the overall picture is one of bits and pieces rather than overall structure. A harsh critic might say 'You have told me that people ate and made pots in the past. Now tell me something I didn't already know'.

The processualists would counter by arguing that we must understand the range of potentially relevant causal processes or we can say nothing about variability. They would regard the scientific approach as safeguarding against the creation of a false past in the image of the present – although, as we shall now see, a belief that science automatically confers a degree of objectivity and reliability is in fact problematic.

FEMINIST ARCHAEOLOGY

The development of a feminist archaeology provides a good example of the limitations of the scientific method. In contrast to many other disciplines where feminist approaches grew quickly, in archaeology the start has been slower (Nelson 1997). What began as a long-overdue critique of androcentric notions and bias when interpreting the archaeological evidence (Conkey and Spector 1984) soon developed into an exploration of gender. However, as Gilchrist (1993: 3 – 4) has argued, the continuing criticism from processualists that such studies need a methodology in order to identify gender from the evidence is misplaced. She asks why there is a need to find women among the archaeological evidence when because of existing assumptions there seems to be little need to find men.

The late arrival in archaeology of feminist critiques in general and gender studies in particular seems strange to many commentators given that gender is about male and female categories that are socially constructed rather than biologically given. Archaeology with its vast time spans and large comparative samples would seem to have much to offer on this issue. As Alison Wylie has pointed out (1991), the long gestation of gender archaeology cannot be explained by the old methodological chestnut that gender doesn't survive in the archaeological record. Instead, it is best explained as a result of the conflict between the ideologies of powerful archaeologies. A processual approach, with its systems, categories and universal values founded on the authority of the scientific method, literally could not see a gendered archaeology. Vision was not restored until a feminist critique took place of such assumptions as 'all men hunt, all women gather', or the notion that everything being equal (which it never is) women make pots and men make ploughshares. These are very obvious essentialist assumptions about the correlation of biological sex with status and activity. They have very little to tell us about the social construction of gender categories. Instead, they tell us a good deal about a powerful academic ideology such as processual archaeology. Since this approach was not looking at the ways in which such categories were constructed, it could claim, with great methodological rigour, that no information existed. A case of 'what you don't believe in, you won't find'. As a result archaeology in particular was a latecomer to the feminist debate.

The advent of gender archaeology was aided by critiques of authority mounted by interpretive archaeologists (see below), particularly in Europe, Australia and South Africa. When combined the advances are already considerable (Gero and Conkey 1991; Wadley 1997). By questioning the scientific method, and with it the processual interpretation of the past, archaeology has become a less secure discipline in terms of understanding itself and protecting its interests. But it has also become a much more intellectually exciting one. The great gain has been a return to the study of people rather than systems. Furthermore, these are often different people to the ones whose voices we normally hear in accounts of the past. The gains are well illustrated by Janet Spector (1993) as she weaves together her experience as an archaeologist with the Native American voice and foregrounds the experience of women in the past. Excavated objects provide her focus, and her narrative emerges from a sensitive reading of relationships and experience rather than the hard edge of science and systems.

The value of gender archaeologies will become apparent in the later thematic chapters (see especially Chapters 4, 5 and 8). Their ability to cross-cut other theoretical approaches is one of their enduring strengths and a source of inspiration for the archaeological imagination.

MARXIST APPROACHES

Histories of processual archaeology can sometimes give the impression that it invented archaeological theory and single-handedly opened that umbrella of anthropological archaeology. This was not the case. One figure, the Australian-born Gordon Childe (1893 – 1957), who was professor of archaeology at Edinburgh and London universities, stands out as an innovative anthropological Marxist thinker working within the tradition of culture history.

Childe wrote many books on the evolution of prehistoric and state societies in the Near East and Europe. He adopted a Marxist approach to the study of change and emphasised the relations of production. Not surprisingly given his huge output and long career, his views changed over time (McNairn 1980; Trigger 1989; McGuire 1992), and his own intellectual evolution is a good example of how Marxism offers an interpretation of a changing world.

Childe remains the archaeologist most widely cited outside the discipline because he tackled the big issues of social and economic change. He is the classic exponent of the grand narrative that archaeology can provide. In *Man Makes Himself* (1936) he began to redefine the three-age model using two socio-economic revolutions that occurred in prehistory but which set in motion the development of the modern world. These were the Neolithic revolution, when agriculture and villages appeared, and the Urban revolution that led to the earliest civilisations, with writing, monumental buildings, bureaucracies, cities, trade and an agricultural surplus that was then unequally distributed to create a ruling class (Greene 1999). These issues were explored, revised and repeated in his many books, including *What Happened in History* (1942) and *Social Evolution* (1951). He also asserted archaeology's broader intellectual aspirations, as in *Archaeology as a Social Science* (1947) and *Society and Knowledge* (1956a).

By the time Childe died in 1957 at the age of 65 he had moved archaeology away from the simple progressive evolution of Lubbock and the people-free typologies of Thomsen and Montelius through the scope and scale of his writings, and provided an antidote to the racist agenda of his contemporary the German archaeologist Kossinna. However, nearly all his work was written before the advent of radiocarbon dating, which provided the first truly independent check on the Montelian scheme. Such absolute dating saw the demise of the strong diffusion model of people migrating from the Near East that Childe favoured to explain changes in European prehistory, and allowed a fuller investigation of his socioeconomic narrative (Renfrew 1973a).

BOX 8 A SEVEN-POINT PLAN FOR ANGLO-AMERICAN MARXIST APPROACHES IN ARCHAEOLOGY.

- Marx's writings are a starting point rather than an end point.
- Social relations are at the core of research in Marxist archaeology.
- Society is treated as a whole not as parts.
- Contradiction and conflict are regarded as crucial features of human society and these act as internal sources of change. This emphasis on the dialectic rejects the idea that society is simply a set of functional adaptations to external factors.
- Human action, or *praxis*, is given a significant role in the process of history. Notions of environmental, material or technological determinism in human society are therefore rejected.
- People make knowledge, and knowledge of the past depends on the social and political context of the time.
- The power relations of the modern, capitalist world are questioned and alternatives proposed.

(Adapted from McGuire in Thomas 1998: 388–89)

Marxism is not, strictly speaking, a theory about the ancient past. However, because it provides a powerful mode of analysis of human society it has proved very influential in the study of that central archaeological question: change (Box 8).

The wide impact of Marxist approaches on world archaeology can be found in many edited volumes (Spriggs 1984; Champion 1989; Miller, Rowlands and Tilley 1989) which cover all periods of prehistory, as well as in regional studies which continue to explore many of Childe's interests in society and systems of production (for example, Kristiansen 1998). A comprehensive review of Marxist archaeology is provided by McGuire (1992).

INTERPRETIVE ARCHAEOLOGY

So far the four types of archaeology I have discussed – culture history, processual, feminist and Marxist – all have major follow-ings on either side of the Atlantic and indeed worldwide. My last two approaches that fall under the umbrella of anthropological archae-ology – interpretive and neo-Darwinian – do not command such widespread support. Rather they reflect different interests between schools of thought, particularly between North America and Europe. Interpretive archaeology, often known as post-processualism because of the approach it challenged, is more often than not dismissed as irrelevant in North America, while neo-Darwinian approaches can mean very different things either side of the Atlantic.

Under the heading of interpretive archaeology we find a wide variety of theoretical positions and an unwillingness to set out any single goal for the discipline. This interpretive diversity began to appear in the 1980s and shows no sign of abating. Robert Preucel and Ian Hodder (1996: 7) present the variety as a fulfilment of the trend started by processual archaeology. However, this does not impress those who still hanker after a unified discipline and a scien-tific agenda with the goal that archaeology should aspire to be science with a capital S (Flannery 1973: 53). For them interpretive approaches are nothing more than 'anything goes'.

What this tells me is that the wheel has come full circle and that authority and status are at stake. This has happened before, with the reaction of the culture historians to the new archaeologists in the

1960s. Then, in 1973, Flannery, a leading processualist, made fun in a poacher-turned-gamekeeper kind of way of the 'law-n-order' new archaeologists and their belief in self-regulatory systems. Processual archaeologists, like all good scientists, are basically interested in control, order and respect.

The particular tension in this familiar struggle is between the vast majority of North American archaeologists, now reared on either straight processualism or modified culture history, and a smaller band of mainly, but not exclusively, European archaeologists.

Interpretive archaeology is particularly concerned with two of the components of contemporary archaeology (Box 1): the mutual character of social life, and the reflexive attitude of archaeologists to their data and profession (Box 9).

BOX 9 FIVE ELEMENTS OF AN INTERPRETIVE ARCHAEOLOGY.

Symbolism: The key early work is *Symbols in Action*, in which Ian Hodder (1982) presents an ethnoarchaeological study of material culture in East Africa. He examines the culture concept (see Chapter 3) in terms of ethnicity, boundary maintenance and the power of individuals. In his book, those elements dear to the processual agenda such as diet and subsistence are hardly touched upon.

Material culture: This is not just seen as the things we create – extensions of ourselves – but as integral components of our personalities, inextricably linked to our social lives. Material culture is an active part of how we build our social relationships rather than a mirror reflecting the positions of authority and class in society. Pots, bronzes – even something as complicated as a city, with its structures and public monuments – have biographies. Their multiple 'lives' are mutually involved in our activities. They are not just instruments for use, but part of that surrounding environment from which individuals are indivisible (Chapter 4). 'Pots as people' sums it up nicely (Chapter 5).

Hermeneutics: This is literally the study of interpretation and meanings in texts but applied by some to material culture (Shanks and Tilley 1987b). More importantly, this approach questions the one-way interpretation of the scientist by contrasting it with a double hermeneutic – an exercise in translation between 'us' and 'them', subject and object. We move from our own frame of meaning, which could be scientific, to that of the people being studied. Rather than imposing our view of how their world worked onto the archaeology, we have instead a dialogue of difference. But what exactly the frame of reference of someone in the Bronze Age might be remains a problem (see Gosden 1994).

Narrative: The way we communicate is by telling stories. Facts get their meaning by being used in these narratives. The hypothetico-deductive programme of the processualists is just one form of narrative structure; the ethnic explanations of culture historians another (Alexandri 1995). Any narrative is structured in time and both simplifies, and imposes its own order on, reality (Gosden 1994: 54). When writing about the past it is important to examine the sources of social authority that are being used to make an argument about change and patterning.

Social theory: Archaeology is not alone in the move to critical self-awareness. Most academic disciplines have gone through a similar loss of innocence since 1945. Four social theorists have proved highly influential in framing our debates about the mutualistic character of social life and the need for reflexivity. These are Martin Heidegger, Michel Foucault, Pierre Bourdieu and Anthony Giddens (for recent reviews see Gosden 1994; Thomas 1996; Jones 1997; Dietler and Herbich 1998; Meskell 1999; Dobres 2000; Dobres and Robb 2000). A common thread to their work is the notion that much of what we do is practical, unthinking, habitual action. This is a form of practical consciousness, as opposed to a discursive consciousness when we are fully engaged in thinking about a problem. The French archaeologist André Leroi-Gourhan, who is best known for precise excavations and a structuralist theory of cave art, anticipated these concepts in 1964. But his book *Gesture and Speech* was only translated into English in 1993 and was much too far ahead of its archaeological time.

POST-PROCESSUALISM

I will illustrate interpretive approaches by briefly looking at one self-proclaimed catch-all grouping. Post-processualism, it must be said, lacks the consistency of a strict creed and a single appointed intellectual messiah, which was provided for processualism by the trinity of laws, science and explication, and by Lewis Binford. It does, however, have four British apostles: Ian Hodder, Christopher Tilley, Michael Shanks and Julian Thomas.

Post-processualism began as a thorn in the side of processual archaeology. It provided a critique of what archaeologists did and why. In the books of Shanks and Tilley (1987a, 1987b), and through the movement known as the World Archaeology Congress, it sought to contextualise the knowledge of the past. On the one hand this involved asking what purposes were served by the production of archaeological knowledge: who was it for and how had it been used? On the other hand it raised the possibility of alternative views of the past based on the opinions of indigenous peoples on whose lands archaeologists were often digging. The authority of the archaeologist to be the sole person qualified to talk about the past was therefore challenged.

This did not go down well. It was seen as nothing more than opening the floodgates to a subjective view of the past. How could knowledge be verified? How could the weaknesses in other inter-pretations – even those as bizarre as those of the lunatic fringe who believe in extra terrestrial interventions to account for Stonehenge or the Nazca lines – be refuted? In particular, the issue of who owns the past was raised. Archaeologists soon found that govern-ments were swayed by political minorities more often than previously when deciding on who had access to and control over sites, landscapes and objects. The archaeologists' lofty claim that they were investigating the cultural heritage of humankind did not always win either at the ballot box or in the corridors and lobbies of power.

When the dust had settled a bit Hodder (1991: 1) identified three results from this work that might be taken as the post-processualist platform for the 1980s:

- Material culture was meaningfully constituted and not just a simple reflection of how society was organised, by which he meant that it has an active role to play in how we make social rela-tionships.
- The individual needs to be part of theories of material culture and social change.
- Archaeology has its closest explanatory ties with history (rather than the physical sciences as processualists had held).

Interpretive archaeologists have continued to build on this foundation.

INTERPRETIVE ARCHAEOLOGY: POINTS FOR AND AGAINST

Will interpretive archaeology ever become the default setting of what archaeologists do? Possibly yes, though most will not realise it has happened because it will probably bear little relation to the current position. When it was a critique of other approaches interpretive archaeology evoked strong passions for and against. Now much of it has seeped into general practice, particularly the reflexive stance (Box 1). Once the archaeological imagination got out of the bottle marked 'science', it could never be the same again. A diversity of theoretical interests combined with many different dialogues is now, like it or not, the norm (Preucel and Hodder 1996: 15).

Since the advent of interpretive approaches, archaeology has been overtly politicised, the World Archaeology Congress being a prime example. Many groups other than archaeologists now have an interest in the past. Issues such as the return of museum collections to their original owners will not go away. Archaeologists now have wider responsibilities than making sure they die with no unpublished backlog.

On the less positive side, what has interpretive archaeology really achieved apart from a critique of processual archaeology, and bringing the discipline up to speed with what other academic subjects have been doing? Feminist archaeology has gone further faster for the simple reason that its objectives and focus are much clearer. Marxist approaches have greater maturity and more to say about change. The excavations and analyses of today seem very similar to those of processual archaeologists in terms of sampling, quantification and the explication of research designs (Chapter 3), which are the lasting inputs from processual archaeology. As Tim Darvill has pointed out to me, interpretive archaeology still relies on field methods designed to achieve quality culture history. One response has been Hodder's (1999) innovative experiment in excavation and interpretation which gives everyone on the project at Çatalhöyük, a Neolithic town in Turkey, a voice, as described in Chapter 1. But the business of too much subjectivity worries many archaeologists, partly because the past, through its surviving objects, exists for them as a reality rather than as a narrative.exercise.

NEO-DARWINIAN ARCHAEOLOGY

True to its label, my final approach that falls within anthropological archaeology is evolving. It owes much, as do Marxist and interpretive archaeologies, to a wider intellectual debate, but this time in the biological rather than the social sciences. In the broader scientific field neo-Darwinians acquire their 'newness' because of the science of genetics, which was unknown to Darwin. As part of this scientific movement archaeologists aim to apply the principles of neo-Darwinian evolution to the past, not only to human physical evolution but also cultural evolution.

BIOLOGICAL AND CULTURAL TRANSMISSION

In 1859 Charles Darwin provided a very powerful mechanism to explain change. Natural selection works because individuals within a population vary. Without that variation there can be no evolution, that proceeds by natural selection and the differential survival of offspring into the next generation (Box 10). What happens is that biological information, in the form of genes, is transmitted between generations. The key point about this transmission process is that it is undirected. There is no goal in evolution, no driving force for things to get better. The social Darwinists of the nineteenth century ignored this basic point and instead turned human history into a catalogue of progress and a celebration of Western achievement (Lubbock 1865; Spencer 1876–96). As a result they gave social and cultural evolution a bad name in both archaeology and anthropology.

BOX 10 KEY CONCEPTS IN DARWINIAN EVOLUTION.

Natural selection is the differential contribution of offspring to the next generation by individuals who belong to the same population but who have different genetic types (Wilson 1975: 589).

Selection pressure is any feature of the environment, both physical and social (e.g. food shortage, predator activity, mate choice etc.) that causes individuals of different genetic types to survive to different average ages, to reproduce at different rates, or both (Wilson 1975: 594).

Archaeologists are well aware of such historical pitfalls. If avoided, then Darwin's immensely powerful theory can be harnessed to the explanation of cultural change as shown by the work of evolutionary psychologists Rob Boyd and Peter Richerson (Boyd and Richerson 2005, Richerson and Boyd 2005). For example, cultural transmission is likened by Stephen Shennan to a system of inheritance (1989b, 1993, 2002). The information contained and transmitted by imitation and teaching through the many media of culture (language, performance, gesture, ritual, material objects etc.) affects what an individual looks like and does. It is, if you like, another part of our individual phenotype; what we see, for example skin colour or stature – as the expression of the invisible genotype.

The neo-Darwinian part comes in when we consider the population of ideas, or representations, that are available for transmission (Sperber 1996). It is these ideas that make up that all-important pool of variation for natural selection to get to work on. This involves us in *population thinking* (Box 11).

Applying such principles is all about investigating how ideas and representations, what archaeologists would usually call styles and types, are distributed within the populations of objects we are studying. What is their frequency? Why will natural selection favour some and not others as the generations roll by? Shennan's approach investigates the conditions under which we expect transmission to occur and in what directions it will drift, change and 'mutate'.

BOX 11 POPULATION THINKING.

In basic terms, any aspect of culture that is imitated is more or less common in the population of cultural representations. When it comes to copying those aspects the result is either to decrease or to increase variation between groups. Moreover, it is the frequency of the item being copied that determines which it will be. Of course, very faithful copying of the frequencies results in stability in cultural representations. This does not imply that natural selection is not working, only that selection pressures (Box 10) are constant.

NEO-DARWINIAN ARCHAEOLOGY: POINTS FOR AND AGAINST

The neo-Darwinian approach to cultural evolution has great potential for archaeology. But it is not a unified field (O'Brien 1996: 4). There is currently little agreement on which units, such as the individual or the population, should be used to measure the effects of selection. Alison Wylie (1995: 208) has also raised doubts about the ways in which the hopes of some of the practitioners are predicated on the power of biological explanation. Does this necessarily make the inferences based on archaeological evidence with all its problems any more secure?

Moreover, so keen are some neo-Darwinists to drive out what they consider to be unscientific concepts such as *intent* from the explanatory process (Dunnell 1978; O'Brien 1996) that they produce an automaton view of human sociality, more akin to the sociobiologist for whom social life is mandated by our genes as shaped by natural selection. But as Shennan has pointed out:

> Assumptions about individuals are in fact behind any attempts at understanding past socio-economic change, or indeed social evolution. The basic ingredients required are *social actors* with *intentions*, who may or may not stand for more than themselves; *conditions of action*, acknowledged and unacknowledged; and *consequences*, intended and unintended.
>
> (Shennan 1993: 56, my emphasis)

The point about humans is that we negotiate what the social structure will be. The precise form of society has never been inherent in our species. Therefore intent, while difficult to measure, is part of the explanation.

Neo-Darwinism, if interpreted broadly, does allow us to explore those all-important processes that integrate the micro- and the macro-scale of human activity, such as individual and society, village and civilisation, a year and a millennium. It is a strong explanation which is very powerful when used, as Shennan proposes, as a biological metaphor for cultural stability and change (Chapter 7). It is also the case that the co-evolutionary processes that led to language (Deacon 1997) and domestication (Rindos

1985) have been very important in human evolution (see Chapter 7): a good case of question and theory being adapted to each other.

WHERE ARE WE GOING?

At the end of his 1962 paper Binford warned archaeologists that 'we cannot afford to keep our theoretical heads buried in the sand' (1972a: 31 – 32). Part of the process of removing them has been to recognise a diversity of views, aims and ambitions for the study of archaeology. The position almost 40 years later is that no consensus exists on theoretical perspectives, which is a healthy sign for the archaeological imagination.

I have shown in this chapter that there are many archaeologies, but basically there are two. There is the archaeology of dates and data, culture history, which has been with us since Thomsen in the nineteenth century. Then there is the archaeology of ideas and imagination which has many forms but is at most only 40 years old, following the widespread appearance of an anthropological archaeology.

Both approaches need data. Both need ideas and theories. However much you might want to, it is not possible to break with past traditions of doing archaeology for the simple reason that we have to incorporate existing facts into our on-going syntheses. Just because we might not like the theories and excavation techniques employed by archaeologists a century ago, that doesn't mean that we can ignore their data. Archaeologists do not start afresh. Rather they add to what is already known. Those facts, those objects, are already coloured with the theories that give them significance to archaeologists.

The point about anthropological archaeology is that it has actively encouraged archaeologists to be theoretical. Hence Marxism, which has a much longer history in archaeology than the scientific methodology of processual archaeology, has been extended to consider global issues in the ancient world (Chapter 6). Feminist approaches have successfully challenged entrenched ways of thinking, and by focusing on gender have added to our understanding of the active role of material culture in creating power (Chapter 8). Interpretive approaches may have more adherents in Europe than anywhere else, but the social theory they draw on has wide significance and provides archaeologists with an entry to debates other than those of science. Finally, the neo-Darwinians, a diverse group ranging from the hardest of hard scientists to those wrapped in a thin coating of biological metaphor, remind us that we need to develop our own theory and methods rather than be simply borrowers.

So, the archaeological imagination is now developing on several fronts. This can be seen in the different approaches that define the nature of what we study, the archaeological record (Chapter 3), in a variety of ways (Patrik 1985). Even so, while drawing the lines between approaches I have been very aware in this chapter of just how overlapping rather than territorial their positions really are. Although frowned upon by some (Johnson 1999a: 118), what is emerging is a more eclectic, rather than evangelical, approach to the use of theory. For example, prehistoric case studies by Christopher Tilley (1996), Alasdair Whittle (1996) and Richard Bradley (1997) now combine the synthesis of data favoured by culture history with many of the techniques advocated by processualists to produce strongly interpretive accounts. I have found this in my own work on Palaeolithic Europe. What began as a processual description full of adaptive, functional solutions to capricious and repeated climatic conditions (Gamble 1986), a game played by groups against their environment if you like, has now become a story of individuals creating social networks in well-trodden landscapes of habit (Gamble 1999). Much still remains of my earlier approach. But the addition of insights from novel theoretical perspectives has allowed me to expand the range of evidence that is normally used and to suggest fresh ways of looking at old data and reasons for acquiring new data. Within archaeology many of the basic concepts, methods and principles remain very familiar, as I will show in the next chapter. What is changing is the archaeological imagination that uses these tools for novel purposes.

SUMMARY

- Different archaeologies are distinguished more by the theoretical standpoint each favours than by the type of data.

- The boundaries between these standpoints are more fluid than is often implied in the literature.
- Interpreting the patterns in archaeological data from rational and relational points of view does produce a different understanding of the same evidence: you have to choose between them.
- Archaeology is basically driven as much by theory as by discoveries in the field. The hard part is marrying the two together.

3

BASIC CONCEPTS

It is now time to meet the archaeology. Exposure to the data is the most important aspect of doing archaeology. However, I resisted opening this book with an account of how we go about finding things and, once found, how we organise them for a good reason. Until I had given you a taste of the varieties of archaeology, which includes both themes (Chapter 1) and theories (Chapter 2) there was no point in discussing how we handle data. There is nothing more silent than a piece of archaeological evidence. Pots, stones, bronzes and bones do not speak to us. They make no sense by themselves. They only acquire significance when interpreted. It is always necessary to appreciate the themes and theories if any useful answers are to be forthcoming.

We now have some of the basic framework that structures archaeological enquiry. What I have shown is that there are many ideas about the past, usually several interpretations of the same data, as we saw in Chapter 1 with Çatalhöyük, and definitely more than one answer to the same question. What all this is telling us is that archaeologists can disagree because they have developed ways of gathering and organising data that allow them to differ. Fieldwork and analysis run to a set of conventions. Participating in the excitement of archaeology requires a knowledge of the concepts that underpin those conventions. In this chapter I will look at those that deal with data gathering and analysis. Later chapters will expand on other issues, but in the present one I will concentrate on a framework for practical archaeology which will lead us into a consideration of the nature of the archaeological record.

STARTING OUT WITH A RESEARCH DESIGN

Doing archaeology starts with questions. As we saw in Chapter 1, with the latest campaign at Sutton Hoo, these are now formalised into a research design that sets out what we want to know, the methods we plan to use and the contribution the answer is expected to make. This is all part of being explicit about the business of archaeology, stripping away, if you like, some of the mystery that surrounds the process and that often amazes visitors to excavations who ask 'How did you know to dig here?'.

Explication – setting out what we plan to do, why we want to do it, how we will do it and what we expect to achieve – lies at the heart of a research design. Put like that some research designs sound very obvious. Too obvious for many, which is why few were written down before the appearance of processual archaeology in the 1960s. Of course, prior to this, the culture history approach had research designs, but they were rarely very elaborate. Usually they involved selecting a region or site for survey, excavating and recovering data, a process which was usually, and in many cases still is, to sort out issues of dating, sequence and the relationship between archaeological cultures.

For example, questions at a regional scale might ask what relative impact each of the Southwestern United States cultures Hohokam, Patayan, Ancestral Puebloan, Mogollon, and their antecedants, had on each other during the almost 9000 years of co-existence (Willey 1966: figures 4.1 and 4.6). Regional survey and excavation would then be employed to get the answers. At a smaller scale the question might be about the constructional history of York Minster in England. Did the layout of the cathedral follow the earlier town plan for the city as established by the Romans and the Vikings?

Answering these questions, which are posed at very different spatial scales, undoubtedly adds to archaeological knowledge. A lot of very good archaeology and many excellent syntheses have resulted from answering similar questions that deal with local and regional culture history.

However, the criticism mounted by processual archaeology was that in many cases such approaches were unsystematic. While data were recovered, the question was how *representative* of past activities were they? This is what was meant by the new archaeology's call for explication in the 1960s. Research designs had to be stated, goals set, procedures outlined and methods detailed before samples could be recovered.

There was a lot of fuss when this strategy was first proposed (Binford 1964). Comments such as 'we don't know what we will find until we start digging' were matched by a reluctance to set down all those ingrained, internal procedures, the experience and knowledge of being an archaeologist. Some of them just seemed too obvious to commit to paper. It was tantamount to revealing hard-won trade secrets. It has also become apparent since that writing down a research design does not necessarily make for good archaeology. Research designs do, however, expose poor questions and ill-conceived methods very quickly.

Research designs are now standard. In fact you will not get funding without one. The scientific model that Binford and others were following now dominates to the extent that it is a professional fact of life, and as a result archaeologists have a much better idea of what we are doing and why. The rise of contract- and developer-funded archaeology has also made explicit research designs essential. Business as well as government wants to know what it is paying for, and why. Greater accountability has resulted in the formal management of archaeological projects (Andrews and Thomas 1995; Cooper *et al.* 1995), which seems a far cry from earlier approaches (Wheeler 1954). But archaeology then was still predominantly a pastime rather than the international profession it is today. The jargon of mission statements (Box 3), performance indicators, project milestones, value for money, assessment and evaluation are a very necessary part of securing funding at a scale that 50 years ago would have seemed inconceivable.

THE REPRESENTATIVE SAMPLE

The shift that research designs typified was from digging for things to digging in order to answer questions. The objective was the recovery of a representative sample of material that would allow the research design's questions about site function and organisation, and any changes they underwent, to be answered. As a result, it was necessary to develop an explicit theory of sampling: not just because archaeologists lacked the time and money to dig and analyse every site or to survey and record every valley, but to meet the criteria of the representative sample (Orton 2000).

The culture historians' complaint about research designs did make at least one good point: we do not know exactly what we are going to find. This is clearly a problem for systematic sampling, where a representative sample usually depends on knowledge of the population being sampled. Opinion polls and market surveys have an acceptable degree of accuracy because the number of voters is known. Moreover, the larger the population and the greater our knowledge of its size and structure, the smaller the samples can be to get at that representative result. Pollsters do not have to ask every voter about their intentions. They sample.

Archaeologists do not know before they start how many sites they will find in a valley survey. Neither do they know how many potsherds, and what frequency of types, will come from an excavation. If we cannot specify our populations beforehand, how can we recover anything but a grab or haphazard sample?

The answer is a clever use of space. Binford (1964) broke the problem down into four populations that need sampling:

- cultural items (artefacts);
- cultural features (buildings, pits, temples within sites etc.);
- ecofacts (in his terms culturally relevant non-artefactual data, e.g. animal bones, sediments, carbonised seeds);
- sites (as activity foci containing the three populations listed above).

Beyond these lay the region that contains populations of sites. The region, as will be discussed in Chapter 6, also has to be larger than the past activities being studied if a representative sample of those activities is going to be recovered.

So the use of space is the solution to the Catch-22 of only finding out about what we want to sample by sampling it. Before we walk that first field transect, lift the turf or make the first dive on a wreck site, we can establish our spatial units and sample them

Key: ■ Known sites   ● New sites   ▨ Sample transects

Figure 3.1 A sampling strategy. The Cycladic island of Melos was systematically surveyed using fieldwalking transects and many new sites added, shown by the black circles. A 20 per cent sample of its surface was covered (lower, shaded areas). The choice of sampling design took into account topography and vegetation. For comparison, an alternative strategy using a random set of quadrants, rather than transects, is also shown (upper). In both cases the sampling strategy can be extrapolated to the areas not surveyed and a representative island-wide picture of prehistoric settlement built up (after Cherry in Renfrew and Wagstaff 1982).

as something we do know about (Figure 3.1). This can be applied to most archaeological materials and landscapes.

The spatial units can be arbitrary: a 50 metre square, or a 20 kilometre square grid subdivided into transects for the surface survey. Alternatively, a *stratified* sample can be drawn up to take into account base map soils and the geology of the region or prior knowledge of the site from geophysical prospection or aerial photographs. But the point is that the spatial grid used is determined by the kinds of questions being asked. It is space rather than the objects it contains that is being sampled: within the space of interest, the material, those four populations listed above, are being *cluster* sampled. It is on that basis that we systematically recover representative samples which can then be quantified.

SURVEY AND EXCAVATION

The past 30 years have seen a move away from excavation as the archaeologist's main method for finding out about the past. Non-destructive survey, principally aerial photography, has been a powerful tool for over 80 years and is now backed by satellite remote sensing. Indeed, with the pace of urban expansion, the dewatering of wetland areas and, most importantly, changes in forestry and farming practices, such as widespread deep ploughing, the aerial record is now an immense archive of what has been lost since the second half of the twentieth century. Landscapes from all periods, with their settlements, fields and cemeteries, have been obliterated and continue to be under threat. Non-destructive techniques, particularly geophysical survey and other methods such as ground penetrating radar and the controlled use of metal detectors, now allow the rapid (by the standards of excavation) plotting of buried features, as was the case when surveying Portus, the ancient port of Imperial Rome (Keay *et al.* 2006). Computer enhancement of the results can produce plans of buried cities and landscapes that are very accurate. These serve as a basis not only for finding out about what is there, and analysing it, but also for deciding on a strategy for excavation designed to answer questions about the dates, relationships and sequence of different elements of the site. Systematic field-survey, where transects are selected according to a sampling design and then walked to recover artefacts from the ploughed soil, has also been instrumental in building up a wider picture of settlement and its changes through time. In many cases material discovered on these surveys is no longer brought back to the lab but recorded on computer in the field and left where it was found. The geographical information systems (GIS) revolution provides a framework for integrating both on-site and off-site data. It grants rapid access to computer-recorded data and allows archaeologists to change their field and excavation strategies on a daily basis if necessary (Wheatley and Gillings 2002).

Excavation is costly and is increasingly seen as a last resort, particularly in the contract- and developer-funded arena. Often discussions to mitigate the outcome for both sides will change the plans for the road or building so as to preserve the archaeology *in situ*, as in the case of the Rose theatre (Chapter 1). Preservation by record, which is what excavation boils down to, has to be a well-argued case of last resort.

RECOVERY

Total excavation is nowadays rarely either an option or desirable, and for a very good reason: the archaeological record is highly repetitive. There is a great deal of redundancy in terms of aspects such as what was made, how people used their landscape and where they buried their dead. Such repetition makes sampling possible.

Sampling will not guarantee the recovery of either the rare or the unique. Some wonderful find may well be in a pit that remained un-dug when a 10 per cent sampling scheme was applied to a site. This reflects contemporary archaeology's interest in the general rather than the unique. Of course we all like to find gold torcs or the skull of a Neanderthal. In the early days of the subject, when that was all archaeological diggers were after, what suffered were the ordinary pots, bones and stones which were simply thrown away. Rare finds grab the headlines and they do no harm. But archaeologists need to concentrate their marketing skills on generating excitement in the less newsworthy but equally important small Roman villa, medieval farmstead and prehistoric stone quarry.

Recovery is something that we can control (Figure 3.2) or at least be systematic about. In the quest for the representative sample the use of sieving and the broader consideration of preservation has received much attention. The recovery of small elements such as

Figure 3.2 Recovering samples. This diagram shows what happens to animal bones at each stage in the archaeological process. Similar diagrams have been produced for other materials. The point of this visual jargon is to remind us that what we do, as much as what happens in the ground, affects how representative our samples will be.

the foot bones of sheep or the remains of fish is something that can be addressed, so that their absence is information about either excavation procedures, inimical soil conditions or past human activity.

ARCHAEOLOGICAL ENTITIES

The material remains that we discover and recover from our spatial grids still need to be organised. These are the entities that we spend a great deal of time analysing, reassessing and shifting around the museum, workroom and laboratory to address the key archaeological question of why cultures vary in time and space. There are three basic entities that allow us to consider this issue. In ascending order they are: attribute, artefact and assemblage.

Artefact types are classified by the attributes they possess: shape, colour, material, decoration and so on. Assemblages are defined by the frequencies of different artefact types, and cross-cut by stratigraphic context and dating. At a higher level of classification we will encounter archaeological cultures, culture groups and technocomplexes (see Chapter 6).

Attribute, artefact and assemblage have of course been around since the start of systematic archaeology with Thomsen and Montelius (Chapter 1). They were the building blocks for relative chronologies and underpinned the success of culture history, and the subject has been structured by them ever since.

These terms were comprehensively defined for an anthropological archaeology by David Clarke (1968: 37), who also formalised an observation that is fundamentral to archaeological classification (Figure 3.3).

When it comes to using such entities in archaeology it is rare to find that they are *monothetic*, where all the expected attributes and artefacts are always present like students at a nine o'clock lecture. Rather, as the class register reveals, it is the case that attendance is variable as in the *polythetic* group. This is important because we must expect fuzzy rather than clear-cut boundaries to our classifications. Archaeologists spend much of their time deciding how many aspects of the archaeological record determine membership of such a group, and in what frequencies. This is an aspect of the principle of popularity described below. Often the usual suspects of differential preservation and haphazard recovery of the data are

Monothetic Group					Polythetic Group				
Artefacts					Artefacts				
A	✓	✓	✓	✓	✓	A	✓			✓	✓
B	✓	✓	✓	✓	✓	B		✓		✓	✓
C	✓	✓	✓	✓	✓	C	✓	✓	✓		
D	✓	✓	✓	✓	✓	D	✓			✓	
E	✓	✓	✓	✓	✓	E		✓	✓		✓
Attributes					Attributes				

Figure 3.3 Polythetic and monothetic systems of classification. The top row of pots are respectively always or partially present as attributes in the culture, or assemblage, A–E (after Clarke 1968: Figure 3). Most classifications in archaeology are polythetic; for example a group of sites whose contents make up a regional culture. The more items that are found in all the sites the stronger the classification will be.

blamed for any inconsistencies. However, the data are the data and like children should not be blamed for being difficult. Neither should we get too hung up searching for ultimate classificatory units as a monothetic approach requires. They will remain elusive. Classification only exists to help answer questions and is not an end in itself, although if you read much archaeology you might conclude otherwise.

ATTRIBUTES

Artefacts are examined through their attributes. These can be observations on composition, raw materials, form and decoration as well as the techniques of manufacture and the contexts in which the artefacts were found (for example a pit, a house or a burial) and also what they were found with – bodies, animals, other similar or dissimilar artefacts. Quantity is also an important attribute as is independent dating evidence.

Attribute analysis is also applied to higher-order classifications such as those created by Childe's urban revolution, or the neo-evolutionary stages of chiefdoms and state (Chapter 7) proposed by Ellman Service (1962). Here a checklist is drawn up and the attributes of the archaeology of the particular culture or assemblage in question, for example Minoan Crete or the Mississippian site of Moundville, compared to it (Box 22).

Such an approach establishes a set of descriptive correlates so that a chiefdom or an urban civilisation can be identified from archaeological evidence.

ARTEFACTS

Artefacts can range in size from a glass bead to the continent it was exchanged for. They range in number from the isolated potsherd to the contents of the city of Teotihuacan or the Roman Empire. The term 'artefact' embraces a wide range of objects, many of which are not traditionally thought of as such. The familiar would include hand-held and human-scale objects; for example knives, beds and houses, as well as the built environment of towns and cities, with monumental architecture, sculpture, bridges and factories. The less-familiar usage of artefact includes the landscapes that people lived in. Many wild areas much loved for their natural beauty turn out to be human artefacts. In southwest England, Dartmoor, a National Park, is seen by many as wild, untamed moorland, in contrast to the farmlands that fringe it. However, the Dartmoor we experience today was created in the Bronze Age when an elaborate system of boundary banks was laid out and the forest cut down. Subsequent exploitation for tin, granite and grazing for sheep as well as tourism and the area's use as a military training area have added to and preserved a prehistoric artefact.

Dartmoor is therefore a large piece of material culture. But the scale of the artefact can get still bigger. Consider Australia, the continent of hunters and gatherers. Erroneously, hunter-gatherer lifestyles are thought to be shaped by nature rather than to affect it (Chapter 8), a view that owes everything to the evolutionism of the eighteenth and nineteenth centuries when Australian Aborigines were thought by some to not even possess society.

Fifty years of archaeological research has totally reversed that passive view. Long before Captain Cook the Australian continent was a cultural landscape. Stone artefacts, the oldest of which date back some 60,000 years, are found everywhere, even in southwestern Tasmania where nobody lives today. The widespread practice of burning the country, traced archaeologically through charcoal deposits, transformed the vegetation in favour of the fire-resistant eucalypts. Many animals, especially the megafaunal marsupials, became extinct either through habitat change or direct human predation. Finally, Australia is one giant canvas of rocks which have been painted, engraved and pecked with signs and representations of animals and humans – artefacts which depict artefacts which contain stories, tracks and paths as artefacts of the landscape.

ASSEMBLAGE

The third level in the basic classification of archaeological entities is the assemblage. This was defined by David Clarke as an associated set of contemporary artefact types (1968: 188), and it is a small step from there to a type list that defines an assemblage excavated from a stratigraphic level or chronological unit.

The most celebrated debate concerning the interpretation of archaeological assemblages involved, among others, François Bordes and Lewis Binford, and was based on the interpretation of stone-tool assemblages excavated from stratigraphic layers in the many caves and rock shelters used by Neanderthal people 100,000 to 40,000 years ago in southwest France. One of the most famous is the rock shelter at Le Moustier, after which the widespread Mousterian culture, based on distinctive tools and techniques, is named. The assemblages were studied by François Bordes, who devised a type list with 63 elements such as stone scrapers, points and borers, and a series of technical indexes that described the method by which the tools had been knapped (Bordes 1972). Each assemblage contained different proportions of types and the variable application of different flint-knapping techniques, and although Bordes had expected a continuous spectrum of variation, what he found from his analysis were only five assemblages, or variants, of the Mousterian.

The Mousterian debate, as it is known, revolved around the differing explanations for that clustering. Were these assemblages the ethnic markers of five different Neanderthal tribes, as Bordes claimed, or toolkits that varied according to function as Binford proposed (Binford and Binford 1969)? Or were they instead, as others argued (Mellars 1970), stages in a chronological development? Similar assemblage studies based on type list and type frequency also abound in studies of archaeological ceramics and metalwork.

ARCHAEOLOGICAL CULTURES

Cultures, like the Mousterian, are the next brick in the wall of entities. Traditionally, and for the foreseeable future, they are the archaeologist's basic building block. Two classic definitions of the culture emerged from very different philosophical and political backgrounds. The earlier comes from the ultra-nationalist Gustav Kossinna, whose settlement archaeology was enthusiastically applied after his death in 1931 by supporters of the Third Reich:

> Clearly defined, sharply distinctive, bounded archaeological provinces correspond unquestioningly to the territories of particular peoples and tribes.
>
> (Kossinna 1926, in Veit 1989: 39)

The second, and better known, was penned by Gordon Childe, who defined the archaeological culture concept in the following classic manner:

> We find certain types of remains – pots, implements, ornaments, burial rites and house forms – constantly recurring together. Such a complex of associated traits we shall term a 'cultural group' or just a 'culture'. We assume that such a complex is the material expression of what today would be called a 'people'.
>
> (Childe 1929: v–vi)

Childe's innovation was to pave the way for a social account of the past. His 'culture = peoples' hypothesis took into account the mosaic-like character of the archaeology of Europe. He disagreed with Kossinna, who put everything good and innovative down to his own ancestors, the northern Aryans, but agreed with the Swedish typologist Oscar Montelius in his acceptance of diffusion from the Near East. Embracing the concept of *ex oriente lux* ('from the east light') also provided Childe with an explanation of change within Europe in his early work.

ANTHROPOLOGICAL CULTURE

The definition that Childe gave us describes the archaeological reality of pots, stones and house types. But within anthropology culture has a much broader meaning than this. E. B. Tylor mapped out the field in the nineteenth century:

> Culture, or civilisation . . . is that complex whole which includes knowledge, belief, art, law, morals, custom and any other capabilities and habits acquired by man as a member of society.
>
> (Tylor 1871: 1)

As such, it is acquired and transmitted:

> Culture . . . refers . . . to learned, accumulated experience. A culture . . . refers to those socially transmitted patterns for behaviour characteristic of a particular social group.
>
> (Kessing 1981: 68)

It can be viewed in very adaptive, functional, terms:

> By culture we mean an extrasomatic, temporal continuum of things and events dependent upon symboling. . . . A mechanism whose function is to make life secure and continuous for groups and individuals of the human species.
>
> (White 1959: 3, 78)

For Leslie White culture was our extrasomatic (literally outside the body) means of adaptation. Although he referred to the use of symbols he did not mean, as Clifford Geertz later proposed, that culture was a network of interpretations:

> Believing that . . . man is an animal suspended in webs of significance he himself has spun, I take culture to be those webs, and the

analysis of it to be therefore not an experimental science in search of law but an interpretive one in search of meaning.

(Geertz 1975: 5)

These poles-apart positions – culture as patterning in the archaeo-logical record; culture as an adaptive mechanism; culture as interpretive networks – are one of the reasons that the concept of culture is regarded as highly problematic by many anthropologists, even though it is historically their core concept. Thorough discussions are provided by Michael Carrithers (1990), Tim Ingold (1994), Christoph Brumann (1999) and Adam Kuper (1999).

THREE ANALYTICAL PRINCIPLES

The entities attribute, artefact, assemblage and culture are the foundations of archaeology. They are used to build classifications and to present interpretations. As we saw in the Mousterian debate, these interpretations might differ. But even here the major protagonists agreed that assemblages exist. They only disagreed over what they signify. Three analytical principles help us to understand why such different archaeologists are agreed on the basics of their particular period of prehistory. These are:

• style
• popularity, and
• stratigraphy.

THE PRINCIPLE OF STYLE

Archaeological classification depends upon stylistic principles. While many definitions have been put forward for this important but slippery term (Chapter 5), it is all too often taken for granted, even ignored by some (Renfrew and Bahn 2005) as one of archaeology's key concepts.

The stylistic principle expects objects to vary in terms of their attributes. But this variation is not infinite or random, but instead follows set patterns that are associated with particular times and places. Knives are knives, but they vary enormously in terms of materials, size, weight and decoration. However, styles of knife can be grouped into geographical and temporal traditions. The bottom line in a stylistic analysis is the assessment of the degree of resemblance between objects. The identification of shared attributes results in the classification of repeated types that are stylistically similar.

THE PRINCIPLE OF POPULARITY

Much of what I have described in this chapter so far depends on the principle of popularity. This has been applied to items as well as types and to styles or traits of manufacture, decoration and use. Fluctuating popularity reflects a change in the archaeological record that is explained by invoking either the diffusion of peoples or the spread of ideas. Popularity changes with time and across space. The principle of popularity also supposes that things are similar because people share the same ideas and cultural premises. This sharing is

Figure 3.4 A Harris matrix for a section in an excavation. This would be combined with those for all the other sections in the trench as well as with the plans drawn from above as the excavation proceeded. The matrix of boxes on the right records the stratigraphic relationship between the layers, walls and pits that the excavator uncovered during excavation.

presented as a basic aspect of all humans. It started in the Palaeolithic and continues today. For culture historians like François Bordes a stone-tool type is therefore as understandable as a Frenchman's beret or an Englishman's bowler hat. They are all expressing the same cultural imperative whereby sharing norms of behaviour establishes group identity. But this imperative is never analysed. Rather it is assumed as the basis for understanding why archaeological units vary and why they changed. It was this lack of clarity that led some, such as Binford, to a serious rethink about what popularity was measuring.

THE PRINCIPLE OF STRATIGRAPHY

Popularity and stratigraphy are two principles that go hand in hand. Stratigraphy turns 'walls of mud' into a record of time and past activity. Most importantly, thinking stratigraphically makes you *look* at time vertically to see deposited sediments as stacked up like so many different-coloured bricks. You need to add that *vertical* dimension to your everyday experience of time as *linear*, whereby minutes turn into hours into days, and as *cyclical*, when your birthday comes round once a year (Chapter 6).

The essence of stratigraphic analysis is determining discrete, superimposed layers or features and then examining their contents. A very systematic and thorough mode of analysis is provided by Edward Harris (1989), whose logical matrix analysis (Figure 3.4) is a widespread convention in field archaeology, an example of visual jargon that archaeologists understand but whose rules need to be learned. Stratigraphic differences may be geological – variation in soils and sediments that appear as textural or colour changes in the sediments – or they may be features of human activity produced by, for example, the digging of pits and ditches, building of walls and dumping of waste material. Stratigraphy is therefore about the building up of layers and features, as well as their cutting away and reworking as a result of human occupation. A stratigraphic analysis unravels the sequence of the creative process of living in the land-scape over periods of time.

Stratigraphic excavations began in the middle of the nineteenth century and some of the best exponents were J. J. A. Worsaae, who excavated prehistoric sites in Denmark, and Giuseppe Fiorelli, who applied a stratigraphic approach to Pompeii in 1860. Not everyone followed suit and not all stratigraphic excavations were well recorded. Moreover, the breadth of interests that Worsaae pursued in his excavations, including the recovery and analysis of organic evidence to reconstruct the environment and subsistence economy, was often lacking. Most digs were just that – digs – with the sole aim of recovering pots, metal, art and burials. The exceptions stand

Site	%	%	%	%	%	%	%	%
A	4.1		6.4		85.4		4.1	
B	3.8		5.7		86.7		3.8	
C	4.1		6.2		85.4		4.3	
D	6.4		14.4		75.2		4.0	
E	7.7		18.5		71.2		2.6	
F	18.4		48.0		29.8		3.8	
G	23.3		53.8		20.0		2.9	
H	32.3		48.2		5.2		14.3	
I	38.7		43.1		0.4		17.8	
J	49.0		29.6		0.2		21.2	
K	61.5		20.3		0.0		18.2	
L	67.5		3.1		0.2		9.2	
M	69.5		0.8		0.0		9.7	

Figure 3.5 A series of battleship curves organised to show gradual changes in the popularity of four pot types in 13 sites (A–M). Each row adds up to 100 per cent and the shape of the curves relies on the assumption that cultural items start rare, become popular and then fade away. In the absence of absolute dates, such as radiocarbon or dendrochronology, this exercise in seriation might serve as a chronological chart for culture historians. The changing fortunes of each pot type might then be explained as the influx of a new human population with a different culture.

out, such as Ferdinand Keller's pioneering work in the well preserved Neolithic Swiss lake villages which he started excavating in 1854. In England the military training of General Pitt-Rivers and his unshakeable belief in evolutionary science led to a model of good practice (Bowden 1991). He both excavated sites and published the results from his Dorset estate (1887). In 1882 he became the first Inspector of Ancient Monuments for the country after Parliament passed legislation protecting some important sites. This position undoubtedly helped the dissemination of his excavation methods.

Sound stratigraphic observation provided archaeologists with a means of comparing their results and building their relative chronologies. Regional traditions of archaeology went through their stratigraphic revolutions at different times around the world. In North America it took place later than Europe, between 1915 and 1927, and centred on work in the pueblos of the Southwestern United States.

SERIATION DATING

Combine popularity and stratigraphy and you arrive at seriation, a standard archaeological procedure that sorts series of attributes and artefacts and then interprets them. Seriation is a technique for ordering stylistic units, such as types, into a relative chronological sequence. We have already encountered an early application with C.J. Thomsen's three-age system (Chapter 1). Another example provides a visual representation in the form of battleship curves (Figure 3.5). As described by David Hurst Thomas (1998: 246), seriation is based on the assumption that cultural styles (what he calls 'fads') change, and that the popularity of a particular style or decoration can be associated with a certain time period.

One of the best-known examples of seriation comes from the southwestern United States. The main question that faced archaeologists investigating the prehistory of this region and its monuments, such as Pueblo Bonito in Chaco Canyon, New Mexico, concerned its relative dating. A ground-breaking paper published in 1916 by the anthropologist A. R. Kroeber used frequency seriations of pottery to provide a chronology. Kroeber made the distinction that variation

BOX 12 SOME OF THE MOST IMPORTANT SCIENCE-BASED DATING TECHNIQUES, THE MATERIALS THEY DATE AND THE AGES THEY COVER.

Dating technique	Materials	Upper limit (years)	Lower limit (years)
Potassium/argon (K/Ar)	Volcanic rocks	30,000	All of human evolution i.e. 5 million
Thermoluminescence (TL)	Burnt flint, ceramics. Unburnt sediments	Present 5,000–10,000	100,000–500,000 50,000
Electron spin resonance (ESR)	Tooth enamel	Present	> 1 million
Uranium series	Stalactite, stalagmite	5000	350,000
Radiocarbon (C^{14}) using accelerator mass spectrometry (AMS)	Bone, charcoal, shell, fibre	Present	50,000, possibly 70,000 in the future
Radiocarbon (C^{14}) conventional methods	Bone, charcoal, shell, fibre	Present	40,000

in the proportion of types could be due *either* to time *or* to geography. Remember, seriation produces a sequence not a scale, and cannot indicate how long any phase lasted. That would come first from dendrochronology (tree-ring dating) in the southwestern United States and universally through radiocarbon dating after 1945 (see below). Seriation works particularly well with abundant pottery sherds from long stratigraphic sequences.

Kroeber was not alone in developing such techniques but appears to have made the breakthrough independently (Lyman, O'Brien and Dunnell 1997: 55). Nels Nelson, Clark Wissler and Leslie Spier also produced seriation chronologies for the American Southwest. The excavations in the Pecos pueblo by Alfred Kidder during the 1920s, using natural rather than arbitrary stratigraphic units, confirmed that these shifts in the frequency of pottery types were indeed chronological.

ABSOLUTE DATING

Stratigraphy provides a sequence; B came after A but before C. Varying popularity, when used in a seriation, allowed archaeologists to elaborate on the process of culture change. You could now ask 'Who came from where?', based on the popularity of types. However, what archaeologists, and especially prehistoric archaeologists, wanted was a way of measuring time not through changes in relative frequency but in terms of absolute years. How long did those battleship curves last? How rapidly did cultures change?

The absolute measure of time beyond written records and king lists was first achieved by counting annual lake varves and tree rings. Such continuous records are extremely valuable. They provide very accurate dating but of course depend upon either the preservation of suitable materials, such as wood, or the deposition of artefacts in lake muds. What was needed was a technique that could date the kind of items that were found on most archaeological sites – charcoal, bone and shell.

The major breakthrough came after 1945 with the development of isotope-decay methods. Radiocarbon was the first, soon to be followed by a number of related techniques which used different isotopes associated with the elements uranium, potassium, argon and thorium. Now there are also dating methods using geomagnetism, thermoluminescence, electron spin resonance and amino acid epimerisation. Different techniques have different time spans and apply to a range of materials. Box 12 lists the materials upon which each technique is based. A full account of this very important but highly technical branch of archaeology can be found in Aitken (1990) and Brothwell and Pollard (2005).

The absolute measurement of time by scientific methods is undoubtedly one of the great achievements of interdisciplinary research. It was primarily a combination of physics, chemistry and archaeology. Willard Libby, working in Chicago, pioneered the radiocarbon technique in the immediate post-war period. His breakthrough was recognised by a Nobel Prize in 1960. Older techniques such as tree-ring dating and varve counting were later used to refine and calibrate the results when it was realised that some of Libby's original assumptions about the stability of carbon in the atmosphere did not adequately allow for variation over time. A review of the power of dendrochronology and its importance in calibrating radiocarbon is provided by Michael Baillie (1995).

Radiocarbon (C^{14}) dating is very useful for archaeologists because carbon is so widespread. Charcoal, wood, bone, fibre, shell and seeds can all be dated, though the chemical pretreatment of samples varies and different laboratories prefer different materials. The applicability of this technique worldwide allowed archaeologists to compare global cultures and processes with a standard chronology. Archaeological findings were incorporated into global history and the scene was set for a generalising, comparative approach. Science-based dating such as radiocarbon dating was part of the quantitative revolution in archaeology after 1950, and it is quite possible that without it the anthropological archaeology of the 1960s (Chapter 2) would have been delayed. I believe it would still have happened but probably not quite in its original form as a hard-nosed, scientific and processual investigation of the past.

THE ARCHAEOLOGICAL RECORD

I have now described some of our basic archaeological units. I have also shown how, prior to absolute dating, archaeologists used the principles of popularity and stratigraphy to order their materials, thus allowing the analysis of change.

However, the absolute measurement of time did not make the archaeologist's job of interpretation any easier. Instead it contributed to a major debate concerning the composition and nature of the archaeological record: 'What exactly is it, how was it formed and how should it be investigated?'

After 1969 Binford became disillusioned with his new archaeology (1983). He was concerned that all that had happened was that archaeology had become a more statistical and increasingly computer-literate culture history. Archaeology might have been recast as an anthropological enquiry with a concern for real-life processes, but this still left a yawning chasm that needed a bridge of inference to span it. Quite simply, how could you go from the static facts that could be dug up to the dynamic but invisible behaviour that produced them? The new archaeology, for all its insistence on testing hypotheses, the deductive method and the collection of samples in a more rigorous manner to enable such testing to occur, had difficulty with this crucial methodological point. It had to be addressed if a scientific approach was to succeed. But how?

MIDDLE-RANGE THEORY

Binford's answer was to set out principles that could act as a bridge between the statics of the archaeological record (those bones and pots) and the dynamics of past human behaviour (the now invisible actions that produced and organised them into spatial and temporal patterns). He called this a *middle-range theory* (Box 7). In practice it was based on experiment and on the observation of people and animals doing things in the modern world, which would allow us to learn about how patterns are created. The issues are well described in Johnson (1999a: Chapter 4).

Binford undertook his own studies among the Nunamiut hunters of Alaska and the Alyawara people of central Australia (Binford 1983). He also studied carnivore feeding and denning behaviour in Africa and North America to try to understand how these animals use bones and how this affects their patterning in the archaeological record (see Box 13). Similar modern-day studies became common.

BOX 13 WHAT IS TAPHONOMY?

Closely related to both middle-range theory and site formation processes is the field of taphonomy, literally the laws of burial (*taphos* = burial; *nomos* = law). It is the study of a subset of the archaeological record which deals with organic remains (Lyman 1994: 1). Taphonomy has been particularly important in studies of animal bone assemblages, crop residues and other environmental evidence such as geoarchaeology, where it is invaluable in sorting out the varied agents and processes, natural and cultural, that have contributed to and shaped archaeological samples. For example, taphonomic studies of how Palaeolithic stone tools are moved around in rivers and become incorporated into gravel bodies as assemblages (Hosfield 1999).

BOX 14 DOING MIDDLE-RANGE THEORY IN THE PALAEOLITHIC.

- Understand the dynamics of behaviour by undertaking a detailed ethnoarchaeological study of a modern hunting society to learn about the decisions they face and how the archaeology they create is organised in time and space (Binford 1978a, b, 1980).
- Hone the skill of recognising relevant patterns in the data. Build a middle-range theory to form the bridge between data and the behaviour, now invisible, that produced it (Binford 1983).
- Compare human hunters with carnivores. Examine how carnivores regularly feed on a carcass and carry food back to their dens. Since the behaviour of wolves and hyenas has remained the same, while humans evolved new adaptations during the Palaeolithic, they provide a yardstick for measuring those changes (Binford 1981a).

In all of this Binford's aim was to determine the range of potentially relevant causal processes for his chosen area, the study of prehistoric hunter gatherers. His strategy was threefold (Box 14).

Not everyone followed Binford's strategy because not everyone was interested in hunters and gatherers. What use were hyenas and modern hunters to the study of sedentary farming societies? Ethnoarchaeological studies have certainly been carried out among agricultural, horticultural and urban communities (Skibo, Walker and Nielsen 1995; David and Kramer 2001). But these have started from rather different premises. Modern material culture such as the Garbage project (Rathje 1992) that started in Tucson, and Hodder's work among the Baringo in East Africa (Hodder 1982) are just two well-known examples that raise challenging alternatives to how we think culture works in time and space and how such patterning reveals people consuming and interacting through the medium of material culture.

SITE FORMATION

Michael Schiffer, once a student of Binford, developed an approach that privileged the study of human behaviour – especially making, using and discarding artefacts. Schiffer (1976) was interested in

Key: ● Opportunity for storage and/or transport

Procurement

Preparation

Consumption

Recycling

Lateral cycling

Discard

Systemic context

Archeological context

Refuse

Figure 3.6 Making archaeology. The formation of the archaeological record with the passage of materials from a systemic into an archaeological context (after Schiffer 1976).

making explicit the multiple role of laws in archaeological research; not middle-range theory as much as the study of how the archaeological record was formed. These formation processes were of two types: natural and cultural. 'N' and 'C' transforms affected objects and their associations in predictable ways as they moved from the past, systemic context into the present archaeological context, where they became refuse (Figure 3.6).

If a difference exists between Binford's middle-range theory and Schiffer's formation processes it lies in the broader archaeological goals they are pursuing. For Schiffer and his colleagues 'the subject matter of archaeology is the relationships between human behaviour and material culture in all times and places' (Schiffer 1976: 4). They identify four strategies which illustrate nicely what they hope to achieve (Box 15).

For Binford, however, the purpose of archaeology is to understand evolutionary transformations such as that from hunting to farming,

BOX 15 THE FOUR STRATEGIES OF BEHAVIOURAL ARCHAEOLOGY (SCHIFFER 1976).

Human behaviour	Material culture	
	Past	Present
Past	Archaeology and the study of *particular* past cultural systems , e.g. rise of palace societies in the Aegean Bronze Age	Ethnoarchaeological studies to inform general archaeological interpretation, e.g. hunter -gatherer settlement patterns
Present	Archaeology's contribution to understanding *general* aspects of contemporary as well as past behaviour, e.g. population pressure as a cause of cultural change	The study of *particular* industrial societies, e.g. the Tucson garbage project as an investigation of material consumption

the replacement of Neanderthals by modern humans and, most recently, asking under what conditions low-density populations among hunters and gatherers become high density (Binford 1983, 2001). Further differences between their positions are explored in the next chapter.

HAS ANYTHING CHANGED?

In this chapter I have gone from research designs to the archaeological record. Both of these concepts represented a major shift in the way archaeology was conceived and practised. At one time the archaeological record was not seen as a problem. Indeed, it is still sometimes claimed that our goal as archaeologists is getting the stratigraphic facts right (Harris 1989: xiii). But, as we have seen, the archaeological record is more than just an offshoot of geology and its laws of superposition. Instead it provides an active, interpretive problem that begins, in Hodder's (1999) phrase, 'at the trowel's edge'. In the same way, being explicit about research designs is another means by which we came to grips with our samples. Obtaining a representative sample has nothing to do with the principles of stratigraphy. Instead it has everything to do with our assumptions about, and approaches to, investigating human behaviour and action through material remains as they are distributed in time and space.

Consequently I have introduced some of the entities, such as attribute, and principles, such as popularity, that archaeologists commonly use. I have provided you with definitions of culture, taphonomy and many other terms. I have acquainted you with these conventions because they structure the practice of archaeology and so make it intelligible to initiates. These conventions are the shorthands that you will find in site reports, conference papers and textbooks. Suitably armed, it is now time to see what we can do with them.

SUMMARY

- All archaeology depends upon samples and sampling.
- Archaeologists depend upon the principles of style, popularity and stratigraphy to organise and analyse their data.
- The building blocks of archaeological classification start with the attribute and then proceed to the artefact and assemblage. Beyond these lie the culture and technocomplex.
- Dating based on seriation and scientific dating allows archaeologists to ask different questions of change.
- Understanding the composition of the archaeological record is a theoretical exercise in its own right and can be approached along a number of avenues.

4

PEOPLE

Getting at the people is the core activity of archaeology. Finding objects, and then analysing and interpreting them, is what we do most of the time. What we must never lose sight of amidst the excitement are those people. It is all too easy to find both dispirited and perfectly content archaeologists who, like Arthur's knights in search of the Holy Grail, have either given up or forgotten that they were even trying to look for them. As a result the people, individually or collectively, can very soon get lost in the details of report writing, the catalogues of coins and carp's tongue swords, the syntheses by region and period, the textbooks by topic and theme: the grist but not the grail.

In the last chapter I examined the entities archaeologists use and the concept of the archaeological record. Now the spotlight falls on people in the past. To address them we need to ask three basic questions:

- Who do we want to know?
- What can we know?
- How do we know?

To answer them we will need to examine the use of analogy and the way we build inferences about people in the past, either using scientific methods or as an exercise in interpretation: 'spinning a cable'.

WHO DO WE WANT TO KNOW?

Throughout the history of archaeology there has been a continuing argument about the relative importance of the individual and the group to understanding the past that reflects wider trends in the debate over individual responsibilities, power, freedoms and psyches and the role of society and the state in constraining and shaping them. The study of the past is one way to continue this debate and is a means of self-knowledge about who we are and why we act in so many different and similar ways.

However, at a practical level, can we study the individual without those written documents which give us a sense of the person, of his or her thoughts, feelings and intentions? Must we always look to an aggregate such as the culture, the system or society to study people in the past? What role did the individual play in making decisions, whether they were to push forward the idea of urban living or imperial expansion, or just what to eat for dinner?

THE INDIVIDUAL

In prehistory the individual is usually regarded as a shadowy figure lost in the long corridors of deep time. Even though prehistoric villages may have had few inhabitants and the campsites of hunters and gatherers even fewer, there is a prejudice against looking too hard for them. This may seem strange given that there are many archaeological instances, stone knapping would be one (Gamble and Porr 2005), of well-preserved, individual actions and therefore, by inference, individual decision making. In fact I suspect that the earlier prehistoric record has rather more snapshots where we can easily see the individual at work than in the later text-assisted periods.

For example, records survive that chart the changing ownership of properties for many of the medieval streets in English towns. Inventories of house contents were often made when an owner died. From these a picture of the comparative wealth and status that accrued from the trade practised in the house or shop can be built up. This is information about the individual. An archaeological excavation of one of these houses, probably deeply buried by subsequent renovations and rebuilds, usually fails to add much more than the size of the living room, how it was built and the contents of the latrine pits in the back garden. This is not the fault of the archaeology, with its coarse-grained time signatures (Chapter 6). Rather it is the error of expecting the material record of the past to furnish information in the same form as the more familiar text-based evidence. Room size and pit-contents, as we shall see in Chapter 8, can be every bit as illuminating of wealth and status as an inventory written down for probate purposes. Furthermore, in his study of eighteenth-century Bristol, Roger Leech (1999: 30) shows how changing architecture and the ordering of space within houses permits a different identification of individual lives from that possible from most text-based accounts. He shows that rather than investigating status through the numbers and size of rooms in houses, it is instead possible to trace distinct lifestyles through separate and peculiarly urban genealogies of architectural form.

THE INDIVIDUAL AND THE SYSTEM

The question is what we mean by the individual. For culture historians it is still the identification of the historical person. Who was buried in the Sutton Hoo longship? Was it really Raedwald, who died around AD 625? And if it was, what do we know of him from the few texts that survive? Very little, is the answer. Not even that he was buried in a ship on dry land with a silver spoon in his mouth.

This game of spot-the-individual was rightly criticised by Colin Renfrew, who observed that we don't want to know *who* was top dog, but *what kind* of dog he was (1973b: 12). However, rather than teaching the dog new tricks many processualists have continued to let it run with the pack. Kent Flannery's statement is typical:

> Obviously individuals *do* make decisions, but evidence of these individual decisions cannot be recovered by archaeologists. Accordingly it is more useful for the archaeologist to study and understand the system, whose behaviour is detectable over and over again.
>
> (Flannery 1967, in Leone 1972: 106)

According to this view, the system rather than the individual governs what happens. Systems have their own trajectory and cannot be deflected by individual action. Raedwald, whatever personal qualities he might have had, was irrelevant to the process of change that was soon to sweep paganism from his kingdom and replace it with Christianity. Systems, as I examined in Chapter 2, are said to run according to basic laws and principles, such as those of thermodynamics or natural selection. These cross-cut prehistoric and historic periods and uncovering them is the aim of scientifically minded archaeologists.

From this perspective individuals become nothing more than the servants of systems. An example from elsewhere reiterates the point and should warn some neo-Darwinian archaeologists (Chapter 2) to be cautious with their dismissals. The biologist Richard Dawkins maintains that individuals are just a means by which genes and their cultural counterparts, memes, replicate themselves (1976). This view of the system as paramount has been nicely parodied by the philosopher Daniel Dennett. He points out that from a library's point of view a scholar is just a way to make another library (1991: 202). Taken to its logical conclusion systems reproduce themselves through the unthinking actions of individuals. If we follow this line then we can abandon the individual among the dusty stacks of unreadable time.

THINKING PEOPLE, DUMB SYSTEMS

Happily the prevailing paradigm continues to shift between those that prioritise the individual and those focusing on the collective. The individual, correctly in my view, is currently seen by some as the unit of selection, the locus of change (Chapter 7). The argument that we can't see individuals' actions or decisions in archaeological evidence has been tackled by Steven Mithen. He uses an evolutionary approach to decision making among prehistoric hunters. He ascribes to the individuals he studies a knowledge of the world and a capacity to plan and make decisions, so that they are able to respond creatively and intelligently to the challenges of their social and physical environment (Mithen 1993: 396). Without these attributes there can, in his opinion, be no satisfactory explanation of the past. Emphasising basic systems, as advocated by Flannery, involved steamroller explanations for change such as group selection and population pressure. The study of the individual never had a chance.

Mithen's description of the individual harmonises with the interpretive approach, although its adherents would probably fault him for filling those individuals up with *essence* (Chapter 1) in order to get them to make up their mind. Post-processualists are very keen to reinstate the individual in archaeological studies (Shanks and Tilley 1987b). But at the same time this is not just swapping the system for the individual. The interpretive twist is to insist on the influence of an individual on the creation of the wider social structure *and* the importance of that structure on the creation of the individual.

In this approach, giving Raedwald a name and elevating his elaborate ship-burial to the status of a historic event is unimportant. 'Raedwald' and all his fine accoutrements are instead an object (Chapter 5), influencing the structure of his society and in turn being influenced by it. Raedwald the 'person-thing', rather than the 'king-person', is both active in a material sense and a symbol for action by others. But then so too was every other individual and artefact in his kingdom and outside it. Here is Renfrew's dog howling a new tune.

PREHISTORIC PERSONS

It remains true, though, that individuals become much more interesting if they are given an identity. Not a label such as that of king, priest or farmer but instead a sense of self and personhood. These concepts are difficult for archaeologists because they are hidden, part of the inner landscapes of our minds and bodies (Fowler 2004). But they are undoubtedly important because the modern world provides examples of at least two different forms of personhood that have implications for archaeology (Gosden 1999).

The first will be familiar to you since it takes the form of a rational account of a Western individual. This is the notion of the person as someone who literally stops at the skin. Such persons are individual units in both a biological and psychological sense. This kind of personhood is an individual matter, distinct from the social ties that link people together in networks.

Less familiar is the version of personhood that comes from anthropological studies of non-Western societies, particularly in the Pacific. The personhood of a Melanesian individual, as explained by Marilyn Strathern (1988), does not stop at the skin. Rather than being singular, as is the case with Western personhood, Melanesian personhood is distributed across many individuals. The Melanesian individual, or *dividual* to emphasise the distinction, is an example of the relational, rather than the rational approach to building categories that I described in Chapter 2. Such differences are important: for example, power in such societies arises from relationships and is not a possession as it is among Western individuals.

While it might be tempting to divide the world's societies into the two camps, in practice, as Edward LiPuma (1998) reminds us, the line is in fact blurred. Neither is there any implication that Melanesian forms of personhood are older or more 'original' when compared to their Western counterparts. The take-home message for archaeologists is that humans have never throughout their history and prehistory been constructed according to one set of social and psychological principles.

THE SOCIAL USE OF SPACE

At the moment it is the rational approach that carries more weight in our accounts of how society works in all times and places. This has not always been the case. Nurit Bird-David's (1999) study of Nayaka people in southern India, who would traditionally be classed as hunters and gatherers, reveals the alternative, relational style. But not so long ago, during Europe's Middle Ages, the relational approach was also common. Individuals were not recognised as separate entities, as we see each other today, but were instead seen as indivisible from the world (1999: 88). The Nayaka and the Normans have more in common than an archaeologist interested in the difference between hunting bands and military states would ever believe possible.

An archaeological expression of this difference can be found in Matthew Johnson's (1993: 349) study of the medieval open hall (Figure 4.1). The arrangement of rooms, he argues, could be related to a conception of the dispersed self, an example of the way that people did not see themselves as separate individuals but rather as related. The hall is a symbolic frame with all the various

Figure 4.1 The changing use of space. The internal layout of a medieval open-hall (upper) and post-medieval lobby-entry house (lower). Access and privacy are very differently conceived in each (after Johnson 1993: Figure 7.3).

roles – landlord, servant, peasant head of household, lord – on view in face-to-face interaction within the building. During the major changes in society that led to the rise of capitalism, this face-to-face community became partitioned. The conceptual space of the hall was physically divided, as alterations to so many buildings in England in the post-medieval period show. Everyday life now shifted to a recognition of the indivisible, the bounded individual caught up in social relations based on class. When a peasant now visited his landlord at home he saw and experienced an alien spatial and symbolic system where previously he had been included, albeit with demarcations based on status, within a single body of space. The performance and participation in lives changed fundamentally from a web of relatedness to the net of modernity.

THE INDIVIDUAL IN ARCHAEOLOGY

Does this mean that individuals will only be found archaeologically where preservation is good and time signatures fine grained? I would answer no. We should not confuse precision in our methods with knowing people (Gamble and Porr 2005). Neither should we expect our knowledge of individuals to be accessible in similar ways through either the object- or text-based record of the past. We know about individuals through interaction and involvement, using all our senses. We engage with others in all the varied activities of our daily lives. That involvement comprises material culture as well as flesh-and-blood people.

We use those same senses and rules of social engagement when we go about investigating the past *with others*. But those others, trowelling next to you in the trench, sitting across from you in class or the library, or walking around the museum, are not the individuals of the past. We cannot engage with the Minoans in the same way that we can with fellow tourists at the Palace of Knossos. That is patently impossible. But what we can do is to credit them with actions, make them knowledgeable, as Mithen suggests – and before him Grahame Clark, who declared that just because prehistorians cannot identify individuals is no reason why they should ignore their existence (1957: 248). The critical point to emphasise concerns change. With the individual correctly identified as highly variable, and hence operated on by selection, we make change an internal,

Figure 4.2 Top-down and bottom-up approaches to the study of society. This model sees the individual baboon, chimp or vervet monkey as negotiating and performing society into being. They do this through building alliances, and when fights break out, you find out who your real friends are. These are finger-tip societies. The ties that bind are literally groomed into existence. Many primates spend up to 25 per cent of their waking time grooming each other and through this mechanism establishing long-lasting emotional bonds.

human process. The alternative is to rely on an external steamroller to iron out the wrinkles in our past.

HOW TO GET ON IN PRIMATE SOCIETY

What exactly is the relationship between the individual and the wider social structure within which we all live? Opinion swings between stressing the importance of the individual and the primacy of the social system, from the micro- to the macro-scale. How we conceive of the problem is very important for how we go about trying to get at those people in archaeology.

Let me come at the problem by examining what we make of the societies of apes and monkeys, our primate cousins.

One reason for drawing the comparison is that monkey watchers have had, like archaeologists, to work out the structure of a society (in this case the primate society) for themselves. They cannot converse with their subjects and they definitely have no written records to guide them. They take either a bottom-up or a top-down approach (see also Chapter 7) to society, those collections of individuals who associate with one another (Figure 4.2). Appropriately for primate societies, a bottom-up approach to explain how society is created is currently the most popular.

The main point, however, is that these individual apes and monkeys are active agents in the construction of their social worlds. The intensity of grooming may to some extent be predicted from their genetic relationships to each other, but it is by no means solely determined by that blueprint. Social life is neither biologically determined, as sociobiologists have claimed, nor inherited in finished form. Moreover, read any primate-watcher's study (Waal 1982; Goodall 1986) and you will be impressed by the personalities, biographies and sheer individuality of the 'animals' they are studying. This is not crude anthropomorphism. It is, however, a major change in the way we conceive of society, from one based on pre-ordained rules and roles to one open to active participation and interpretation. Of course there are limits, but there is no hard-wired, innate structure to primate societies. And of course it is all done without words and normally without material culture.

The alternative is a top-down view of society. Here institutions precede the actors. You are born into a society. You inherit its culture. You act out your life according to rules determined collectively and somehow existing outside of human action. The institutions of the state, the law, business and education continue, unlike you and I who are their temporary stewards. The system therefore *seems* to be more important than the individual, as Flannery explained above.

INSTITUTIONS AND SOCIAL ARCHAEOLOGY

In practice, both bottom-up and top-down approaches must be considered. We may negotiate what sort of society we want, but we do not have a completely free hand. Karl Marx pointed that out. Individuals are part of wider groupings and those institutions do carry on, many of them beyond the lifespan of an individual. It is this reciprocal relationship, the give and take of social life at the micro- (individual) and macro- (society) scale that needs to be appreciated (Figure 4.2).

The dominant model in social archaeology has emphasised the top-down, institutional approach. Examples would include Renfrew's early state modules (1977), equal polities locked together in competition for prestige. Closely allied are the chiefdoms of the neo-evolutionists, who use their checklists of attributes to distinguish them from states and tribes (Kirch 1984). Then there is the 'institution' of hunting and gathering, which is treated as being different in essence from farming or horticulture (Service 1966). Finally, there is the condition of being a modern human as opposed to a Neanderthal or any other of the myriad early hominins (Stringer and Gamble 1993).

Such top-down models have been very useful in pointing archaeology towards big questions (Chapter 7), because they exploit the dimensions of time and space to discover repeated regularities that then need explanation.

However, the bottom-up and top-down approaches must work together (as shown in Figure 4.2), and so long as it is recognised that only a matter of emphasis privileges one over the other, the situation is tenable. More importantly, the contrast between the individual and the institution is important to an anthropological archaeology. The distinction raises the question: how do we think society works? Without such a model we can hardly expect to get at those people who are the core of archaeological enquiry.

AGENCY: AN ALTERNATIVE THOUGHT

This contrast is important for archaeologists because it returns us to questions regarding the units of analysis and contexts that might allow us to explain change. Let me make a suggestion.

The individual may be a red herring. In fact if we are not careful the individual may only be a small institution, filled with essences (like free will) and attributes (such as the right to bear arms) that we believe are, or at least should be, universal. If that is the case, then we need to avoid putting the individual forward as another ideal type or cipher. Rather than make a checklist of those attributes we feel belong to the individual, it helps to follow the social theorists and attribute individuals with agency, the ability to act (Dobres 2000; Dobres and Robb 2000). With agency comes that all-important capacity for involvement. If that did not exist, then there would be nothing to talk about. Therefore agency can be universal without being one of those unhelpful essences. A historical discipline like archaeology can use a universal property like that.

NETWORKS

Network analysis provides another pointer to help us round the conceptual problem of society. As Charles Orser argued (1999: 280) in his discussion of the components of modern-world archaeology (Box 1), network relations between groups and individuals define humanity in a much more satisfying manner than our often vague notions of culture. Moreover, it is more immediately applicable to the archaeological record.

Individuals – both human and primate – are all concerned with building social networks. These change throughout our lifetime, for example as we pass from childhood to adulthood. By old age we might have created huge webs of interaction based on many connecting ties involving such activities as politics and economics as well as the use of various symbolic codes and the construction of gender. Not surprisingly, therefore, we vary enormously in our skill to build and maintain networks. Network size and the types of relationship they contain differ from person to person.

One way to understand this variation is through a consideration of the three resources available to construct your social networks – emotional, material and symbolic. Network analysis shows that most of us use emotional networks to build small, intense and long-lasting networks of between three and seven members. The use of material resources expands that number to about 20, while using symbolic resources – sending someone a card as a token of acquaintanceship or friendship – can extend the number of such ties to over 500. You can check this out from your own experience. Count up the names in your address book on your mobile phone. Then divide them up in terms of how often and for how long you call them. Then ask yourself how many of the names get a Christmas card. You will see that the groups you have made fit the model of an intimate, effective and extended network which you build, negotiate and maintain. Welcome to your very own bottom-up society.

The explanation of why we can identify three major but overlapping networks could be given to us by any baboon: it is largely a matter of time. Baboons are limited in the amount of time they can spend per day grooming each other. Too much and they die happy but very hungry – so too with us. Therefore the number of other baboons they can groom into their intimate network is limited by the very means that makes it such a powerful bond. Emotional resources are expensive, concentrated and exhausting. Maintaining 500 ties at a highly emotional pitch would wear us all down very quickly. So we have devised other ways to perform socially, to engage with that number of people – to construct action and make it predictable. Material resources: food, marriage partners, raw materials and so on are one means. Symbolic resources, that elision between style and social technology, provide an even more plastic and extensive mechanism (Gamble 1998).

Networks are relevant to the archaeological record because they vary enormously in terms of size and scale from person to person. Potentially networks flow in all directions and could go on for ever. The trick, then, is to discover how we cut networks down to size. According to anthropologist Marilyn Strathern (1996), the answer is through transactions, which can of course be of material and symbolic kinds.

The existence of limits does not imply that, once negotiated, networks are fixed for all time. We can – and constantly do – change the members of our networks, promoting some, divorcing others. Very little of this is based on genetics, and almost all of it on action and involvement. The result is that we all construct overlapping social fields. These are defined not by institutions but by the web of networks we spin and which in turn spin us.

BACK TO ESSENCE

You might argue that this notion of networks is just a vague universal function supported by a large dollop of essence. After all, what is a relationship if not the essence of something we express as friendship, love, altruism, hate and indifference? This is partly true. Networks are only useful in exposing the flows of action in society. What, to my mind, overcomes the problem of essence and universalism is the sheer variety of experience that the formal structure of a network, rather than just a loose blanket term like 'society', allows us to encompass. Without variation, as Darwin pointed out, there can be no change. If individuals and populations were identical there would be nothing for natural selection to get to work on and no people to get at. Networks tell us what we know but have difficulty expressing: that our social powers are limited though we strive to overcome them.

WHAT CAN WE KNOW?

The second of those three big questions about how archaeologists can approach individuals in the past is basically about where ideas come from. These ideas are what make our archaeological imagination tick, and to answer it we need to examine the issue of analogy. This will involve a brief examination of some of the pitfalls that surround its use.

Many of these problems are so fundamental that to many people's minds they create limits to inference – boundaries to archaeological knowledge about people. As a result, as Alison Wylie (1985: 101) has pointed out, many archaeologists have a 'chronic ambivalence' to using and developing appropriate analogies.

ANALOGY

Analogy is basically about using the present to interpret the past. The first step is to identify a similarity between two entities. For example, these could be artefact styles, site layouts or settlement systems within a region. The similarity is then measured in space and time. I would call this a process of *pattern recognition* that is only possible from a knowledge of the data and a sense of the problem (Chapter 6).

The next step is to infer the relationship. That can be deceptively easy. I notice that the first domestic plants and animals in Mesoamerica and Mesopotamia coincide with the expansion of villages in both regions. I infer a common process of population pressure on resources to account for the intensification of subsistence in the first place and the continued growth of settlement size once turkeys and sheep, maize and wheat are available.

So far so good. That analogy seems reasonable based on a supposition, believed to be universal, that population pressure is inevitable and will only result in growth if carrying capacity can be boosted. The backing for such an inference stems from the way in which we consider the world to work.

The problem comes when you are asked to justify that inference. Why should the past run according to the same processes as the present? Should the past be interpreted in the light of the present simply because we can measure some similarity between the two (Hodder 1991: 148)?

ETHNOGRAPHIC ANALOGY

This highlights a pitfall to which many have succumbed because of an injudicious use of ethnographic analogy. The misuse of the ethnographic parallel is something for which the founding fathers of the discipline have never been forgiven. Wilson (1862) and Lubbock (1865) illustrated their works on prehistory by drawing parallels with the customs and morals of modern peoples. The lesson they drew was a living archaeology, where examples of the European Neolithic could still be found in the nineteenth century Pacific or among the Native peoples of the United States.

The most famous example was published in 1911 by an Oxford professor of geology, W. J. Sollas. His book *Ancient Hunters and Their Modern Representatives* illustrated the three stages of the Palaeolithic (Old Stone Age) by using the Tasmanians as living examples of the Lower Palaeolithic, the Australian Aborigines as the Middle Palaeolithic and the Bushmen (San) and Eskimo (Inuit) combined as the Upper Palaeolithic. For Sollas the superficial similarity of the stone tools made and used in each group was enough to draw the analogy. His inference was no doubt based on a ladder of progress where the simpler your technology the lower down the evolutionary scale you belong.

You might have thought that the reaction to such rampantly progressive schemes would have been total. They do live on, however benignly they are now presented, in neo-evolutionary models (e.g. Johnson and Earle 1987). Here simple and complex hunters are arranged in ascending order of their distance from the 'goal' of becoming an agricultural society. The Tasmanians serve as examples of those near the bottom of this scale, and the Inuit of those near the top (Keeley 1988; Woodburn 1991).

ETHNOGRAPHY WITH A SHOVEL

Ethnographic analogy cannot provide insights unless the relationships that are implied by the similarity are thoroughly understood.

Robert Ascher tried to narrow the field by limiting analogies to cultures that manipulate similar environments in similar ways (1961: 319). However, this was still too broad for new archaeologists, particularly Binford, who were rightly concerned about the subtle power of analogy to simply recreate the past in the shape of the present. If this happened, then there would be no independent place for archaeology. The past would be what we said it was, justified by what went on in the present.

If broad categories such as habitat and economy were to be used, then the reasons why they produced similar cultural responses had to be understood rather than assumed. The fact that the temperature was the same in a modern and an archaeological situation did not by itself justify the use of an analogy. The best warning of this pitfall came from Martin Wobst (1978). He coined the phrase 'ethnography with a shovel' to warn us against the problem and advised us to backfill the pit before we fell into it. He was very clear about what we were throwing away if we continued to wield the ethnographic shovel, and this is the opportunity to examine data on human behaviour in all its many dimensions, people, space and time – from single individuals in private to the largest groupings, from the smallest catchment area to continent-wide spatial distributions, and from single events to millennia.

ETHNOGRAPHIC CLUES

But once aware of the dangers we can also be aware of the importance of ethnographic analogy for our archaeological imagination. Gordon Childe pointed the way:

> Ethnographic parallels in fact afford only clues in what direction to look for an explanation in the archaeological record itself.
>
> (1956a: 49)

This is how I interpret Ascher's approach. It was also the guiding principle that sent Binford on a learning experience to work with the Nunamiut in northern Alaska. From this came his exercise in building middle-range theory (Binford 1978a) (see Chapter 3 and Boxes 7 and 14).

We would of course be unwise to ignore ethnography and the variability and action it can give us insights into just because of some inappropriate uses (for a full discussion see Wylie 2002). What we have to remember is that the ethnographic variation we can see today is only a tiny fraction of all that has gone before. This includes the material objects. It also includes the structure of relationships and society. This was a point the new archaeologists were very clear on: the end product of archaeology was not interpretations or even syntheses of interpretations, but rather generalisations concerning how cultural systems operated and why they evolved. As Binford observed (1972a: 49), you will never find this out by observing the present. Ethnography suggests ways of thinking, not the answers to such questions.

DIRECT HISTORICAL ANALOGY

There has always been a division between the use of analogy in the prehistoric and historic periods. Ascher (1961: 319), and many others, pointed to the comparative logical ease of drawing analogies when the time gap is short and space, in the form of common geography, is constant. As soon as these gaps widen, as they must in prehistory, the job of the archaeologist changes. The key word in applying direct historical analogies is continuity. Where prehistory grades into recorded history or ethnography, as in the pueblos of the Southwestern United States or among the Australian Aborigines or from the British Iron Age to Roman occupation, then, according to Ascher, interpretation proceeds by analogy to living or historically recorded groups.

Christopher Hawkes (1954) had previously gone much further. He identified two modes of thinking that he believed strongly conditioned archaeological interpretation of time periods for which texts were available. These were the *distinctness* and *proximity* of the recorded history to the prehistoric world (1954: 159). Hawkes was an expert on the pre-Roman British Iron Age, which explains his interest in ascertaining how the few lines about the British in Julius Caesar's *Gallic Wars* could help in the interpretation of hill forts, burials and tribal boundaries. In this instance distinctness is well attested by the contacts between Julius Caesar and the British when he invaded for a few weeks in August 55 BC and a couple of months in 54 BC. By invading and jotting down a few notes for the benefit of those in Rome the proximity factor is catered for in a direct historical analogy.

Never underestimate the power of text, especially for the culture historian. Take one example, Strabo's throwaway comment that preconquest Britain produced much grain and hunting dogs for export. Notwithstanding that we do not know which part of this large island he was referring to or the quantities involved, this line has been used to summarise all of British agricultural production before the Romans arrived. On the other side of the scales, the analysis of several million animal bones and thousands of carbonised grains from many archaeological excavations seem to count for nothing. All this confirms is the primacy that some archaeologists traditionally give to the authority of the written word, a curious view that the past becomes interesting only when put down on paper.

HAWKES' ONION

'Archaeological theory and method: some suggestions from the old world' is often held up to indicate how difficult some inferences are for archaeologists. His ladder of inference, as it is usually called, is

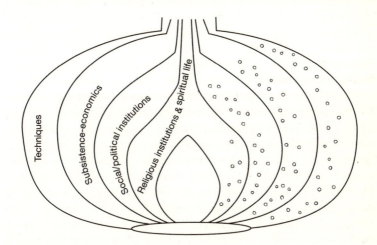

Figure 4.3 Hawkes' onion. The layers of archaeological inference.

really better described by the analogy of peeling an onion with four skins (Figure 4.3).

For Hawkes, inference became progressively more difficult as he peeled from skin one through to skin four. The core of his concern lay with the relative difficulty of inferring activity in the absence of texts. Each peel brings tears to your eyes as you realise what has been lost because it wasn't written down. Getting at religion was the hardest of all, unless aided by texts that keyed you into the minds and beliefs of the people who built the temple and buried their dead.

And then just when you think the worst is all over and you can put your handkerchief away you reach the heart of the inferential onion. The move from techniques to spiritual life represents to Hawkes the move from the animal to the human. Therefore our real object of study – people – is the most difficult. As Hawkes put it 'the more human, the less intelligible' (1954: 192).

These limits to inference have been very influential. Hawkes' onion has been peeled many times and his ladder propped against many theoretical walls. The limits he identified confirmed the primacy of text-aided archaeology. They still confirm to many culture historians their belief that processual and interpretive approaches are just speculation unfettered by analogy and therefore best not attempted. Having dug the ditch around their onion fields they could return to collecting and describing data.

OBJECTS, ESSENCE AND INFERENCE

The big problem with Hawkes' onion was that it accepted only one source of authority for interpreting all his skins of activity contained in archaeological evidence. These were texts. To a much lesser extent the environment and ethnography could provide analogies for his first two skins, but this just confirmed to a classical scholar why the study of hunters and gatherers was best left to others. In the absence of direct historical analogies (an impossibility for the Palaeolithic of even 20,000 years ago), could the inhabitants of the Palaeolithic world ever be brought into the human fold? As a result, Hawkes' ladder of inference was also the familiar ladder of progress. The creation of texts tipped you into being human because only texts allowed us to get to the heart of the matter and deal with the most human bits of being human.

I would counter this by returning to our earlier discussion of essences (Chapter 1). For many culture historians, especially those nestling close in time to recorded history, texts have the power to animate. What they breathe life into is by definition human; its human essence being defined by those very same attributes and properties contained in the texts. They have an authority like a magic wand, transforming everything they touch.

The same could be said of the organisational system that formed the framework for the processualists. These had essences such as self-regulation and cyclical patterning.

While abandoning the authority of texts in order to peel the onion, the mistake they made was to trust so blindly in the universal qualities of science. Generalisation allowed processualists to abandon such notions as distinctness and proximity and to argue instead for repeated basic functions of the system. Patterning, they argued, was so strong that it must refer to repeated solutions governed by understandable processes of adaptation and change. This is the line that some neo-Darwinian approaches have continued to take, underpinned by the biological structure of change and variation.

PICKLING THE ONION

I believe that the answer to the difficulty of analogy is to recognise that this is an onion that has passed its sell-by date. What is at fault is the very idea of layers of human activity or subsystems within an overall systemic structure. Instead the social is bound up with the technical, just as the religious is part of subsistence. It may be an analytical convenience to divide up human action in this manner, but not if all it does is to close off large chunks of the past to interpretation. So, don't peel the onion. Either eat it whole or pickle it in a jar labelled 'history of the subject'. I think you will find that the limits to inference suggested by this analogy will then become less of a problem.

THE ANALOGY OF CHAINS AND CABLES APPLIED TO EXPLANATION

Onions and ladders are only two of the analogies used to help us understand how we infer and explain human action from archaeological remains. The process is also commonly described as forging links in a chain of logic (Figure 4.4). The strength of the link is usually based on a scientific approach to hypothesis testing and one where the method of deduction (see Box 16) is often preferred.

However, methods and explanation do not necessarily need an explicitly scientific framework, particularly if we now accept that the archaeological record is much more complicated than we once thought (Chapter 3). Part of this complication is the problem of biased survival, but more important is the question of how the archaeological record preserves human action. If these issues remain unresolved within the subject (Patrik 1985), then just how appropriate are scientific methods for their investigation?

Is there an alternative? In particular, can we capitalise on the combined insights of the traditions and approaches beneath the archaeological umbrella (Figure 2.1) and by entwining them produce greater strength in our methods and explanation?

I think we can. The integration of these approaches in order to enhance our archaeological imagination is a very positive development, described by Alison Wylie (1993: 24) as a cabling, or tacking, exercise. The way we construct theory in archaeology cannot mimic the links in a well-forged chain, where each link is logically joined to the next by the strength of the hypotheses we are testing (Figure 4.4). Instead, we build theory in a historical discipline such as archaeology by spinning many-stranded cables. This way we do not have cast-iron links but rather more flexible explanatory structures that depend for their strength on many frames of reference rather than just one.

Figure 4.4 Links and cables: two approaches to building explanations.

Tacking is another way to describe the process, and at the same time retain the nautical analogy. The analogy is with a yacht tacking into the wind; between problems and theories, data and interpretation (see also Figure 7.2). The result is very much the same: a many-stranded cable of explanation. The concept of tacking also acknowledges the spatial- and time-scales with which we deal as we infer action from our inert data. We tack from immediate, small-scale, individual actions such as eating or making stone tools, which might have taken minutes, to the layers in which they are contained, which might represent 1000 years and 10,000 people. At the same time we are often tacking between the individual and the group and between the site and the region. Recognising that this flexibility is entirely positive, and how we compensate for variation in the quality and quantity of our information, allows us to steer a course through the rocks of the archaeological record.

HOW DO WE KNOW?

My third and final question about finding individuals in the archaeological record brings us back to basics. With some of the approaches discussed above we might have begun to drift away from the notion of archaeology being about people but concerned only with objects. Somehow we have to return to that rich texture of ethnographic variability that the processualists wanted to locate in the archaeological record. Contextual archaeology might provide this, as described by Ian Hodder:

> Without the general theories there would be few questions asked of the past and fewer answers given. Without a contextual approach, the present and the past become reduced to an assumed sameness.
>
> (1991: 149)

TWO DETECTIVES

Hodder's point is so basic to the future development of archaeology that I will illustrate it further with my own analogy: archaeologists are often likened to Sherlock Holmes, the master of induction and deduction (Box 16).

No clue is too small or insignificant for the trained observer to see how it leads to an inescapable conclusion. To Holmes the mud on the boot of one of his visitors to 221B Baker Street is a guide to his or her travels around London. His cursory inspection of trusty Watson's family watch is an opportunity to diagnose that his brother, now dead, was an alcoholic. Holmes has a fine archaeological imagination and an ability to tease out the underlying system from a detached description of the facts, rather like someone watching a play.

BOX 16 THREE APPROACHES TO BUILDING THEORY.

Induction: a generalising approach to understanding the world based on a number of specific observations. *Bronze* metallurgy always precedes iron. This statement could of course be contradicted by new discoveries.

Deduction: a truth-preserving approach that begins with a premise which, if correct, must mean that the conclusion is also true. *Bronze* metallurgy is a less complicated process *and* this is why it always precedes iron. Complex is a difficult premise. It could well be redefined as the wider notion of progress is rethought. It could be falsified by replication that showed that in fact bronze metallurgy was the more complicated process. In both cases it would lose its ring of truth and fresh deduction would be needed.

Abduction: the construction of theory. The leap of faith from the data to the theory that explains it. Bronze Age artefacts embody the principle of *individualism* over collective social action. Such leaps of faith have a short half-life but move the subject onwards much faster than induction and deduction.

Contrast Holmes with another detective in another continent and another city, Philip Marlowe. Not for him a seat in the stalls – more a view from backstage, if not the backstreets. Stuck in his empty office with a large bluebottle, he ignores the clues to trouble sitting in front of him when Orfamy Quest (the perfect name, I always think, for an archaeological project) comes to hire him. The reason is that Marlowe is not detached from the world, he is fully involved in it. Through his involvement he has a moral sense which acts as his guide in unnavigated waters. Marlowe, if he thought about it at all (which he doesn't), has an abductive approach to problem solving. His leaps of faith are not based on probability and that sense that night will always follow day. Rather they are based on an understanding of how people work – that curious co-ordination in collective human action which works because of some implicit contract that exists between us. This allows us to guess what other people will do and – most of the time – get it right. The alternative, working it out step by step every time we encounter someone, does not bear thinking about unless we have the brainpower of a Holmes.

Furthermore, Holmes starts with an inductive model of how the world works. He knows intuitively what the system should be because he is by his class and upbringing the product of a top-down approach. Marlowe, by contrast, is very often in the gutter because he didn't see the sap coming. There is only one way for him and that's up. Both are successful even though their methods are so different.

Holmes represents the general system. It is significant that his exploits are related to us through the eyes of another, Watson. The observer, observing the great detective. In contrast, Marlowe stands for the contextual richness of lived-in experience that he passes on to us in the first person.

As an archaeologist you basically decide what type of detective you want to be. But if you are sensible, as Hodder indicates, you learn from both. 'Am I right, or am I right?', as the singing detective, who shares a name with Raymond Chandler's hero, once sang.

FROM THE PRESENT TO THE PAST

If Marlowe and Holmes had become archaeologists these differences would probably have surfaced in the way they made use of the present to study the past. Holmes would have been in his deductive element proceeding from the known to the unknown by carefully researched steps. The remains of the past are static. Reconstruction of the behaviour that produced them and the variation in time and space they possess requires some careful inferential steps. These are steps to the archaeological imagination that we need to make explicit.

THE PRINCIPLE OF UNIFORMITARIANISM

Such an approach recognises two main procedures. The first is the principle of uniformitarianism, long recognised by geologists, where the key to the past is contained in the processes we can observe in the present. The processes of tectonics, weathering and sedimentation are assumed to be uniform between the present and the past. The laws of physics, chemistry and geology remain the same. Explanation is to be sought in the repeated workings of these processes to explain drifting continents, mountain building, ice ages and all the varied landforms studied by the geologist.

Uniformitarianism has also been applied to the historical sciences, including archaeology. The principle has been most successful when dealing with absolute limiting factors such as the need to eat and reproduce. Failure to do either results in no archaeology, as Eric Higgs pointed out to me when I was an undergraduate in the 1970s. The application of models developed in evolutionary ecology that recognise the selective imperative of reproductive success provide an example of the principle in action (Bettinger 1991; Kelly 1995). By contrast, uniformitarian assumptions about the details of ritual or social life soon start cracking like a bad analogy.

LIVING ARCHAEOLOGY

Actualistic studies provide insights into the complexity of living systems (David and Kramer 2001). These may be ethnoarchaeological studies examining boundaries, the use of technology, patterns of mobility or the arrangement of settlements. Termed 'living archaeology' by Richard Gould (1980), they have transformed our understanding of those societies most unfamiliar to Western city dwellers, those of hunters and gatherers. In Binford's (1978a) classic study of the Nunamiut people of northern Alaska he revealed the complexity of the decision making processes involved when it comes to even a small group of people tracking, killing, processing, transporting and consuming their staple food: caribou/reindeer. More than any other work this study confounded the idea that hunters and gatherers are simple and easily explained by common sense.

Archaeologists have also studied how other species exploit their environments and interact with each other (Box 13), and Binford has once again been instrumental in such work (Binford 1981a). Attention has focused on those species that create their own archaeological record in the form of bone accumulations in caves and under overhangs. These include hyenas, leopards, wolves, porcupines and owls, and once again the interest has been in earliest prehistory, where such studies have unravelled the various agencies that contributed to a bone deposit (Brain 1981; Stiner 1994). Very often it has been found that the human component of these Pleistocene sites is comparatively small. In much of Europe, for example, glacial climates produced both rich grazing conditions but also severe penalties for failure. In many regions in this continent we find that the dominant species, as revealed by the consistent accumulation of bones in caves, were hyenas rather than humans (Gamble 1986). This discovery should not be regarded as wasted effort. It was Binford's insight that by learning about carnivores in the present we could sharpen our observations about the people we really wanted to study. Recognising the competitive relations between carnivores and humans is one route to describing more accurately the capabilities of early hominids such as the Neanderthals.

READING THE RECORD RIGHT

But what sort of data do we want, ideally? The problem is that, generally speaking, ethnoarchaeology and living archaeology seek to understand the system. They search for systems rather than individuals. For some, this colours the way they interpret the archaeological record and the people it contains. In his critique of Schiffer's formation processes, Binford (1981b) returned to a comment by Robert Ascher:

> In a certain sense a part of every community is becoming, but is not yet, archaeological data. The community becomes archaeological data when replacement ceases. What the archaeologist disturbs is not the remains of a once living community, stopped as it were, at a point in time; what he does interrupt is the process of decomposition.
>
> (Ascher 1961: 324)

Archaeologists who thought they were obtaining a snapshot of the past, like watching a shark swim past the glass window in an aquarium, were guilty of what Ascher called the 'Pompeii-premise'. Human history is not arrested and preserved in the archaeological record like a giant jar of pickled herrings. Neither should we necessarily try to strip away the taphonomic overprint from our samples, to remove all those hyena-chewed bones and owl-introduced rodents. Diane Gifford (1981) pointed out that to do so would in fact remove information. We learn about the selective forces on humans by seeing the full constellation of agents with which they were involved. The record is not blurred by these other agents but rather put in context.

To understand what we have in the archaeological record we need another analogy. To rework Ascher's words, the archaeological record is constantly in the process of becoming. There is no single point of view. A better analogy would be the multiple drafts of a book on a word processor. As I know only too well, there is a timeline to their production. There is a history to their development. They only become fixed – that is, published – when, as Ascher pointed out, replacement finally ceases. This is also the case with the archaeological record. Each new field project expands and changes our understanding of it. Every new analysis and synthesis alters what we thought we knew. The archaeological record is about the most unfixed thing I know. And even as I write that, it has changed.

WHO DID WE MEET?

Studying the people of the past will always need more than digging. Here I have examined some of the terms that are bandied about, and contrasted various positions such as group and individual, networks and systems, analogy and inference. The two fictional detectives Holmes and Marlowe, like the contrasted rational and relational viewpoints on what is social, remind us that there is always an alternative way to crack a case. What I have identified here is that we need to adopt an anthropological approach to the task of studying people. This does not necessarily mean that the key lies in more ethnoarchaeology. What we need to consider instead are the questions we want to ask and the approach to change that we take. This will be examined in Chapter 7. We also need to return identity to these people, whether it is as individuals, groups or nations, and this will be my task in Chapter 8.

Archaeology as anthropology has been with us in several guises for about 40 years. It has proved an immensely productive way of investigating the past and has fostered the development of several alternative approaches. It transformed and broadened the archaeological imagination. New questions were devised and methods developed to answer them. This is an ongoing process and replacement has not yet ceased. However, as we will now see as we turn to objects and material culture, the approaches can be as different as a deer-stalker and a trilby hat.

SUMMARY

- What you study, individuals or groups, depends upon the questions being asked and the initial standpoint being taken.
- There is no single model of society for the archaeologist to follow.
- Bottom-up and top-down, relational and rational approaches offer insights into the workings of personhood and social life; but don't expect them to be compatible.
- Analogy is central to knowing anything in archaeology, but aim to spin strong cables rather than rely on links in a chain of reasoning.

5

OBJECTS

We have now seen that there is nothing self-evident about the past. The enterprise of archaeology is not simply confined to the things of the past but, more importantly, deals with questions, approach and interpretation. Archaeological debates and disagreements are not just about the dates of this pot and that city, but are far more fundamental. They concern approaches to gaining knowledge about human action in the past, which in turn produce expectations about what is known, and can be known, of activities in the past. Because such activity is invisible, objects are crucial to all our debates. The way we investigate and interpret objects is therefore important and I will now explore these issues.

OBJECTS AND THE ARCHAEOLOGICAL IMAGINATION

In Chapter 1 I introduced Julian Thomas' concept of the archaeological imagination – the aspect of our everyday lives that makes the investigation of the past possible. The simple example he gives is of finding crumbs in a cake tin (1996: 63). From this we can infer not only that once there was cake, and even what sort of cake it was, but also that someone, or something, has been there before us. The only alternative is that the cake was beamed-up onto a passing spacecraft, which requires an imagination that is definitely not archaeological!

MATERIAL CULTURE

Thomas' cake tin is an example of material culture, which can be defined as the objects, environments and worlds with which we interact and that surround us. The world we are born into is very much a material one that shapes and creates us. We will also contribute to it in our turn, by creatively adding, arranging and subtracting elements within it. And that is the point: we are both created by and creators of material culture. As Randall McGuire puts it:

> material culture not only exists in a context, but it also helps form that context. It is not just backdrop; it is instead the stage and props for human action.
>
> (1992: 104)

Neither is there any reason to suppose that this relationship has not been going on for a very long time. As a result these objects, this material culture, has a history. That cake tin endures. It began life as part of a *production* process. It might change *function* and become a box in which to store your photographic memories. Its *context* of use might also alter as it moves from the kitchen to the living room. It might be *exchanged* for another object as an act of *consumption*. It could *transform* into an heirloom and then become an antique, its value judged by attributes other than function alone. It still remains a tin box but now it supports a raft of possible social relationships and activities. The crumbs it contained, and the activity of eating that we infer took place are less important than its history and its personality.

The key words of production, function, context, exchange, consumption and transformation will be examined later in this chapter (The Biography of Objects). For the moment, notice that when treated separately these words sum up our common-sense attitude to material culture – 'It must mean or do something, other-wise what's the point?' Individually, these words represent our usual approach of conceptually breaking down the object we are studying into discrete parts and analysing them separately before the mental task of re-assembly takes place and conclusions are drawn. In this sense the process resembles the much larger project of systems analysis (Figure 2.2), where whole societies were reduced to their component subsystems. While this proved a useful device to tackle a complex problem, somehow Humpty-Dumpty never quite got stuck back together again.

Archaeologists are not alone in breaking eggs and scrambling the result. Many other disciplines are also object- rather than solely text-centred. They also employ similar customary definitions to analyse their objects, as provided here by a distinguished art historian:

> Material culture is just what it says it is – namely, the manifestations of culture through material productions.
>
> (Prown 1993: 1)

The goal, he goes on, is to uncover the thoughts and beliefs in peoples' heads. Why did they make a teapot with a short rather than a long spout? In silver rather than china? Plain brown instead of covered in flowers?

Now this is only one view of material culture and, as we saw in the last chapter, a rather traditional one. It attempts to explain culture *by* culture. The shape of the things we make (material culture) is to be explained by the shape of the beliefs (cultural norms) that we all have in our heads, and share, so long as we come from the same culture.

MENTAL TEMPLATES

These norms are the mental templates that Binford criticised so effectively in the 1960s' new archaeology (Chapter 2), and the paradigm whereby culture is shared represents the normative view. Thirty years later Binford might have used a computer metaphor to beat them with, perhaps describing culture as hard-wired into the brain. Certainly the French archaeologist François Bordes, with whom (as was mentioned in Chapter 3) Binford debated the meaning of variation in stone-tool assemblages made by Neanderthals more than 40,000 years ago, would have argued in this way. For Bordes, cultural choice was ingrained, non-negotiable (1950: 419; 1973): the classic view of the culture historian. For Binford, culture was our adaptive process of survival (Binford and Binford 1966; Binford 1973). It was therefore under selection and would vary as environmental conditions, rather than minds, changed. Cultures varied not because people shared similar cultural values and expressed these in terms of material culture, but because people participated in culture in different ways. Culture, as the principal means of human adaptation, was not spread evenly over the geographical range covered by either a person or a group. Ecological circumstances resulted in local variation as different survival responses were made in different places and at different times.

INTERPRETING ARTEFACTS

In Chapter 3 I reviewed the basic entities, the building blocks, that archaeologists use to identify repeated patterns in the data. Now we can begin the task of interpreting such regularities in time, space and form. But remember, these patterns are theory-laden from the first.

ARTEFACT CLASSES

Processual archaeologists have recognised three behavioural realms that artefacts participate in. These are:

- material – artefacts coping with the environment;
- social – artefacts dealing with social organisation;
- ideational – artefacts that address ideas, values and belief systems.

Binford originally referred to these as technomic, sociotechnic and ideotechnic artefacts respectively, and stressed how they primarily functioned in different contexts (Binford 1962: 23–25). In fact all artefacts cross-cut these three realms of behaviour, though they may appear to play a more significant role in some than others. Take, for example, the crown a monarch wears. It is possible to interpret this object in all three classes. Technomically it is a hat that keeps the head warm or, depending on design, it might equally make a protective crash helmet for a cyclist. Sociotechnically it is also an item of display which communicates information about status and rank. Furthermore, how it is displayed, on the head, acts to privilege the 'head' of state above the 'body' politic. Ideotechnically the crown is a symbol of the abstract concept of monarchy and the rites and duties of allegiance and obedience owed to it.

Partly in recognition of this ability of artefacts to blur the distinctions between realms of behaviour, James Sackett later reduced the three classes to two (1982: 70). These are the *utilitarian*, which include tools and weapons in the material realm, and *non-utilitarian*, such as ritual paraphernalia and artwork, which are suspected to have expressed social relationships and beliefs. Both of these classes are therefore implied to have functions.

ARTEFACTS AND MEANING

The phrase 'symbols in action', which was also the title of Hodder's ethnoarchaeological study of culture (1982), neatly summarises the emphasis attached to objects by a post-processual, interpretive approach. Hodder's great complaint is against imposing universal functions on artefacts just because they look the same. Hence a teapot or a crown, a lamb or a tiger may have very different functions in very different settings.

However, Hodder readily admits that some functional meanings are inescapable. Hammers are intended to pound and doors to shut. But these are regarded as trivial, 'So what?' meanings. Instead, artefacts escape from the mundane to become symbols in action in specific historical contexts. The density of meanings contained either in a medieval city street or in the contents of a rubbish pit are so great as to defy universal description and comparison, one street with another, pit by pit, layer with layer has become an immense, and some would say, unproductive task. Furthermore, universal meanings quickly run into the cul-de-sac of the single interpretation (Box 9).

Hodder's original solution for the material culture in the archaeological record was to treat it more like a 'text' waiting to be read (1991: 125). The dual concept of 'text' and the double hermeneutic, backed by Giddens' notion that we have a dual position in the world (1984), were designed for each other (Box 9). Moreover, from this perspective the reading that takes place depends on data, not theory. The more data, the better, for such a contextual approach.

But there is a contradiction here. On the one hand, Hodder is highly critical of universal functions being attributed to artefacts and vociferous against universal measuring devices as proposed by middle-range theory and its links between statics and dynamics (Chapter 3). But while insisting on the importance of examining specific contexts on their own merits (1991), he nonetheless remains entirely happy with universal principles of meaning as contained in notions such as the *habitus* and power (Chapter 8).

ARTEFACTS WITH PERSONALITIES

However, we can move on from these normative processual and post-processual statements, and a lead is given by Marxist and feminist approaches. Once again I return to Thomas' idea of the archaeological imagination. It is because we interact with the material world today that we have an in-built appreciation of how objects and people interacted in the past. We do not have the people. They are long gone. But we do have the artefacts, sites, monuments, landscapes and even worlds. These may only be partially recovered and much has been lost, but what remains is intelligible. Not by lifting that pot to your ear and listening. Nor by standing in a street in Pompeii and empathising what it must have been like to be a Roman citizen on the day before the volcano blew up, but through the understanding that comes from making, using, interpreting and interacting with objects on a daily basis. As anthropologist Daniel Miller has written:

> Artefacts are a means by which we give form to, and come to an understanding of, ourselves, others, or abstractions such as the nation or modern.
>
> (1994: 397)

Karl Marx made the point much earlier with his notion of objectification, the process by which objects and things become components of social relations (McGuire 1992: 103). This is a crucial point for an object-centred subject such as archaeology. It is also one that keeps being rediscovered. As Roberta Gilchrist (1993: 15) puts it, the great contribution of post-processual archaeology in the 1980s was to return to this position by reaffirming that material culture is *active* in social relations rather than just a *reflection* of society. She continues, 'material culture can be seen to construct, maintain, control and transform social identities and relations' (1993: 15). This is very different to Sackett's utilitarian and non-utilitarian classes, described above, or even Binford's three behavioural realms. Grasp this point and you will appreciate what some of the longstanding disagreements between different archaeological schools boil down to.

However, before we get too carried away, Hodder (1991: 69) makes the point that material culture, while a type of social reality, is not the only one. People may have 'love affairs' with Lamborghinis and talk to the cat as though it were a human member of the family, but what we cannot do is understand those relationships by just looking at the car and the cat. We have to interact with those artefacts and that is the problem that faces the archaeologist (see Chapter 3, The Archaeological Record). You and I can interact with artefacts when we visit rock-art sites; during excavations, when we carefully lift that Anglo-Saxon glass claw-beaker from the ground (and then view it on display in the British Museum), and by walking the streets of any city or monument-strewn landscape. But that is our experience and just the latest page in the biography of those artefacts as we interpret them. What remains hidden is their previous lives, supposedly the very subject matter of archaeology.

This raises two issues for the study of objects in the past: dualistic approaches and the archaeological concept of style.

DUALISMS

One problem that has dogged the study of material culture is the familiar dualism, or opposition, that separates out the constituent essences of objects. The most prevalent of these is the dualism between 'natural' and 'cultural' objects and you will be familiar with others such as subject and object, internal and external.

NATURE–CULTURE

In practice this dualism may seem straightforward. A railway engine is a cultural thing, while Australia's Great Barrier Reef is natural. In practice such oppositions only work in extreme cases –

which, being extreme, are of little value. Most distinctions are decidedly fuzzy. A domestic sheep is a cultural object even though it has the credentials to be considered a natural thing. A wild sheep may seem more natural, but if it is part of a hunter's world then it is also cultural because it is available for exploitation. And consider that most durable of natural things, stone. When nicely shaped into masonry and used to make cities it is cultural. But what about all the unmodified stone that makes up Neolithic tombs, serves as ballast in ships, or just litters the landscape as named rocks and places? Nothing we touch remains natural. Nature is what we say it is. It is an unhelpful concept, impossible to define.

SUBJECT–OBJECT AND THE CARTESIAN THEATRE

The division between subject and object is one of the foundations of Western analytical thought, usually traced back to the French philosopher and mathematician René Descartes (1596–1650). The division separates the world into inanimate (rocks) and non-sentient (sheep) things, and humans who are animate and sentient. It also divides a person into mind and body, thereby detaching thought from action. We become thinking machines, applying our subjective reason to the objects of the world. This conjures up the unlikely scenario, known as the Cartesian theatre, whereby your mind sits in the audience, analysing your body's performance on the stage. You may also find you are sitting next to Sherlock Holmes analysing a case (Chapter 4).

In terms of material culture what the subject–object dualism promotes is the separateness of things from people. The full inclusion of objects in our individual and collective worlds is denied. All that can be achieved is a single interpretation (Box 9), a one-way street to understanding.

INTERNAL–EXTERNAL AND THE ESSENCE OF THINGS

The last dualism I mentioned, internal–external, continues this division. When applied to objects, it proposes hidden meanings and different levels of understanding (Tilley 1993: 5). Traditionally it has placed limits on the inferences we feel safe in making about the past (Chapter 4). For example, it is supposed that an object like a teapot has an external appearance and a hidden internal essence. On the outside we can read the shape and form, the teapot's style (see below), as a functional thing. A teapot functions as a teapot – everyone knows that, even the Mad Hatter. The internal essence is, like the dormouse, harder to tease out because not everyone knows, or can be bothered to consider, that a teapot is also a symbol of global consumption – imperial ambitions expressed through production and exchange of an exotic crop – and a local way of life. Teapots can also trigger strong emotions, as Bill Bryson records in his travels (1995), when he discovered that the British can get genuinely excited about the prospect of a hot beverage. The eagerness for regularly consuming a tropical product was a result of colonialism related to the transformation of the world under capitalism. British workers now drank a hot mild stimulant to have the energy to stand at their looms (Mintz 1985). And all this inferred from a small pottery object.

STYLE

You cannot go far in your archaeological reading without coming across the concept of style. Very soon, however, you will wonder why something so basic has to be so complicated. Opinions are sometimes contrary and a marked lack of agreement exists about what style is and what, in fact, it does. Let me give you some examples (Box 17), in their proponents' own words, from the archaeologies we looked at in Chapter 2.

BOX 17 THE MANY FACES OF STYLE

CULTURE HISTORY

'A style is a norm.' (Hawkes 1954: 158)

'A highly specific and characteristic manner of doing something which by its very nature is peculiar to a specific time and place.' (Sackett 1982: 63)

'What do I mean by style? The configuration of a single object is its form. When groups of objects share formal characteristics, those resemblances or resonances constitute style ... When style is shared by clusters of objects in a time and place, it is akin to a cultural daydream expressing unspoken beliefs.' (Prown 1993: 4–5)

PROCESSUAL

'The working definition . . . equates style with that part of the formal variability in material culture that can be related to the participation of artefacts in processes of information exchange.' (Wobst 1977: 321)

'Formal variation in material culture that transmits information about personal and social identity.' (Wiessner 1983: 256)

'Style from a unified perspective [is] a means of non-verbal communication to negotiate identity.' (Wiessner 1990: 108)

INTERPRETIVE

'Style must concern structure as well as function.' (Hodder 1982: 205)

'Style is defined here as: "the referral of an individual event to a general way of doing".' (Hodder 1990b: 45)

'In order to understand style – more broadly, the meaning of material culture-patterning – we have to understand the social conditions of its production.' (Shanks and Tilley 1987b: 144)

'Style is a form of social rather than individual practice.' (Shanks and Tilley 1987b: 155)

'Style is not a characteristic of material culture, but is a result of a contemporary way of conceptualising material culture.' (Boast 1997: 174)

NEO-DARWINIAN

'Style denotes those forms that do not have detectable selective values. Function is manifest as those forms that directly affect the Darwinian fitness of the populations in which they occur.' (Dunnell 1978: 199)

Some common concepts emerge, indicating that there might be more common ground than at first meets the eye. These are 'similarity' and 'variation' in forms and types, the notions that were so skilfully exploited by Thomsen and Montelius. But as the few quotations show, there is much more disagreement in the definitions over the function, informational and individual, and social aspects of style.

Robin Boast sums up this confusion and points to its source:

I have not resolved the question of style because it is not resolvable. It is a social categorisation of the world, one among many, that grew out of a set of assumptions about how the world works. It exists as part of

our social and intellectual tradition, an 18th-century western tradition
that has become doctrine.

(1997: 191)

The doctrine that supports the archaeological concept of style is the
Cartesian separation of the world. Without dualisms such as
external–internal there is no place for style. As Boast also shows,
what stems from these divisions is the idea that objects have an
inherent social character. In other words there is a basic purpose to
things *before* they become social (Boast 1997: 174). We are back to
essentialism, which I highlighted as a basic concept of archaeology
in Chapter 1.

The problem we face is that such ways of thinking about the
world are so ingrained that we regard them as entirely reasonable and
natural. That's fine. But unless challenged, our archaeological imagination will never escape from its chains because they cannot be
seen. The reason why style is so complex is not only because we are
blind to the causes but also because the major approaches, as shown
in Box 17, cross-cut four different archaeologies, making simple
pigeon-holing difficult. Style is eclectic and so is its interpretation
and explanation. Let me now sketch the chains that bind.

ISOCHRESTIC AND ICONIC STYLE

Polly Wiessner (1990: 105) tries to unravel the spaghetti by pointing
out that you can't ask 'what is style?' without asking 'what is stylistic
behaviour?' This moves the issue away from definitions, where I
think everyone is agreed that there will be no general agreement, and
back to the all-important aspect of style as 'doing', as action. The
key question then is 'what is understood by such action?' Is this in
turn functional behaviour, being ethnic or a notion of human agency
(Chapter 4)? Adherents of the different approaches have all argued
their corner at length in order to answer the following question:

• How does the action of style, variously described, relate to artefacts
  and material culture generally?

The answers are numerous but dominated by the conclusion that
at its heart style is linked to identity and in particular to ethnic

identity (Chapter 8). This is of course what Childe (Chapter 3) played on in his famous definition (1929: v–vi) of an archaeological culture, recognised through repetition and similarity, and his translation of that entity into a people. James Sackett is very clear about the reasoning behind this equation when he accounts for similarity in style by intensity in social interaction. The most important aspect producing similarity is proximity in time and space (1982: 74).

Sackett has developed this concept of style further by asking where style resides in the formal variation of artefacts. Which elements of shape and form can be said to be the result of stylistic behaviour? To answer this question he has explored the choices open to anyone making and using artefacts. In many instances there are several, often many, ways to achieve the same end result. Think of the variation in styles of toothbrushes, screwdrivers, cars, books, houses and so on. Not all of this variation is dictated by functional requirements alone. So, according to Sackett, the artisan has a choice of equivalent alternatives for the finished product, each of which will still be able to brush teeth or drive down the motorway. He calls this an *isochrestic* approach to style, a word he coined and which means equivalent in use. This approach provides an answer to his question of where style resides in those pots and toothbrushes. Whenever isochrestic options exist, which is most of the time, then factors allied to ethnicity dictate the choices that are made in practice (1990: 33). Such choices may be based on habit – they are probably largely made unthinkingly in what might be simply termed tradition. In other frameworks they would be regarded as aspects of practical consciousness or *habitus* (Chapter 8).

Set beside these is Sackett's iconological approach to style, where choice is purposeful and style is consciously added-on (and therefore known as adjunct style) to reinforce identity. Designs are added to clothing, pots, bronzes and sculpture in order to make the point that 'we are who we *look* we are' as much as 'who we *say* we are'. Once again, in another interpretive framework this would be seen as a discursive, thinking process.

INFORMATION AND STYLE

Sackett is at pains to be clear that he is not providing a theory of style but only showing where it resides in the shape and design of artefacts. Wiessner and Martin Wobst are more explicit in their discussions of the role style plays in the visual exchange of information that turns out primarily to concern identity. Wobst's model (1977) was based on the principle that since information contributes to survival, then style, which expresses that information, will be under selection. Choice is therefore determined by transmitting messages efficiently and unambiguously so that social encounters generally pass off successfully. This is in marked contrast to Dunnell's view, quoted in Box 17, where style is presented as superfluous to Darwinian evolution. It is 'noise' rather than 'information' because it is not under selection.

Wiessner, using her ethnographic study of projectile points in the Kalahari, bases her explanation on the psychological benefits that accrue from belonging to social groups. She proposes two kinds of style: *assertive*, where individuals express their individuality and skills, and *emblemic*, where group identity is expressed. Both will be under selection from the social domain. Sackett regards approaches such as those of Wobst and Wiessner as stressing the *active* voice of style (1990: 36–37). Style does something; it has a function. It is an add-on, as in his iconological approach. By contrast, Sackett himself is a supporter of the *passive* voice of style. In this mode, signalling still takes place but it does so as a set of habitual isochrestic choices where ethnicity acts as the unseen selective force.

EXPANDING STYLE

The link between style and ethnicity satisfies some as an explanation. Among the interpretive archaeologists, however, ethnicity is too narrow a concept to account for style. Instead style connects all those social, political and ideological relations in different social and historical circumstances. It does not just refer to what we look like (Shanks and Tilley 1987b: 144). This aspect has been explored by Siân Jones (1997: 119) who, in contrast to Sackett and Wiessner, emphasises that all material culture is active in the process of creating those social relationships that we label ethnicity (see Chapter 8).

And this raises another very pertinent question:

- How big a concept is style? Is it more than the shapes of artefacts?

Sackett again provides an important lead (1990: 35). For him, style is not just the finished, hand-held artefact, the city plan or the landscape littered with tombs and monuments. The term must incorporate the choice of raw material, the techniques of production, the tradition of apprenticeship by which these are learned and what he calls the 'themes' – for example the standardisation, specialisation and efficiency – that guide all these choices. The latter may sound rather like shared norms, but it is his inclusive approach to the thoughts and actions involved as well as the objects that is important. In broadening this analysis he is also proposing a unified approach to style. Instead of making the distinction between style and function among artefacts that evolutionary archaeologists such as Dunnell insist upon as a basic dichotomy, Sackett brings them together; which is a view that most interpretive archaeologists would support.

CHAÎNE OPÉRATOIRE AND STYLE

It does appear, however, that this unification could have occurred much earlier. The French archaeologist André Leroi-Gourhan provided a theory of technical processes that achieved just that in 1966 when his book *Le geste et la parole* ('Gesture and speech'), appeared (Leroi-Gourhan 1993). His ideas came from a very different tradition of thinking about technology and style than his Anglo-Saxon contemporaries. His influence outside France remained limited while knowledge of his work was confined to his seminal analysis of cave art and excavation of well-preserved Palaeolithic hunting camps, until *Le geste et la parole* was translated in 1993.

Leroi-Gourhan's basic idea is that technical acts are at the same time social acts. Calling on the French anthropological tradition most closely associated with Marcel Mauss, he emphasised the importance of the human body as a source of meaning, power, symbol and of course action. He used the term *chaîne opératoire* (operational sequence) to examine how actions can, literally, speak louder than words.

LEARNING THROUGH THE BODY

A good way to illustrate Leroi-Gourhan's concept is to consider how we learn to make things. He would say that it is through attention to the gestures of manufacture and doing, for example watching potting, stone knapping, weaving, butchering animals, threshing grain, ploughing fields, and then trying it for ourselves. It is by seeing the body in action, imitating and copying these rhythmic gestures, that we learn to walk, eat, embrace and indicate moods. Much of this, Leroi-Gourhan pointed out in advance of either Bourdieu or Giddens (Box 9), was part of habitual, unconscious action. As put by Thomas (1996: 19), we don't 'live in' our bodies as those dualisms would suggest. Rather the body is an aspect of the self that we 'live through'.

Our life's everyday routines do not take up much of our conscious thought. The trick to learning is to throw away the rule book and fully enter the activity. Walking is a good example: think about it too much and you will probably fall over, as can happen when you are faced with crossing a high, narrow plank and vertigo kicks in, making you unsure of what you normally take for granted.

LEARNING IN A SOCIAL CONTEXT

Learning how to use the body and disciplining it to act in customary ways is a style every bit as indicative of who you are as a coloured shirt or a fancy spear point. Artefacts are therefore extensions of the body, the result of sequences of gestures applied to material, and so truly social as well as technical. This recognition presents us with the opportunity to dispense with a dualistic approach to understanding what we do and why.

Let us now consider an alternative and more familiar view of learning by going back to that Cartesian theatre. Remember, in this theatre mind and body are split. Thought is applied to materials which are also separate from the body. Here the concept of the mental template comes back into its own. The potter starts with a mental image of the pot he or she is going to make and then works towards that goal. The apprentice potter is instructed by reference to that image and tries to copy it. The finished pot is very much an object, external to the person who made it, as a good dualism requires. What has been forgotten in this scenario is the sequence of gestures, the rhythms of the *chaîne opératoire*, which link act and object in a continuous flow. Far from separating action into cognitive and technical domains (or material, social and ideological domains as above), everything becomes social. Thus the *chaîne opératoire* is more than just a suite of muscle memories about how to do things without thinking about them. It is the acts themselves and the linkages they provide across time and space that matter.

Randall McGuire provides the Marxist perspective, which nicely sums up the position:

> Material culture entails the social relations that are the conditions for its existence. It is both a product of these relations and part of the structure of these relations.
>
> (1992: 102)

THE BIOGRAPHY OF OBJECTS

I will end this chapter on archaeological objects by considering their biographies through those six keywords – production, function, context, exchange, consumption and transformation – that I promised to return to. The point of a biographical approach is to re-animate those objects through inquiry and interpretation. Remember this is not an autobiographical approach where these same pots, temples, shipwrecks and tin mines speak to us eloquently about their pasts. Rather it is, as Thomas pointed out, an approach that acknowledges just how important artefacts are in creating us. He writes:

> Ways of engaging in the world are not simply stored 'in the head': they are immanent in the relationships between people and things.
>
> (1996: 19)

Artefacts have histories just as we do. They have life cycles. They participated in other lives. Their analysis provides an example of cabling and tacking between data and ideas (Chapter 4). These points are well illustrated by one of the commonest forms of archaeological evidence: pottery.

POTS AS MATERIAL METAPHORS

One of the most obvious things about pots is that they break very easily. But what if, as John Chapman (2000) argues, such breakages were more often than not intentional? This could either be achieved by smashing the pot or making it in such a way that it broke more easily than otherwise it might. Chapman's point is that artefacts are a means of expressing social relationships in a metaphorical form. Now the essence of lingusitic metaphors is to express one thing in terms of another (Lakoff and Johnson 1980), for example through metonymy where a part stands for the whole: 'it's good to have some new faces round here' uses one part of the body to stand for the new colleagues.

But metaphors can also be material, as Christopher Tilley (1999) has shown. Without uttering a word you can understand one thing in terms of another. Think of your passport photo or your finger-print that stands for you, a part-for-whole relationship. Chapman's point is that by intentionally breaking things, such as pottery vessels, sets of relationships between people were being created (Figure 5.1). Such fragmentation goes hand-in-hand with the distributed character of personhood, those *dividuals* I discussed in Chapter 4. The purpose of fragmentation is to enchain, or link, people together through their involvement with material culture. Often the results of this process take the form of exchange networks (Chapter 6) and activities such as sharing and gift-giving. It also results in the accumulation of materials at sites as varied as cemeteries and settlements. This is what Andy Jones (2002) found in his metaphorical approach to the Neolithic sites of the Orkney Islands. The result is a nuanced understanding of the identity of individuals, their distributed personhood, in these prehistoric land-scapes.

THE LIFE OF POTS

I could cite an example from anywhere, but I have chosen a modest rescue excavation in a quarry in the heart of England (Hearne and Heaton 1994). The Shorncote Quarry site is Late Bronze Age in date, which puts it in the ninth to eighth centuries BC. Several timber roundhouses once stood on the site and there were some large pits containing broken potsherds which added up to at least 31 vessels, a clay weight probably used in making textiles with a loom, and a few fragments of clay moulds for bronze casting. A small collection of animal bones and crop remains was also present. Elaine Morris studied the pottery (in Hearne and Heaton 1994: 344).

Sherd

Bowl

Bone

Body

PART

WHOLE

Tessera

Mosaic

Grave

Cemetery

WHOLE

SET

Figure 5.1 The relationships between parts and wholes according to Chapman (2000: Figure 1.4). Fragmentation lies at the heart of this metaphorical relationship while enchainment and accumulation are two ways by which people form relationships with other people and artefacts.

PRODUCTION AND MANUFACTURE

The evidence for production is lacking. There is no obvious potter's workshop or even workspace. The artefacts used in smoothing and finishing the pots – bone spatulas, for example, or ornamental stamps – were not recovered. Neither is there any evidence for pottery kilns, not even a simple bonfire firing, at this small site.

Absence of evidence, however, is not always evidence of absence. The pots themselves are all handmade, built up with a distinctive slab and coil technique. The microscopic analysis of each potsherd's fabric, the clays and the mineral inclusions they contain, however, point mainly to local production. Most of the clays and the material used as temper, which stops the pots cracking, are found within 7 kilometre of the site. This distance matches those in a global ethnographic survey of local pottery production by Dean Arnold (1985).

Not a single complete pot was found at Shorncote. Nonetheless a variety of shapes and forms were present in the collection, as determined by comparison with complete examples from elsewhere in the region and by the reconstruction of complete profiles from the fragments. As a result we know that jars dominate the collection and that bowls and other forms such as dishes are rare or non-existent. The lack of bowls could be a result of sample size – the assemblage comprised less than 1000 sherds – since larger collections from nearby sites do have this additional form. Alternatively, the lack of bowls could be a clue to the activities performed at the site.

Each of the pots has one of three types of decoration: none, finger tipping (which produces little indentations) or the application of cordons or strips to their surfaces. Of the 31 pots that comprised the assemblage, 24 had no decoration.

The different shapes, manufacture and decoration demonstrated by the pots all point to something more than their being functional or constructed according to some cultural template found only in the Late Bronze Age. Ethnography can help here by opening our eyes to the possibility of variation. In her study of traditional potting in Northern Cameroon, Judy Sterner (1989) found that, contrary to expectation, the most decorated pots, large jars, were the most rarely seen, being kept in houses and compounds. She also found that the shape of the pot was more important than the decoration it carried for making a visual statement. It seems that, as with much material culture, it is the overall features of the object rather than the fine detail that has significance.

FUNCTION

The fine wares, highly burnished forms, are very rare in the collection but seem to have been used for holding acidic liquids, as shown by pitting on their interior surface. Most of the pots fall into the archaeological category of coarse wares, even though some of them are decorated. The jars could have been used to store many things. Food residues were found as sooty deposits on the inside of pots, and elsewhere these have demonstrated the storage of products such as milk, honey, fish and pig fat. At Shorncote, Morris found that such evidence occurred on only three of the ten fabrics, or wares, analysed. These three fabrics accounted for over 50 per cent of the sherds and were likely to have been the cookpots. From sites nearby we know that cookpots at this time are usually medium to small in size, whereas storage jars are medium to large.

CONTEXT

The potsherds were clustered in significant areas of the site. The overall pattern was of low density but Morris found that there were concentrations in the top layers of the big pits and in one circular gully feature. The two roundhouses had no pots. She put this patterning down to three factors. The roundhouses may have been built for different functions and used at different times. The big pits were closer to one house, making it easier to throw broken pots away rather than leave them in the gutter. We don't know for sure, but refuse disposal is a theory-loaded concept at the best of times – one person's dust heap is another's fortune – and simple explanations probably miss the mark. Potsherds at Shorncote might have been intentionally deposited in selected parts of the site, as they were on many other settlements in later prehistory – a social action that was just as significant as the more familiar ritual of sweeping a broken jar out of the home.

EXCHANGE

Interestingly, when Morris analysed the fabrics in the potsherds she found that some of the rarer forms in the collection had been manufactured from different raw materials, hinting at different production centres. Not everything was locally produced after all. This was expected since prehistoric pottery in this region has been known for many years to have been exchanged over distances of up to 100 kilometres (Peacock 1968). This was not in the form of commodities, like us buying mugs made in Taiwan at a petrol station. Rather, such exchange was based on creating social relations out of social relations (Chapter 8). To exchange or trade a pot was to exchange or trade a part of yourself.

CONSUMPTION

Pots can hold more than just water. For example, the Middle Bronze Age (fifteenth to eleventh century BC) is well known for its elaborate cremation urns. It is known that these started life as domestic pots and only later became used in burials. In her ethnoarchaeological study Sterner (1989: 454) found that individuals had their personal soul pots, empty but brim-full of meaning. These pots embodied and brought to life the underlying beliefs about the living and the ancestors, and the relationships between these categories. Christopher Tilley (1996: 323) goes further, arguing from his case study in Neolithic southern Scandinavia that pottery was metaphorically related to the corporeal aspects of human existence. The soft, malleable substances of clay and water have to be built up and shaped. The parallel with the soft outer flesh of the human body and the way it is shaped over the skeleton is striking. Skin can be decorated with tattoos, paint and cicatrices and pierced for ornaments, which may explain the frequent decoration of pottery surfaces. Then fire makes the clay hard. Fire also reduces the body when it is finally cremated to its hard components.

These contexts, Tilley reminds us (1996: 323), show that the process of production is a relationship between people and objects rather than a cause. It is through production, exchange and consumption that people establish relationships with other people and so negotiate the form and meanings of their world (Miller 1995). As Mary Douglas and Baron Isherwood (1978: 72) point out in their study of consumption 'goods that minister to physical needs – food or drink – are no less carriers of meaning than ballet or poetry'. Just because it is common, and survives well, does not make the consumption of pottery a mundane, functional activity. At Shorncote the potters and pot-users were not just meeting a need, making a container to cook barley in. Instead the potters were the facilitators in a *chaîne opératoire* (see above), where the properties inherent in the clay and water were cross-cut with analogies drawn from bodily processes. These included growth and decay and technological processes involving the shaping and building-up of those jars from the material in hand.

TRANSFORMATION

Finally, the Shorncote pots incorporated a deeper past into their fabric even as the wider world of the Bronze Age changed. Morris found that some of the temper, or filler, that was added to the clay to improve its mechanical properties during firing was not simply ground-up shell or limestone but ground-up Bronze Age pottery as well. This is known as grog-temper. There are two explanations for its use. The first emphasises practicalities: the potters needed some temper so they ground up some pots there and then. Alternatively, as Sterner (1989) found, the decision may be deliberate. The pot you are grinding into grog is a person, an ancestor. Pots are repaired with other pots. New pots are made which include older pots in the constant cycle of social reproduction. In the Middle Bronze Age, before Shorncote was built, large food vessels were often turned into cremation urns. These pots contained people, or at least their ashes, just as today in Cameroon soul pots contain souls. By the time Shorncote was built the burial rite had shifted from cremation to excarnation, the exposure of the dead body to the elements. But during this transformation of a key ritual the older tradition of regeneration survived. Those pots Morris analysed contain grog – other pots. But rather than seeing this just as pots within pots, it can also be seen as another way of putting a person in a pot, just as previously the large urns contained the ashes of the deceased.

During the simple act of pottery production some of the vessels at Shorncote took on the attributes of persons dead and persons living. Grandmothers, uncles and great aunts, all gone but still incorporated into the everyday activities of the living which make life continue such as cooking and the storing of food and drink. Thus the individual pot became a sort of family tree, reworked by each new generation. A ceramic tape of social memories and a reminder of ancestral obligations.

The incorporation of the tradition of regeneration through the medium of pottery manufacture, repair, and the process of cooking and consumption shows, as Morris reminds us, that simple functional explanations only deal with one aspect in the lives of even the scruffiest of pots from the smallest and most forgotten of excavations.

THE DEATH OF STYLE?

In Chapter 1 I defined archaeology as basically about three things: objects, landscapes and what we make of them. It is quite simply the study of the past through material remains. I have shown in this chapter how archaeologists have used their analyses of style to make something of the material they study. Style both orders and interprets the differences in architecture, stone axes, bronze pins, burial rites and the layout of towns and fields. But I have indicated that, although style is one of our most trusty methods for recognising patterns among archaeological evidence, it is also one of our most slippery terms. We have relied upon it because it produced understandable results in the great scheme of looking at and interpreting the world as a set of oppositions: for example, nature – culture, internal – external. However, such great schemes have their own history of popularity, and like a battleship curve in a seriation chart they come and go. Much of what is presented as theoretical foment in archaeology is due to changes in the way the world is now conceived and analysed. The certainty of style, however defined, is one of the casualties in that change. As a result we can never look at objects, including the human landscape, which I have only so far touched on briefly, in the same way. The next step is to broaden the enquiry and look at the all-important frameworks of space and time which provide our main route to the interpretation of the past.

SUMMARY

- Objects and artefacts are not passive blobs as a rational perspective insists. They have an active role to play in a relational approach to the study of people, past and present.
- We will always have difficulty in interpreting the meaning of objects if a stylistic approach is adopted, because different archaeologies attach a diverse significance to its role in human social life.
- Metaphor provides a basic device to understand who we are, and why, and can be based on artefacts as well as words. This is an encouraging thought for archaeologists.
- The biographies of objects are similar to the biographies of people. Both depend on appreciating the importance of context.

6

TIME AND SPACE

Time is the big one for archaeologists. Or at least, you would think it should be. But until recently time as a concept, rather than a technique of dating, hasn't been at the top of our list of things to sort out. Indeed, our other dimension, space, has received far more attention both conceptually and as a framework for measuring and comparing archaeological data. In this chapter I will examine these two basic dimensions. We shall see how different concepts of time are every bit as important, if not more so, for understanding the past as getting the age of the Pyramids right by developing a new science-based technique to measure accurately how old things are (see Chapter 3).

Time and space are in fact inseparable. To think of one is to suppose the other. In line with earlier chapters, I present you with a basic choice. Time and space can be used as the struts in an external framework – something that people today, and in the past, rattle around in and bump up against like the wall of the set in *The Truman Show*. Alternatively, you can see them as created by human activity. Space and time are examples of those everyday rhythms described by Leroi-Gourhan (1993) that emerge through our involvement with the world rather than as pre-existing conditions on our actions.

And that involvement is all about the body with its size, senses and varied capacities for doing things. The body, which includes the mind without separating it out artificially, is the basis for our experience and appreciation of time and space. Humans and hominins have always had bodies, and while they may have interpreted their experiences differently we can assume that they did undergo such experiences. In this chapter the concept of the body forms the pivot between time and space and acts as another way to explore an archaeology that sees things either rationally or relationally.

CONTEXTS AND ENTITIES

In order to expand our understanding of the alternatives of time and space we need some further entities to add to the attributes, artefacts and assemblages discussed in Chapter 3.

In the first instance there are *contexts*. This term can mean different things to different archaeologists, as discussed below. Then there are *entities*, or classifications that cross-cut contexts and are built up piecemeal from their contents. These depend on space and time for their definition. The most important, however, are the by now familiar archaeological *culture* as well as some newcomers: *culture group*, *technocomplex* and *world system*.

CONTEXT AND PRESERVATION

When excavating, a context has both a spatial and a temporal meaning. This is what stratigraphy (Chapter 3) is all about. The context from which finds come could be a pit or a grave, a temple or a granary. It can be disturbed, containing items deposited at different times and for different reasons, but for most excavators the ideal is undisturbed, *in situ* preservation of the evidence. This situation is ideal because it would produce a *closed* find-group, and from such contexts come precise associations of artefacts which can be used for dating purposes as well as for the reconstruction of events and activities. These can on occasion involve very short-lived activities – for example the 15 minutes it took to make a flint biface half a million years ago at Boxgrove, West Sussex, England.

Like time, contexts can be vertical as well as horizontal. The archaeological stratigraphy of a tell mound such as Çatalhöyük or a deep urban excavation is built up through the changing picture of the contexts that excavation reveals. Pieced together, these might reveal shifting patterns of activity in particular neighbourhoods, perhaps with alterations in settlement size and its cultural demography. Thus several hundred, or even thousands, of years of continuous occupation in one place is built up as a record of intersecting contexts. These are represented in visual archaeological jargon such as the Harris matrix (see Figure 3.4).

TIME CAPSULES

Precise, *in situ* information is not rare in archaeology. On occasion there are even time capsules such as the Tudor warship the *Mary Rose*, which sank with all hands on board off Portsmouth in 1545, in front of Henry VIII and the invading French fleet. Another warship, the *Vasa*, toppled over in Stockholm harbour on her maiden voyage on 10 August 1628. These are precise time capsules, storehouses of material culture and habits, to be compared with Tutankhamun's tomb, the Copan burials or the town of Pompeii – sealed by what happened in the space of a day.

But not all *in situ* time capsules yield easy answers. The contents of the dry land ship-burial of Sutton Hoo in Suffolk, eastern England, have been much discussed (Carver 1998). They are an eclectic group of local, continental, eastern Mediterranean, pagan and Christian items. Some of them were antiques before they were put in the ground, thus blurring the notion of contemporaneity. Moreover, perhaps the most significant artefact – the body – was either never actually present or just not preserved. In this instance, an *in situ* context has led to much disagreement over the date of the site, whether it is a burial or a cenotaph, and the identity of the person who was either buried or commemorated. This is partly due to the very scrappy textual evidence which most commentators try to tie the find to. I suspect that if the fates of the *Vasa* and the *Mary Rose* had not been written down at the time, similar, rather unproductive debates about whose ship it was and which king or queen's reign it sank in would have followed.

ARCHAEOLOGICAL TIME SIGNATURES

Contextual integrity, the *in situ* ideal, is rather different to the notion of signatures. A *fine-grained* time signature provides a very good match between what went on at a site and what was left behind in the archaeological record. It is the archaeological equivalent of the Polaroid snap. Typically a group of mobile hunters might catch game, gather plant food and use local stone to produce artefacts. If they do all of this locally, and then leave the residue behind, it can become a fine-grained signature even if it is later disturbed by geology, ploughing or any other transformational process (see Chapter 3).

A *coarse-grained* time signature is much more common. Here there is a lag in both space and time between activity and deposition. The process of creation of the archaeological record is more like that of editing a film: starting and stopping, shooting out of sequence and splicing together later. The wheat that went into the granary was grown many kilometres away. It sat in the storage jars for a long time. It was then redistributed, perhaps to people who never grew or processed it. Only then was it turned into bread, after which it began to trickle into the archaeological record. Those wheat grains that fell on the fire and became carbonised might still be lying exactly where they fell 6000 years ago. The integrity of their preservation is not the issue. Time signatures record the temporal rhythms of the behaviour that left something behind.

MEANING = MESSAGE + CONTEXT

The other use of the word context is concerned with a rather different set of meanings. Rather than simply recording objects by aspects of their space-time dimensions, a contextual analysis also looks to interpret their meaning. But what is meaning? I define meaning quite simply as message + context. The notion of message was touched upon in Chapter 5 through the complicated issue of style in material culture. It is difficult to interpret but we made some headway in dissolving the dichotomies between style and function, social and technical. Can we do the same for context?

CONTEXTUAL ANALYSIS

Context has been defined by Hodder as the totality of the relevant environment in which entities such as attributes, artefacts and assemblages are found (1991: 143). This 'relevant environment' refers to a significant relationship that will help us to unpick an object's meaning. The questions being asked by the archaeologist will also shape that context.

What the archaeologist is saying is actually quite simple and follows the basic rule of systematically sampling the unknown (see Chapter 3, The Representative Sample). To get at meanings, contexts must be bigger than the entities being studied. If an artefact is under the interpretive lens, then its context has to be the time and space dimensions from which it comes and from which other similar or dissimilar artefacts might come. If meaning is the goal, then the artefact, the culture or any other entity cannot be abstracted from this framework, what Hodder calls the 'relevant environment', and studied in isolation: if this is removed, then the message is lost.

A contextual analysis seeks to unpick those strands of symbolic references whose well-spun webs signify the context and give the object meaning. To go back to the 'text' metaphor, a contextual analysis depends upon many readings. It thrives on a high density of data, the richer the better. Good examples of this relationship are the detailed excavations of rooms and houses at the Neolithic town of Çatalhöyük (Balter 2005; Hodder 2006). These investigations show that while meaning is specific to a particular context, it may be repeated elsewhere.

CONJUNCTIVE APPROACH

Several of these points were made 60 years ago by Walter Taylor in his conjunctive approach, from which Hodder derives his contextual perspective (Hodder 1991: 189). The conjunctive approach stressed the analysis of cultures from the inside, identifying affinities through associations and relationships, similarity and difference: item to item, attribute to attribute (Taylor 1948: 95–96). It was contrasted with the comparative approach then dominant, which looked for correspondences outside the entity being studied – thus usually comparing culture with culture. Like Hodder, Taylor warned against the attractions of the comparative approach with its interest in universal meanings such as function (Chapter 4).

Contextual and conjunctive analysis also share the basic belief that culture explains culture and that the meaning of objects is contained within them and revealed through their context. They would also agree that:

> Much of an archaeologist's work consists in judging relative similarities or differences between material remains, whether at the level of artefacts, assemblages or whole complexes.
>
> (Doran and Hodson 1975: 135)

ARCHAEOLOGICAL CULTURE AND CULTURE GROUPS

Childe's classic definition of an archaeological culture was set out in Chapter 3. It combines recurrence in time with distribution in space. David Clarke updated it slightly and added a higher grouping, the culture group. Culture was a 'polythetic set [see Figure 3.3] of specific and comprehensive artefact-type categories which consistently recur together in *assemblages* within a limited geographical area', while a culture-group is 'a family of transform cultures; collateral cultures characterised by assemblages sharing a polythetic range but differing states of the same *specific multistate artefact-types*' (Clarke 1968: 188, original emphasis).

What Clarke is saying in the language of the time is that culture groups are *weak* cultures. We can see that patterning exists but it is not very robust. There are contradictions with the culture model, where greater correspondence is expected in the popularity and presence of artefact types within and between assemblages excavated and recovered from different sites.

Clarke's important point about the polythetic structure of artefacts establishes that culture groups will have less overall affinity than cultures. He suggested about 30 per cent affinity for specific artefact types, for example particular forms of pottery beaker or clothing pin, but about 60 per cent affinity among the larger sets of artefacts, graves and pots. By contrast, a culture would have much higher percentages of both types and sets of types.

FUZZY TAXONOMY

The overlapping, fuzzy-bordered nature of these entities' distributions is to be expected. They are after all elements in a polythetic set (Figure 3.3) where not all items are always present and where some spatial overlap, rather than discrete distributions, is the norm. The lesson is that human activity is continuous. It is overlapping and blurred in the present, and so is also blurred in our representations of the past. We impose the edges, or cut the continuum, in order to break down complexity so that we can manage, analyse and re-experience it.

This fuzzy reality is the hard part for the archaeologist as taxonomist. Where do you start to carve this turkey when you can't even see its joints clearly? We are left with the question of whether more work, more data, would turn culture groups into cultures by boosting the level of affinity. Then we believe we would know where to put our taxonomic knife. Clarke's intuition was that the structural bones would be revealed by spatial analysis. He even suggested guesstimates (Box 18), which I don't think are far wrong, to guide us.

BOX 18 THE SIZE OF ARCHAEOLOGICAL ENTITIES

	Estimated range radius (km)
Culture	30–300
Culture group	300–1200
Technocomplex	1200–7500+

(Clarke 1968: 331)

TECHNOCOMPLEX

Clarke proposed another term, 'Technocomplex', for the even vaguer entities existing at scales greater than the culture group. It has been widely used, particularly in the study of stone artefacts. In North and South America it is broadly equivalent to the term 'tradition' as in Paleo-Indian, Old Cordilleran, Desert, Archaic, Northwest Microblade and Arctic Small-tool traditions/technocomplexes.

Technocomplexes are characterised by general *families* of artefact types. If plotted out, the assemblages in a technocomplex might share only 5 per cent of the artefact types but up to 60 per cent of their broader technological families, such as hunting tools, transport technology and storage equipment. This suited the evidence, which comprised rather unstandardised but broadly similar sets of stone tools widely distributed across Europe and Africa, thought to represent different coping strategies for dealing with common environmental problems at a regional and inter-regional scale. Clarke's use of terms such as 'family' indicate his adherence to a biological model for drawing up an archaeological taxonomy that is very functional, highly systemic and ultimately adaptive. While we need to classify, we must also recognise that revealing natural taxonomies cannot be the sole task of the archaeologist. That way lies a degree in stamp collecting.

WORLD SYSTEM

A problem that has faced archaeologists is thinking big. Not in terms of ambition – something that archaeologists have never lacked, as demonstrated by the excavations of the Ziggurat at Ur or clearing the rainforest from Angkor Wat – but rather in the scale of human interaction. The temptation has always been to think local, be parochial, with just a whiff of diffusionism to paper over the unexpected.

When studying the ancient empires there have been surprises such as the extent of the Inca road system down the spine of South America, or the discovery of coins minted in Rome from excavations in Laos. The problem has always been considering the impact of these indications of contact. One of the big achievements of archaeology in the past 40 years has been to expand the scale at which we commonly think people interacted, from the Palaeolithic to the industrial eras.

Archaeology has played its part in demonstrating that life everywhere was international well before Columbus and the European world-empires. A useful model for such a change of mindset is provided by the Marxist historian Immanuel Wallerstein and his analysis of the modern world system (1974, 1980). He deals with the cyclical accumulation of wealth and power at dominant centres and their tributary peripheries. The spatial notion of core/periphery struck a chord with archaeologists, who expanded their studies of the earliest states to include neighbouring prehistoric societies in their consideration of the civilising process (Frank 1993; Kristiansen and Rowlands 1998: 222; Kristiansen 1998). Such archaeological studies soon went beyond the rather general expectations of world-systems theory. Sometimes these imply nothing more than chaos theory at its most banal, where everything is related causally to everything else (Chapter 7); a Roman emperor stamps his foot and a tempest of world religions is the result.

ONE WORLD

But the real value of world-systems thinking is to confirm the subject matter of archaeology as globally interconnected. No one is left out of this world – especially those, like hunters and gatherers, whom the nineteenth century consigned to stagnation and primitiveness. For example, even those hunters at the 'uttermost ends of the earth' from Europe and eastern North America were influenced by, and had some reciprocal influence on, the centres. The transformation of Siberian and Alaskan Inuit society through indirect contact with the Amur civilisations 2000 km away is an example. We know from the excavation of Inuit graves that these prehistoric warrior-hunters went into local battle protected by whale-bone armour made to a Chinese pattern far to the south. Much later their descendants would supply that same whale-bone for the corsets of London and Paris: a good example of the power of material culture to constrain and transform the shape of society.

The lesson from world-systems theory is: think big. Basically, do not always expect local answers to local questions, especially those that involve change (Chapter 7). Never underestimate the scale of the 'primitive' world.

TIME

The discussion of contexts and entities has been necessary because, like action in the past, time remains invisible. Certainly we experience it but we cannot grasp it. We use metaphors to describe those experiences – 'time is like an arrow', 'time is cyclical' – and the rate at which it seems to happen – 'how time flies when one has fun', 'time on my hands' and 'how time drags'. The way we understand the experience of time in the past is not, I maintain, by chronologies alone, but through entities such as artefact, technocomplex and archaeological culture, which we have now examined. These are, if you like, congealed lumps of time. The difference is that we can grasp these archaeological entities because we created them and we can even change their shape by changing our mind about them.

TEMPORALITY

This raises the important issue of temporality, which I define as the varied activities and processes that occur within time. Since the flow of experience is continuous, what we are looking for are those temporal structures that we can use, often arbitrarily, to make the process meaningful. At the same time, by chopping time up we acknowledge that different activities have different temporal structures. Some may well fit the metaphor of the arrow, with its hint of progress and direction to the process, or the wheel that comes round every year in the ritual of Christmas or every generation in births, marriages and deaths. Other activities may better fit the process of ageing, as with ruined, ivy-covered monuments, symbolic of time passing and the eventual decay of all things – even the Pyramids.

But these metaphors are predictable and reduce the flow of time to analytical chunks that often come to be disconnected from the people who generated them. It is possible to compare one arrow with another (Chapter 7), for example the rise of civilisation in the Near East and in Mesoamerica or the development of metallurgy in China and in Africa. It is also possible to contrast different cycles, such as the annual subsistence rounds of hunters and gatherers (this can be done on a truly world scale) or the solar- and lunar-inspired rituals of monuments from many periods (Ruggles, Prendergast and Ray 2001). Valuable as these comparisons might be I would agree with those who espouse the conjunctive approach (see above) that we need to get beneath the surface and see if we can't address the issue of temporality rather than simply the comparative classification and measurement of units of time (see Box 12).

A AND B SERIES TIME

The anthropologist Alfred Gell (1992) neatly dismissed the idea, once held by many, that the cultures of the world experience time differently. This is important as it means that we can assume a similar state of affairs for the peoples of the past (Chapter 4, The

Principle of Uniformitarianism). Gell concluded that we all basically have a choice when it comes to time concepts. These boil down to the following difference:

A-series time = past/present/future
B-series time = before/after

In A-series time, the present is wafer thin, just a fleeting moment. It is a drop in the stream of consciousness and cannot be tied down or adequately described. Adherents to this view have to spend a lot of time referring to the past and the future in order to fix what is going on in the present. B-series time, on the other hand, is congealed by being mapped on to space. It occurs between dateable events.

That is the choice. In practice, Gell argues, the two series work together. A-series time provides us with internal representations of what external, B-series time, is like. Those B-series representations in turn inform the way we think about time in the instant of the present. How does this help the archaeologist? The answer is through objects. They endure (B-series time) and they continue to change because of our relations with them (A-series time).

TIMESCALES AND TIME PERSPECTIVISM

It should by now be clearer why concepts of time, as opposed to measurements of time, never count for much in culture history, neo-Darwinian or processual archaeology (Chapter 2). As Geoff Bailey has shown, we spend a great deal of our resources on measuring time but very little on the concepts of time (1983). Perhaps ironically, time is not seen as a resource that built or shaped the past. It is only seen as something, in the guise of decay, that stops us receiving the full picture in the present. Moreover, given *enough* time – which obviously archaeologists have never lacked for – change by diffusion, natural and cultural selection or systemic transformations could be assumed.

Within this barren time-vortex there have been some considerations of what an archaeological perspective offers to our understanding of human time. Time perspectivism, as discussed by Bailey (1983), looks at the issue of the very long timescales we have at our disposal in the long run of human evolution. Geologists refer to this as 'deep time' and archaeologists have emphasised the long-term perspective that our studies bring to questions of adaptation, survival, stasis and change.

The long term, measured in thousands of years, is indeed an archaeological way of thinking. When faced with dates as long as telephone numbers, many people wonder how archaeologists can think in those time spans.

CONTEMPORANEITY

The answer is that we don't. In the same way that the distance to the stars is mind-boggling, so too is the fact that Chauvet Cave in southern France, whose fabulous paintings of rhinos, horses and lions are dated by radiocarbon to 33,000 years ago, is about the same distance in time from the very famous cave paintings of Lascaux, executed 17,000 years ago, as the latter are from Michaelangelo's Sistine Chapel. All three were painted by people with modern capabilities, but the artists who created the first two shared a long tradition of activity in the landscape governed by the rhythms of hunting and gathering.

Here is an example of enough time by anybody's standards. To comprehend it we don't think of 10,000 individual years. Nobody can. Neither do we even think in more manageable spans of 500 or 1000 years. Both of these scales our outside our ken. You might as well try to imagine each byte in the gigabytes in your computer. What we do is conceptually crystallise time, like honey on the end of a spoon. We average it in order to manage it.

But that is only part of the process of understanding time. What we also need to do, as outlined above, is to make time more human, more personal. This is done by treating the crystallising process as one that respects the archaeological record and the way time has always been experienced.

TIME AVERAGING

Time averaging, that process of crystallisation, is how we deal with the common question of contemporaneity. Historical records are apparently well suited to dealing with this aspect of time. With a bit of digging in the archives we could probably find out what the other European monarchs were doing on 10 August 1628, when the Vasa sank. Laughing, probably. It would be even easier to compare what was going on in Sweden, England, Massachusetts or China in that year and that decade. This would be regarded as pretty good control over contemporaneity, slotting into a human life span.

Thirty-three thousand years ago that precision, of course, escapes us. We could compare what was going on in Tasmania, South Africa and Europe at around that time, but nobody could claim contemporaneity on the scale of a human generation of 20 years. But then why would you want to? The questions relevant to 33,000 years ago are not going to involve the foreign policy and military ambitions of King Gustavus II Adolphus, whose flagship it was that sank on that calamitous day. Although the cave paintings might have taken the Chauvet artists a single week, a month or repeated visits to the cave over 20 or 100 years, we just do not know – the issue of contemporaneity is meaningless. What we have are some precise events and large blocks of time represented by a palimpsest (or jumble) of times, places, landscapes and objects. In the Lower Palaeolithic such time averaging means that 'contemporary' is often a block of time 70,000 years in length. By the Neolithic that is reduced to between 700 and 1000 years. By the medieval period, contemporary time units of 100 or 50 years are common.

So don't expect the past to behave like the present, especially when contemporaneity is an issue. Instead, celebrate that part of our cultivated archaeological imagination that allows us to think beyond our normal restrictions and to recognise that our time frames (yesterday, today, the news breaking now in all the capitals of the world) are not the only way to reckon contemporaneity in human action.

MICRO- AND MACRO-TIMESCALES

This discussion of contemporaneity has highlighted an issue I have already returned to several times, micro- and macro-scale. Archaeology has plenty of temporal data to examine this important issue. In any excavation you will come across evidence of very brief micro-episodes of time: How long does it take to tip food refuse into a pit? Those same plant and animal remains, as well as the pot that got thrown away with them, can be inferred to represent longer periods of time. That leg of pork came from a three-year-old pig, the charred wheat grains from a season's crop, the pot maybe lasted a generation. The pit they were all found in might, however, be dated to no finer than within a 150-year span in the early Medieval period.

When micro-timescale activities are also preserved *in situ*, then our archaeological imagination really feels a *frisson*. The main archaeological horizon at the 500,000-year-old site of Boxgrove, West Sussex, England, was created over probably no more than a human generation, 20 years. Over this time people regularly visited the place, made stone tools, hunted and butchered animals, and left the remains behind. Fifteen minutes to make a biface, a few hours to butcher a horse, contained within a stratigraphic envelope of 20 years and all happening half a million years ago. Here the micro- and the macro-timescales are neatly embedded within each other.

BODIES IN TIME AND SPACE

Our bodily experiences provide us with our sense of time and space. As the day passes we grow hungry, travel distances and fall asleep, while as the years go by our appearance changes as we age. The body has distinctive rhythms, such as digestion, and its structure allows repeated actions such as walking. As a result, a personal temporality is established. We also experience space through our bodies and come to understand what it is to be in or on, behind or in front of. In short, bodies provide those experiences that are commonplace but nonetheless fundamental for building an appreciation of the world. Such experiences lie at the heart of our use of metaphor where we understand one thing in terms of something else; for example when we express our moods by saying 'I'm *on* a high' or 'She's *down* in the dumps'. What this means is that we 'think' through our body (Hamilakis, Pluciennik and Tarlow 2002) by experiencing what it is to be in the world. Our bodies, not just our minds, are strong reference points for understanding the world in both its spatial and temporal dimensions.

How does this help archaeologists? Well, at one level our bodies remind us why those analytical dualisms I discussed in the last chapter are unhelpful. They separate our archaeological analyses from the world of sensations and emotions, turning them instead into cold, rational thoughts. In a rational approach the body has been used to explain the gaps in the spatial patterns of fine-grained signatures as discussed above; for example, seeing where the flint knapper knelt by the blank areas in the scatter of debris (Gamble and Porr 2005) or working out from the size of bodies how many people were seated round an open hearth (Binford 1978b).

But a relational approach takes us further than this treatment of bodies only as instruments for measurement among well-plotted, well-preserved settlement data. Bodies are themselves objects, an item of material culture (Sofaer 2006). Our bodies also make sense of the common forms of tools and artefacts. Containers such as houses derive much of their symbolic power from analogies with the trunk of the body. As many anthropologists have pointed out, the entrances, partitions, walls and roof timbers of houses are very frequently described in terms of body parts (Carsten and Hugh-Jones 1995). Houses are also material metaphors for containment, analogous to the experience of being inside our bodies, seeing out through eyes and windows. Containers abound in material culture. Not only are there houses, but also pots, baskets, graves, cradles, skulls, boxes, canoes, clothes, masks, books, chariots and even flocks of animals – the list is vast – but there are also instruments that draw on analogies with our limbs and digits rather than the trunk. These would include spears, arrows, fishing rods, toothpicks, pins, sticks and axes. Many of these will be composite artefacts, as is the case with ploughs and bows (Gamble 2007).

A relational approach to material culture, and applied to archaeological data, starts with the body and seeks to understand the variety of artefact forms and their associations in terms of the experiences of those people who made them. Instead of the material world being a set of problem-solving devices, like knives to cut meat, material culture was an active agent in structuring how people thought and experienced the world (Knappett 2005).

BODIES, PLACE AND LANDSCAPE

Concentrating on the body as a source for understandings of the ways people in the past related to their worlds brings us to that other archaeological dimension, space. The entities and scales I have previously described above (e.g. technocomplex) and in Chapter 3 (e.g. assemblage and culture) and that I will shortly describe below (e.g. site and region) largely need time as a measure of their duration. In spatial terms they are made up of popular artefacts and repeatable combinations which are left behind as solid markers. Their message is clear: people were here, they did this, they lasted this long, they went and others came in their place.

The alternative is to think rather differently about seemingly ordinary terms such as 'place' and 'landscape'. The trick is to realise that these are not alternatives for those archaeological journeymen terms 'site' and 'environment' that people either built or played games against as part of their adaptive survival. Instead, places and landscapes are constructed from the act of living. These terms are about time and temporality.

The key word is human *involvement*, with its implication of a continuous stream of activity. As Christopher Gosden has insisted, we start by understanding that the times those activity streams generated *are* the landscape (1994: 193). Place in this context can be defined by:

> the experiences it affords to those who spend time there – to the sights, sounds and indeed smells that constitute its specific ambience. And these, in turn, depend on the kinds of activities in which its inhabitants engage.
>
> (Ingold 1993: 155)

Places are not distinct from the landscape but part of that continuous involvement (Tilley 1994). The activities that occur there structure the temporality of the landscape and inscribe it with meaning. The landscape also acquires its own history through the superimposition of traces of human activity that can range from erosion of the soils to the building of a ceremonial centre, from throwing away a bone to burying a loved one.

In the light of this understanding we can now rewrite the meaning equation from

meaning = message + context

to

meaning = object/style + place/landscape

Three further concepts will help to make the point. The first, the *landscape of habit* (Gosden 1994: 182) summarises those habitual, taken-for-granted actions by which we live most of our lives. The landscape of habit is constructed by the actions that normally get things done but which don't really concern us unless something goes wrong – the axe breaks, the snows stay late or the harvest fails.

The second concept, that of the *taskscape*, has been suggested by Tim Ingold (1993). Actions speak louder than words. We hear activity as much as see it or infer it by using our archaeological imagination. Attention – attending to others, attending to the task in hand – is a very important social activity. Our ears confirm that we are surrounded by creative action which we respond to.

Habit, like the distinction between practical and discursive consciousness, is addressed by our third concept, another landscape, this time a *social landscape.* Here the choices are more deliberate, more creative in terms of negotiation with others and with things. Both landscapes – the social landscape and the landscape of habit – influence each other and are firmly embedded in each other. The parallel with the practical and discursive consciousness that all of us have is obvious – these are indivisible but allow distinct ways of acting. An excellent example is provided by Richard Bradley's (1997) study of rock-art sites in Atlantic Europe. The composition and siting of the art is conditioned both by everyday, habitual actions such as the tending of livestock, as well as by a wider social world.

During the course of human evolution there have been significant changes to our social landscape (Chapter 7). Objects and our relationship to them have been central to these changes. Time is inherent in those objects, and it is through them that place and landscape come to symbolise time and space as a result of human action. The concept of *habitus* provides another formulation of these issues, which I shall discuss in Chapter 8.

SPACE

On the face of it space seems much more straightforward than time. The distance between two points can be measured, as can the size of towns or the quantities of goods found away from their source of manufacture. Archaeologists like distribution maps and at a smaller scale excavation plans will always be an essential record of what we do. The quantification of spatial data and systematic sampling based on a spatial framework were two of the great steps forward made by processual archaeology. These advances will now be examined through another of the lasting products of processual archaeology: the research design.

The new geography of the 1960s (Haggett 1965; Chorley and Haggett 1967), which like the new archaeology also dealt with laws, hypotheses, models, sampling, quantification and statistical analysis, provided the impetus for a spatial archaeology (Clarke 1972a; Hodder and Orton 1976). It was more enthusiastically pursued in Britain and Europe than in North America partly because the quantification seemed to fill the gap left behind by a lack of European ethnography. The 'archaeology as anthropology' of North America was, for a short while, 'archaeology as geography' in Britain before the lack of human content in such approaches was fully realised (Gamble 1987). Scales of spatial analysis were thoroughly investigated from the micro to the macro (Clarke 1977). The blending of research design, methods and analysis came together in the intra-site to inter-regional model that has been very influential as a framework for investigation and interpretation. Two early and classic examples are illustrated by Flannery's work in Mesoamerica (see below) and Clarke's (1972b) study of an Iron Age settlement system (Figure 6.1).

But space is not just about research designs, systematic sampling and nested levels of enquiry. In the first place it is about *pattern recognition* where the nested levels are, at a minimum:

- intra-site,
- site, and
- region.

Second, there are at least four *analytical approaches* to space which need to be reviewed briefly because of what they have contributed to archaeology. They are:

- central places and polities,
- the attrition of distance,

Figure 6.1 From the micro to the macro. Fitting the spatial scales into this nest of
concepts allows us to analyse human action at a variety of scales while
keeping sight of the whole picture. The example comes from the Iron Age
settlements of southern England (after Clarke 1972b).

- Geographical Information Systems, and
- the social use of space.

PATTERN RECOGNITION AND SPATIAL SCALES

As accurately described above by Doran and Hodson (1975), archaeologists spend a great deal of time looking for patterns in their data. This is done at a number of scales. Three are very important: intrasite, site and region. Analytically these three spatial scales form, like Russian dolls, the tiers in a nested hierarchical structure.

INTRA-SITE

The first level in the *nested hierarchy* of spatial scales is the intrasite level. This combines many of the aspects of contexts that we have discussed above, but with an important difference. Intra-site analysis looks for spatial patterning among connected groups of contexts and features recognised during excavation. It may be based on the distribution of finds and their quantitative frequency by reference to an arbitrary grid rather than necessarily related to a definable context. This is a common strategy in field walking. Intra-site patterning is very strongly linked to specific questions about activities and aspects of the built environment.

SITE

Sites are the stock-in-trade items for archaeologists. They are what we excavate and are the repositories for information. Successful careers can be built on their excavation alone. Increasingly, however, our information comes not from excavation but from various forms of non-invasive technique (Chapter 3). These include geophysical prospection, aerial photos and the surface survey of artefacts, for example when we systematically pick finds up from the surface of ploughed fields. Excavation is not the way to answer all our questions.

Sites are described in many ways. Functionally, among many others we have: villas, towns, forts, monasteries, pueblos, camps and shell middens. These are described quantitatively by such factors as size, contents, age, duration of occupation or use and complexity.

But sites, like culture groups, can also be difficult to define. Sometimes the boundaries are difficult to discern. Where there are ditches, walls and banks the category seems clear cut and comparisons can be made on size alone. But very often it is difficult to determine where one site ends and another begins – this is especially true of a vast category of site, the unenclosed settlement, often represented by a scatter of materials across the landscape. Within such find scatters there may be chronological indicators provided by some distinctive flints and pots, but very often there are not.

REGION

The last level in the nested hierarchy of spatial scales is the region. These too can be difficult to define. They can be period-specific such as a particular hunting territory, or any of the ancient empires. They may be delimited by the similarity of particular artefact categories. Flint, pottery and coins are the normal items used. But this is unsatisfactory and often difficult for the reasons illustrated in Figure 3.3. In cases where rich linguistic and anthropological data exist, as in the southwestern United States and Australia, these have been used to draw up regional boundaries. The archaeology is then compared between such ethnographic regions to investigate issues of time-depth. This approach can run the risk of re-creating the past in the form of the present (see Chapter 4).

The regional scale of investigation and analysis, as established by processual archaeology, is an important archaeological concept. When behaviour is being studied, the unit of analysis must be larger so that a representative selection of that behaviour can be recovered for study (Chapter 3, Sampling Strategies). That has always been a problem with earlier approaches, where one site was taken to represent much more widespread aspects of cultural behaviour when in fact it could be atypical. Moreover, the size of regions will vary depending on the mobility and scale of inter-group contacts. This is why regions are often determined arbitrarily by means of a grid whose size might vary depending on the mobility and range of contacts the system being studied is thought to have. The contents of each cell are then systematically sampled. The alternative is to delimit natural regions. This carries some weight when the questions being asked are ecological, for example sampling the annual subsistence round of hunters and gatherers. It makes less sense when the focus shifts to more abstract instances of power, exchange or identity.

REGIONAL THINKING

An excellent example of this nested approach is Kent Flannery's (1976) investigation of the archaeology of the Oaxaca Valley, Mexico. This influential, as well as entertaining, study of the rise of civilisation also stands as a parable of the archaeological times. Interspersed with systematic, quantified fieldwork linked to testing dynamic, rather than providing purely descriptive, models is a dialogue between three fictional archaeologists. The differing points of view of Flannery's Great Synthesiser (GS, who relies on other people's data), Real Mesoamerican Archaeologist (RMA, who is a culture historian interested in the Formative period) and Sceptical Graduate Student (SGS, who is strongly quantitative, processualist and a 'pain-in-the-ass – but at least he's *my* little pain-in-the-ass', according to the RMA) do not disguise the fact that they are all part of one archaeological personality. The parable is not about which one gains ascendancy, but rather that after years of either silence or the dominance of single points of view a debate is now taking place.

Flannery's approach to regional analysis was to build from the bottom up. He starts with the household, then goes to the village and on to the region, and finally the inter-regional scale. This model has been very influential. Rather than start with a grand theory or law, it begins with the recovery of information about how people lived their daily lives. Such a nested hierarchy of analytical techniques, changing questions and behavioural inferences shows how a processual archaeology can be built rather than assumed. This same methodological structure can be found in Clarke's analysis of Iron Age Britain (1972b, 1979) and in Colin Renfrew and Malcolm Wagstaff's (1982) study of the town of Phylakopi, on the Greek island of Melos, and its place in the Bronze Age Aegean.

ANALYTICAL APPROACHES TO SPACE

The analysis of space reveals many strong patterns in the data and is a framework for archaeological investigation. But what do we then make of space, and what principles apply? I have selected six models and techniques that illustrate how important space is for archaeology. In particular, the study of social relationships and the construction of gender depend on space.

The link between space, settlement and social organisation has been important in synthesising archaeological data at both a site and regional scale. Central places have particular functions, such as a market, and often geographical explanations for being there, for instance proximity to the richest soils in the region or good communication networks. But natural advantages are not always self-evident. Why was Sutton Hoo on that little backwater in Suffolk? Will someone please explain to me why Stonehenge is on windswept Salisbury Plain?

Central places are about people and the flows of goods and information. The concept has been applied to all periods of archaeology. Glynn Isaac (1978) proposed a central place foraging model for hunters and gatherers based on his archaeological fieldwork in East Africa and ethnographic work by Richard Lee among the !Kung San, mobile foragers in the Kalahari desert. Isaac's model for hominids 2 million years ago had them radiating out from a home base on a daily basis as they foraged for food. He expanded his model to consider such issues as the spatial extent of foraging activity, the division of labour between the sexes, and the transport of food. From this he developed his food-sharing hypothesis to account for human cultural origins.

These properties of centrality were also used by Claudio Vita-Finzi and Eric Higgs (1970) in their model of site catchment analysis, which amalgamated the principles of urban economic geography and the foraging of the !Kung San. They applied a territorial analysis to hunting and agricultural sites. Circles were drawn around sites based on the economies of walking. These had a radius of 10 km for hunters and 5 km for farmers. Beyond these distances returns dropped off in a predictable manner as more calories, or energy, had to be expended than could be acquired. Hence a sort of territorial threshold, or sphere of operations, was established. These thresholds could be established by walking the radii from archaeological sites and noting soils, slopes and the terrain. The catchment of the site was linked to its economic contents, which included animal bones and carbonised cereal grains. Site catchment analysis therefore provided, in an appropriately circular fashion, the explanation for site location. People made camps or built villages to exploit nearby resources.

The notion of centrality has also been widely applied to later monuments and settlements. Here Colin Renfrew's studies of the palace economies of Minoan and Mycenaean Greece have been influential (1972). Palaces such as Knossos and defended citadels such as Mycenae were analysed for their size and functions. In particular, the presence of granaries at Knossos led to its interpretation as a redistributive centre. Furthermore, central places had central people whose status and power stemmed from their ability to organise the redistribution of agricultural and craft surpluses.

POLITIES

Data regarding the relative sizes of these central places has been a powerful tool in characterising the demography and attendant power structures of early state polities. In Mesopotamia there is usually a marked difference in the size of the largest site, for example Warka or ancient Uruk (Redman 1978: 255), when compared to its neighbours. This is known as a primate distribution, where one centre dominates the regional settlement picture. In the later stages of state formation this disparity in site size levels out and the graph shows a continuous distribution for urban sites and villages. At the same time there are changes in the means by which power was concentrated in the hands of the few in a single centre.

The interest in political formation has been investigated as much through the spatial dimension as the artefactual (Renfrew 1977). The attraction of such an approach lies in the comparative basis that the analysis of space provides. Comparing site size and density, and examining differences in a settlement hierarchy, is often easier than assessing the comparative complexity of early states on the basis of the number of gold masks they produced, the size of their pyramids, or the intensity of their agricultural production. Space contains relationships because distance carries costs as well as opportunities.

Islands and archipelagos provide a good example of how space has been used to investigate polities. They often combine a clearly bounded regional approach with an imperative for exchange. This has been done for Hawaii (Kirch 1984) as well as for many of the Mediterranean islands. The framework is reminiscent of a world-systems approach but in this case delimited by natural boundaries and related to objects.

THE ATTRITION OF DISTANCE

By quantifying the spatial distributions they have always plotted out archaeologists have revolutionised their study of trade and exchange. This has been combined with advances in sourcing the raw materials that were used in the manufacture of common items such as pottery and stone, bronze and iron tools. As a result it is possible to examine systems of production, distribution and consumption (Chapter 5). For example, Palaeolithic archaeologists have shown that stone tools from hunting camps are overwhelmingly made of materials that come from less than 5 km away (Geneste 1988). Furthermore, if distant stone sources, those from between 30 and 80 km, are being utilised, the archaeological evidence is almost always in the form of retouched implements rather than waste flakes. In other words we are seeing the movement of finished items, presumably carried by individuals.

Pottery also provides a quantified measure of the difference between local and distant. In his ethnoarchaeological survey of central America, Dean Arnold (1985) found that potters obtained their clays from within 7 km and usually from within 1 km. Of course, this local procurement has to be set beside the long distances over which some pots were subsequently traded. Examples in Europe include Roman wine amphorae and fine table wares, such as Samian pottery, which were traded around the empire.

The quantified evidence exploits the geographical observation known as the attrition of distance. As a general rule a fall-off in the popularity of objects is expected the further one goes from their place of production. In this instance distance represents a cost, especially when translated into transporting heavy, bulky items. This was the model underpinning site-catchment analysis, where villages would be located close to good soils, minimising daily distances to the fields and reducing the costs of transporting the crop at harvest-time.

From an archaeological perspective the interest focuses on observing contradictions to this simple expectation. Particular goods, such as rare obsidian mirrors in Mesoamerica, do not steadily decline away from source. Rather their frequency 'peaks' at places where exchange partners of similar rank or status lived. Much attention has been given to the circulation and distribution of these so-called *prestige goods* which are exchanged between élites (Renfrew and Shennan 1982; Kristiansen and Rowlands 1998). Their distribution provides information about the scale and organisation of polities and the unequal flow of goods between people within them.

The importance of trade and exchange has been stressed in the examination of change, particularly in the question of how state societies and the early civilisations arose (Chapter 7).

GEOGRAPHICAL INFORMATION SYSTEMS

The archaeological love affair with distribution maps has recently received a further fillip thanks to the advent of geographical information systems (GIS). This is the future of spatial archaeology (Wheatley and Gillings 2002). GIS has replaced the laborious business of hand-plotting artefacts on maps with computer procedures. But there is more to GIS than just saving time. The core of GIS is the database and, thanks to advances in computing hardware and software, this can incorporate more data than was possible even only 20 years ago. This allows for the management and analysis of much more complex sets of data than before. One example is provided by Richard Bradley's (1997) regional survey of the rock art found from Portugal to Scotland. Using GIS he was able to calculate for different areas the intervisibility of rock-art sites, known technically as viewshed data. The point of such an exercise is to define a hierarchy of sites in the landscape, to compare whether the most visible are also the richest in terms of the number of motifs and how close sites are to one another. The GIS analysis revealed a structure and patterning to the rock-art data that had not previously been suspected.

An example of using GIS in a relational approach is provided by Fiona Coward's study of the Middle to Upper Palaeolithic transition in Northern Spain. Rather than simply focusing on a traditional economic analysis of the landscapes exploited by Neanderthals and Modern humans in this region, she used scientific palaeoenvironmental data to identify where the particular animal species that each population relied on for food could have been located in the landscape. From the differing frequencies of animal bones recovered from sites in the area, she was able to reconstruct some of the changing patterns of paths and tracks described by their Middle and Upper Palaeolithic inhabitants as they moved between their hunting grounds and camps. These altering patterns of movement, interaction and activity are the basis for a consideration of the differences between Neanderthals and modern humans that does not rely on top-down appeals to the biological 'essence' of either species but builds a bottom-up picture of each group's relations with one another and with other animal species in the landscape as enacted in the daily business of obtaining food (Coward 2005a, b).

Another great potential for GIS in archaeology is predictive modelling. We want to know more about the distribution of sites and artefacts to guide future research as well as the management of the archaeological resource. Through prediction we can test hypotheses about distributions. A recent example is provided by Robert Hosfield's (1999) study of the distribution of Lower Palaeolithic artefacts in southern England. He modelled the activities of collectors during the last century as well as the pattern of mineral extraction. This allowed predictions to be made about the likely occurrence of deeply buried sites incorporated in the river gravels of the region during the past half-million years of human occupation. Such predictions now need to be tested. An archaeological information system would add that important ingredient which is largely missing from GIS, the long-term activities of people.

SOCIAL SPACE AND GENDER

Space is about power. As such it provides a framework for the discussion of gender, the social construction of difference between men and women. Roberta Gilchrist's study (1993) of English nunneries shows how these differences can be approached by analysing the physical movements of religious men and women through the spaces they built, lived in and modified with time. She found that the architectural layout of monasteries and nunneries was very different. In the nunneries the most restricted and difficult to reach areas were the dormitories, while in the monasteries it was the chapter house and sacristy, which were easily accessible in the nunneries. Furthermore, in contrast to monasteries, nunneries were located in liminal surroundings, at the threshold of changes in either the natural landscape or the townscape. A further distinction lay in the fact that nunneries rarely altered the landscapes around them, unlike their male counterparts which relied on self-sufficiency in agricultural produce. As a result, nunneries more closely resembled the houses of the gentry, which, Gilchrist suggests, was the social group that fostered and supported them. They were founded to interact closely with the local community, and consequently their support network lay in that direction rather than in self-sufficiency. Her archaeological study led her to conclude that:

> If nunneries looked different from monasteries, were placed in different landscape situations, and were never endowed in order to achieve self-sufficiency, this is because medieval patrons had a different purpose in mind for medieval religious women.

> (Gilchirst 1993: 190)

Monastic architecture was therefore critical in the social construction of the gender difference between religious men and women – a good example of material culture being active in social relations rather than simply reflecting them.

SPACE AND SOCIETY

Time and space are the framework for archaeological analysis and interpretation. The experiences of our bodies as we go about our daily business provide us with an understanding of these dimensions. Furthermore, we can forge a link with bodies in the past. In this chapter I have looked at the issue of temporality and how it helps us to understand the construction and use of landscapes and sites. I have returned to the issue of obtaining a representative sample, and we have seen that space solves that old problem of not knowing what you are going to find before fieldwork starts. We have a research strategy that samples space for populations of artefacts, sites and landscapes, and these are built up into regions and world systems. Each level has a temporal as well as a spatial dimension, not just in terms of how long a village was inhabited or over what distances a lead ingot was traded, but rather in terms of the rhythms and repetition of human action as people went about constructing their lives.

Understanding how time and space are so intimately connected with the construction of social life opens up a huge field of exploration with archaeological data. The built environment with its constraints and possibilities can be reconstructed from plans and peopled with objects. The analysis of the ways in which space is conceptually structured and related to the body as a source of interpretation and authority provides a very potent means of extending the archaeological imagination in new directions. It will undoubtedly impact on our next topic, the study of change.

SUMMARY

- Bodies are key to interpreting time and space. A rational approach sees them as units of measurement and stomachs that need regular feeding; a relational approach views them as a source for giving meaning to symbols and does not divide them from the world they inhabit.
- Scale affects both time and space from the micro to the macro, and always has done.
- Scales tend to nest inside each other. They are a convenient way to build an analysis from the bottom up, from the site to the region.
- Time and space are not neutral concepts or arbitrary frameworks. They come with a great deal of theoretical baggage on account of the ways in which the sensations and experiences of bodies are interpreted in their cultural context.
- Archaeologists might profit if they spent less time worrying about dates and distance and more thinking about temporality and the 'scapes' of human experience; sensescapes, bodyscapes, landscapes and seascapes, and how these have been expressed through material metaphors using containers and instruments.

7

CHANGE AND STASIS

At the heart of archaeological investigations lie questions about change. These are the big 'why' questions where we try to understand the move to agriculture or the factors behind the spread of people to the New World by at least 15,000 years ago. 'Why' questions can also be much smaller in scope. They may deal with shifts in the species of animal hunted at a site, the transformation from mud-brick to stone architecture or from circular to rectangular houses, changes in burial customs or the appearance of new styles in art or coinage.

But change is only one side of the coin: on the reverse is stasis. When the coin is flipped it is this side that dominates the archaeological record. For long periods on either a prehistoric or historic timescale nothing much seems to have happened. Pottery styles remained constant. The dead were sent to meet their ancestors in much the same way. Crops were harvested and stone chipped in repetitive fashion, often for millennia on end. The question 'why no agriculture?' in a continent such as Australia becomes as inter-esting as investigating the origins of rice cultivation in China.

The contrast to our experience of constant technological and social change could not be more marked. Both change and stasis therefore need explaining. The notion we have that change is the only constant in our lives needs examining. Change is not an essence of the past. But of course it did happen.

QUESTIONS ABOUT CHANGE

In earlier chapters I explored issues of variability in human behaviour and the archaeological record using the dimensions of time and space. This framework is also important when asking questions about change. Change is a multiscalar problem for archaeologists. We need to understand exactly how and where we are pitching our question in order to frame an appropriate explanation.

I will tackle this scalar problem first by looking at six big questions that deal with origins. Then I will move down the scale to less grand questions about why aspects of societies vary. I will examine what we mean by change and ask if we can recognise it as distinct from variation. This will involve considering complexity as a basic issue alongside that of the scales of analysis.

ORIGINS AND THE BIG SIX QUESTIONS

These are questions on which a great deal of archaeological enquiry has focused. Very often they run on a 20-year cycle, which is about the gestation time for large field projects to be written up. The origins cycle runs like this: an international conference is called to tackle an issue of global interest, such as the origins of agriculture (Ucko and Dimbleby 1969), urbanism (Ucko, Tringham and Dimbleby 1972) or modern humans (Mellars and Stringer 1989). Delegates arrive with their fresh data and carefully prepared syntheses. New models and hypotheses are put forward. The raft of information is assimilated. A large proceedings volume emerges and many spin-off volumes then follow as the issues raised are amended, tested in the field and refined by further analysis. Then, after a few years, the excitement cools. Work still continues but not with the headline-grabbing intensity of before. Interest in the question continues to bubble away quietly until the cycle hits its second decade, another international conference is called and the pan boils over once more.

At least five big questions follow this cycle:

- Origins of hominins.
- Origins of modern humans.
- Origins of agriculture and domestic animals.

• Origins of urbanism and the state.
• Origins of modernity.

The first four questions have been there since the birth of archaeology. The fifth is evidence of archaeology's new place in the historical sciences. These issues are now all investigated by interdisciplinary teams. They subsume many themes, such as complexity, specialisation, power and intensification. Their implications are global. They are often referred to as revolutions, most famously by Childe (1951) with his Neolithic and Urban revolutions, the two great stages in human cultural evolution before the Industrial Revolution of the eighteenth century. In addition, I would add to this quintet a sixth big 'how' and 'why' question:

• Global colonisation by the human species.

This question has implications both for the earliest colonisation of habitats, continents and islands as well as their rediscovery as part of mercantile capitalism which gave us, among other things, the triangular slave trade. In other words, this question covers all the other five. As we shall see below, unravelling the process of global colonisation has in fact been one of archaeology's great, but rather unsung, discoveries.

There are of course other big questions, such as origins of feudalism, or the rise and spread of world religions. Language and writing have been treated as origins questions, as have the graphic arts and key aspects of technology such as shipping, wheeled transport and metallurgy.

Much of this only recognises that we can investigate the origins of anything. But these 'big six' questions are widely recognised as fundamental to archaeological endeavour. They also illustrate very well the type of explanation that archaeologists favour. I will return later to the issue of whether such questions have now served their usefulness.

ORIGINS OF HOMININS

This is a question about bodies and brains. We know from genetic evidence that the hominins, which include ourselves and all our fossil ancestors, split from our closest relative the chimpanzee between 5 and 6 million years ago. The reasons for this split need explaining, as does the subsequent path taken by hominin evolution, which led towards upright walking, bipedalism, and a greatly enlarged brain, a process known as encephalisation.

Fossil evidence from southern and east Africa shows that by two-and-a-half million years ago some hominins were fully bipedal, whereas others still retained features such as long, curled fingers and toes, indicating a semi-arboreal adaptation. Moreover, hominin brain size was by this time almost double that found in chimpanzees. Such encephalisation, where brain size far exceeds what is expected in a primate of our size, is unique to the hominins. It was a costly process because brains are very expensive tissues to maintain (Aiello and Wheeler 1995). Our big brains account for only about 2 per cent of our weight but use up nearly 20 per cent of all the energy we consume. They require high-quality foods.

In hominin evolution you don't get something from nothing. A balance had to be struck between the relative size of our key organs: brain, heart, kidney, liver and stomach. The evolutionary trade-off was an expanding brain at the expense of a shrinking stomach. Less gut means less processing of food intake, which means higher-quality foods – a feedback loop feeding on itself (Figure 7.1).

About two-and-a-half million years ago we also find the first stone tools. These simple hammers, choppers and sharp flakes would have assisted the recovery of meat and marrow from animals either brought down by hominins themselves or scavenged from other predators' kills. Between two and one-and-a-half million years ago we find the first hominins outside sub-Saharan Africa in the Near East and Java.

So what need explaining are the Darwinian selection pressures (Chapter 2) that resulted in such an expensive tissue as the brain and such an odd form of primate locomotion as upright walking. Very strong selection indeed is required to make brains bigger, not only because of the extra feeding costs but also because of the longer time that those bigger-brained children, born ever more helpless, needed parenting. As a result there was unlikely to have been a single cause such as a change in the environment, or even competition from the other closely related hominin species who shared the savannah – forest margins. Instead, the evidence favours complex, multi-faceted explanations which deal with the life history

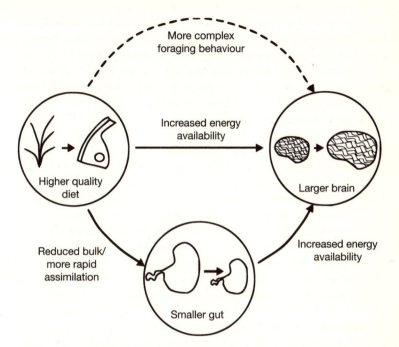

Figure 7.1 A causal feedback-loop between several variables to explain why we evolved larger brains (after Aiello and Wheeler 1995)

of the hominins, the wider community and the environmental changes in which they were involved.

The social brain hypothesis, put forward by Robin Dunbar (1996), makes the case that group size and brains grew together. This is certainly the case with monkeys and apes where the sizes of the brain and of the group are strongly associated (Aiello and Dunbar 1993). One benefit of living in larger groups is better defence against predators. It has also been suggested that the abnormally large hominin brain evolved to monitor increasing numbers of people and organise all the additional social information of living in groups of over 100 individuals. Change was slow and gradual, measured in millions of years, but hominin brain size does show a significant increase 500,000 years ago. Group sizes of 120 are now predicted and to function these would have needed a new form of rapid communication to replace finger-tip grooming that is the primate means of social bonding. Spoken language would fit that need and may well be that old. Archaeologists can test this hypothesis by examining the layout of campsites and in particular the role of hearths in structuring the everyday activities of social life (Gowlett 2005), as well as by studying artefacts such as figurative art that are thought to represent the symbolic ability necessary for language (d'Errico *et al.* 2003).

ORIGINS OF MODERN HUMANS

This is a question about essences and relative achievement. But first of all we have to define what modern humans are; only afterwards can we search the archaeological archives for their origins.

There are three parts to the definition. Modern humans can be defined genetically, anatomically and behaviourally. The first points to an African origin since today people in that continent have the greatest genetic diversity. This is used as an argument of origins since such genetic diversity must have developed over a considerable period of time. The point of origin is believed to be between 250,000 and 300,000 years ago. The anatomical evidence also points to Africa as the continent of origin. To date, the oldest modern-looking skulls come from East Africa and are some 190,000 years old. The behavioural evidence is less clear cut. Traits from the currently accepted checklists are found scattered across Africa from 300,000 years ago. These include changes in stone and bone technology and the use of pigments, exotic stones, camp sites and marine resources (McBrearty and Brooks 2000). A similar scatter can be found in parts of the Old World, especially in the best researched continent, Europe (d'Errico 2003).

However, around 60,000 years ago these disparate elements are combined in some places into a distinctive package that has been called the Human Revolution (Mellars and Stringer 1989). The pace of stylistic change accelerates and differs, often considerably, between regions. Figurative art and novel forms of architecture are present in northern latitudes after 40,000 years ago, while richly appointed burials are found after 30,000 years ago. Moreover, people are found in Australia for the first time 60,000 years ago and in the Americas by at least 15,000 years ago and possibly earlier.

These achievements may seem rather strung out in time. Revolution hardly seems the right word for something that takes place over 30,000 years. But that has to be put into the context of the 6 million years of hominin evolution that has occurred since we split from the chimps. On this timescale, change was rapid and dramatic.

The origin of modern humans also involves the fate of other hominin species, most famously the Neanderthals. These people, with their distinctive faces and bodies well suited to northern climates, lived in Europe and the Middle East. Their fate has long interested archaeologists. Were they replaced by incoming modern humans, *Homo sapiens*, or did they evolve into them? The genetic and anatomical evidence that *Homo sapiens* replaced them is overwhelming. But the behavioural evidence points to at least 10,000 years of coexistence in parts of Europe. The last Neanderthals are found in southern Spain some 25,000 years ago. This was long after modern humans had spread throughout northern Europe. The demise of the Neanderthals must now be seen as protracted and complex rather than short and simple.

Change in this question is usually tackled with evolutionary models. However, historical contingency is increasingly coming to play a part in the explanations being put forward, precisely because the constituent parts of the triumvirate of genetics, anatomy and behaviour do not mesh chronologically. One hundred thousand years ago some people looked like you and me. Their genes had a modern pattern, like yours and mine, and yet they acted according to a much older script. Archaeology, rather than genetics or anatomy, holds the key to understanding our recent origins.

ORIGINS OF AGRICULTURE AND DOMESTIC ANIMALS

This is a question about manipulation, control and progress. Famously termed the Neolithic Revolution by Childe (1935), the package of changes in subsistence, the appearance of settled villages and increase in population numbers has been taken as a turning point in human prehistory. Traditionally the behavioural markers come as much from the widespread use of pottery, polished stone, large funerary monuments and increasingly elaborate settlements as they do from the appearance of domestic animals and cultivated crops. A contrast is often drawn with the preceding mobile hunters and gatherers. For example, early Neolithic villages in the Near East and southeastern Europe often form impressive tells or mounds, as at Karanovo in Bulgaria, and bear witness to intensive and repeated use of particular locations over many millennia.

In the face of these archaeological data the case for progress seemed clear cut. Neolithic peoples in the Old World manipulated the same domesticated cattle, sheep, goats, pigs and dogs, and cultivated wheat and barley, all of which formed the basis for contemporary civilisation. They lived in villages which often became towns, as at Çatalhöyük in Anatolia. They had religious monuments. They represented a break with the past of the hunters and gatherers, described in the nineteenth century schemes of social progress as the stage of savagery.

The key point about the Neolithic Revolution is the control of subsistence production and the possibility of a reliable surplus that this revolution ushered in. The focus of human affairs appeared to shift from consuming to producing. Childe's legacy has been to make many archaeologists look no further back in time for our origins than about 10,000 years ago, when the first evidence for domestic cereals and sheep are found in the Near East. Hence these few relevant millennia have been searched diligently for an explanation (Gebauer and Price 1992; Harris 1996; Redman 1978).

Explanations have included that of climatic change forcing the wild ancestors of animals, cereal grasses and humans together. Differences between geographical regions have also been put forward, with people in the marginal zones intensifying production to keep up in the post-glacial world. The importance of identifying the original home of domestication, either the fertile crescent of the Near East or the smaller Levantine corridor (Bar-Yosef 1998) has been important in evaluating such models.

The result has been to reverse the notion of progress. The farmers were in fact the failures among the hunters and gatherers, losing their key tactic to fluctuating resources, mobility, by settling down (Binford 2001). The latter can also exhibit the trappings of agriculturalists, such as cemeteries, villages and trade routes, while still hunting deer and gathering shellfish. Moreover, we need to break free of the Near Eastern bias and remember that the Neolithic Revolution occurred independently in several other areas of the world, though involving different species in each instance: China (rice and water buffalo), sub-Saharan Africa (sorghum and cattle) and Mesoamerica (maize and turkeys). Indeed, the process of domestication has occurred in many places and at many times, as is now revealed by archaeology and genetics (Bellwood 2005; Zeder *et al.* 2006). Sometimes the domestication of new species occurred in an existing agricultural setting, sometimes not. Examples of the latter include dogs in Palaeolithic Europe, cats in Egypt, llamas in Peru, dingoes in Australia, elephants in India, dogs again in prehistoric North America and musk-oxen in Alaska during the 1960s.

So it is not a simple case of GM foods originating in the Neolithic. Manipulation by hunters through selective breeding eventually produced more than 57 varieties of dog from their wild counterparts. However, the unexpected effects of comparable selection on the productivity of key grass crops such as wheat, rice, finger millet and maize were astonishing. The tiny seeds of these thin little grasses evolved into kernels of concentrated energy and power.

In considering this third question, change has often been put down to a prime mover where one factor is singled out as the catalyst for change. Prime movers that have been put forward over the years include population pressure, climate change and propinquity between grasses and humans. But the convergence on an agriculture mode of life was a global process, which casts doubt on any simple prime mover. A co-evolutionary approach as explored by David Rindos (1989) directly tackles the issue of convergence. He reminds us that evolution works through undirected variation and that human innovations facilitate rather than cause evolution. Bigger ears of wheat provide the means but not the explanation for change.

Alternatively, the move to new forms of production has been attributed to changes in the social requirements of production (Bender 1978). Intensification, which in this instance involved selective manipulation of the resources themselves, rather than just working harder or developing other mechanisms such as storage, has always been a response available to hunters and gatherers. Indeed, archaeological evidence for hunter-gatherer intensification is now commonplace in continents, such as Australia (Lourandos 1997), where what we know as farming was introduced by Europeans. The realisation that the Neolithic is not all that Childe cracked it up to be means that to understand the process we must look again at the historical circumstances of those societies that took up the option. It also requires that we examine those areas where agriculture did not develop indigenously, such as Australia, which at the time of European contact did not have pyramids poking out of the Queensland rainforest, in order to achieve a satisfactory explanation.

BOX 19 CHECKLIST OF TRAITS FOR CHILDE'S URBAN REVOLUTION.

1 *Size:* an increase in settlement size towards urban proportions.
2 *Surplus:* the centralised accumulation of capital resulting from the imposition of tribute or taxation.
3 *Monumental public works.*
4 The invention of *writing.*
5 Elaboration of the exact and predictive *sciences.*
6 The appearance and growth of long-distance *trade in luxuries.*
7 The emergence of a *class-stratified society* based on the unequal distribution of social surplus.
8 *Composition and function of an urban centre,* freeing part of the population from subsistence tasks for full-time craft specialisation.
9 *State organisation* based on residence rather than on kinship and involving territorial definition.
10 The appearance of *naturalistic art.*

ORIGINS OF URBANISM AND THE STATE

This is a question about our civilised origins – not only about how technologically smart we became, but how some centres of power came to dominate. This has been a popular question with colonial archaeologies (Box 24) seeking authority from the past for their activities in the present. Once an agricultural surplus became possible, what could be done with it? Once again Childe's view has been very influential: he suggested that the surplus was turned into people who were then organised through a cadre of specialists (priests, kings, soldiers, bureaucrats).

By means of a ten-point checklist, the archaeological archives could once again be examined (Box 19) to discover when society had moved from the Neolithic stage – barbarism, according to the nineteenth-century viewpoint – to full civilisation. Childe summed it all up very succinctly as a technological package:

> Metallurgy, the wheel, the ox-cart, the pack-ass, and the sailing ship provided the foundations for a new economic organisation.
>
> (1942: 97)

More recently this has been described by Andrew Sherratt (1997) as the secondary-products revolution. Once again this applies to the Near Eastern domesticates. Secondary products include milk, animal traction and an emphasis on wool for clothing. Their appearance points to a further intensification in the agricultural process. Metals were important in the Old World, but apart from copper and gold were less significant in the New, where iron metallurgy was unknown.

Between 3500 and 1500 BC a combination of urbanism, writing and specialisation produced state-level societies in the Near East, Egypt, the Indus Valley and China between the Yellow and Yangtze rivers. In Mesoamerica a similar combination was in place 2000 years ago with the widespread influence of the Mayas, until their civilisation collapsed between AD 771 and 830 (Yoffee 2005). John Baines and Norman Yoffee have succinctly identified the common link between these geographically separate developments:

> The formation and maintenance of elites, and then of elites within elites, lie at the heart of civilisations: inequality is fundamental.
>
> (1998: 234)

These primary states were followed by many other civilisations, for example the Inca of South America, Great Zimbabwe in southern Africa and the Minoans and Mycenaeans of Greece. The last appear to be locked into a world system relationship (Chapter 6) with the civilisations of the Near East, just as the complex societies of south-western North America and the Mississippi Valley were to some extent with Mesoamerica.

Recasting the question to examine the origins of the state, rather than of civilisation, has not been without its difficulties. Agreement over how to define the state also remains elusive (Feinman and Marcus 1998). We all know it when we see it in the form of the Mexican city of Teotihuacan, which housed 200,000 people. But what about less obvious examples such as the complex Hawaiian chiefdoms or the pueblos in Chaco Canyon, New Mexico? Should they also qualify? Opinions differ. One feature of explaining the state is that environmental factors are accorded less importance in accounting for origins, probably because of these fuzzy definitions, and rather more when the issue of their collapse is examined.

Change in this origins question still involves a debate between a generalising approach, the comparative study of the state and historical specificity. For example, what particular features led to elite control? To what extent was the exercise of power dependent upon local circumstances, such as the availability of copper sources or of trade routes to control and exploit? The role of trade, particularly the circulation of prestige goods, has been presented as crucial in setting in motion the cycles of production and social reproduction typical of these state systems (Friedman 1994). Control of production through irrigation was important in the Mesopotamian states, but elaborate and extensive water management in Papua New Guinea led only to tribes without chiefs.

The key, as Baines and Yoffee (1998) argue, is that the elites in archaic states and civilisations did not so much create the wealth that archaeologists dig up by the dumpster-load but transform the meaning of that wealth. This was the role of those priest kings and other potentates who controlled symbolic resources. They, and only they, gave those obsidian mirrors, gold sarcophogi and elephant ivory footstools value and meaning. Elites were only interested in material redistribution in so far as it kept them in power. They were not bound by the cultural requirements of the welfare state. High culture, defined as 'the production and consumption of aesthetic items under the control, and for the benefit, of the inner elite of a civilisation, including the ruler and gods' (Baines and Yoffee 1998: 235), was the focus for the exploitation of wealth by the social order to establish the legitimacy of that order.

ORIGINS OF MODERNITY

This is a question about attitude. The investigation of modernity, the transformation of the world under industrialisation, nationalism and capitalism, has been dominated by historians and social scientists and the expressive powers of authors and artists – modern tunes, modern art and a material girl (Box 20).

BOX 20 WHAT IS MEANT BY MODERNITY?

Modernity is a term of identity. It is used to characterise something essential in our own society and so refers to this particular historical period. The term it is usually contrasted with is *tradition*. Modernity entangles different societies at a global scale and reinterprets their traditions and culture. Modernity, as Jonathan Friedman writes (1994: 143), implies the separation of the symbol from what it refers to.

(after Friedman 1994: 214)

At the heart of the issue lies the idea of separation and a break with the past (Thomas 2004). These separations led to immense gains in analytical and theoretical science, engineering and medicine. Cartesianism came to dominate all aspects of human knowledge, including the study of the remote past. Unsurprisingly, the literature on the origins of modernity is vast. For our basic purposes it is permissible to cut to the chase by citing five propositions that have been applied to other, non-Western cultures, and their view of their own past (Box 21). These propositions, most closely adhered to in archaeology by the culture history and processual schools (Chapter 2), illustrate our traditionally close relationship to modernist approaches.

That having been said, modernity may not be unique to the European Industrial Revolution that began in the eighteenth century. In the fourth and fifth centuries BC, Greece had comparable tendencies to analytical separation. However, this was not supported by industrialisation and the alienation and commodification between people involved in the work process that it produced (Friedman 1994: 229).

BOX 21 FIVE PROPOSITIONS ABOUT THE WORLD THAT A MODERNIST VIEW OF KNOWLEDGE WOULD MAKE.

1. There is only one 'true' version of the past.
2. The past consists of arbitrarily chosen segments of a temporal continuum which ends with the present moment.

3. The structure attributed to the past is the product of a specific kind of research carried out by those competent in the field, that is, archaeologists.

4. The structure of the past is therefore objective, which corresponds to proposition 1. That is, there is only one, not many pasts.

5. All other structures or interpretations attributed to the past are, by implication, ideological in the sense that they are misrepresentations. This allows anthropologists to dismiss the 'natives' point of view' as only a mere folk model, a common-sense explanation. It is never of any scientific value as defined in terms of the above approaches by the competent practitioners mentioned in proposition 3. Archaeologists can be equally contemptuous of New Age interpretations of stone circles and the like.

(after Friedman 1994: 137 – I have adapted them to refer to the study of the past)

Charles Orser (1999) has referred to our study of the industrial period as modern-world archaeology. But why should archaeologists be studying the past 300 years at all? Wouldn't it be more sensible to leave it to the historians and their mountain of written records?

A point that Sarah Tarlow (1999: 265) makes is that the transition from the medieval to the modern led to the commodification of peoples and things. Since the basics of archaeology are concerned with objects, we should be well placed to comment on the changes. However, we first have to convince historians, who seriously outnumber archaeologists working on this period, that they may not be justified in favouring the text over the object to explain the origins of modernity. Matthew Johnson, for one, makes the telling point that:

Most agree that [modernity] has something to do with material things, how they are produced and consumed and the social and economic values people place upon them; and that the changing relationship between things, values and people has a lot to do with the origins of the modern way of life.

(1993: 325–29)

We ignore objects and their transformation into commodities at our peril. Furthermore, by coming late to the modern-world game archaeologists might be able to sidestep some of the origins pitfalls that have previously ensnared them. Certainly there is a good deal of debate about what to call and how to define the period chronologically. More importantly, modern-world archaeologists have the opportunity to assess change in a more reflexive manner than their colleagues studying the rise of Hittite civilisation. The familiar past of the last 300 years is just that – familiar – and it is through objects, those broken willow-pattern plates, street plans and glass bottles, that we can begin the process of de-familiarising what we think is the known past (West 1999: 1). As Susie West makes clear, this is a very different use of material culture from that known in prehistory, where the object of the exercise is to make the totally unknown familiar. In modern-world archaeology those objects challenge the orthodoxy. They won't do away with written records, eye-witness accounts or the works of Charles Dickens. We have to make the two work together to provide those rich insights that the interface between the 'world as lived in' and the 'world as thought', the amalgamation of text and object, can achieve.

A further advantage that modern-world archaeologists have in their study of the origins of modernity lies in their awareness of essences. The push to modernity was first accounted for in a series of important books and papers by James Deetz (1977) and Henry Glassie (1975) as a process of 'Georgianisation' from 1600 to 1800. The changes could be traced in the way food was prepared – individual portions rather than helpings from the common pot – and architecture, where individualism was expressed through new levels of privacy, as shown by the partitioning of rooms. Such Georgian principles help to define the trends but also encourage an essential way of thinking. Something either is or is not Georgian and hence is on the way to or has already arrived at modernity. The state of mind is stressed and curiously that 'world as lived in' quality that comes from objects is lost. The truth is we can never 'see' Georgianisation, just as we cannot 'see' either the Neolithic Revolution or the transition to modern humans. As Johnson remarks (1993: 345), a concentration on the rise of institutions or the desired qualities of social life can miss the point. Too much emphasis on origins takes our eye away from the changing matrices of social relations that created such institutions and qualities. Modernity and capitalism were more about constantly becoming than they were about an origin with a discernible transition and a well-established start date.

GLOBAL COLONISATION BY THE HUMAN SPECIES

My final big question has received nothing like the systematic attention of the other five. Yet by asking how and why we became not only a global species, unique among mammals, but at the same time the sole extant hominin, allows us to put them in perspective (Gamble 1993).

As the world was rediscovered by explorers such as Columbus and Cook, so they found that it had already been peopled. Modernity was part of the process of global rediscovery. The great discovery of prehistoric archaeology has been to show that this global peopling was a recent event in our hominin history and that outside the Old World it was entirely achieved by ourselves, *Homo sapiens*, a finding now supported by the genetic study of the great human diaspora that began 60,000 years ago (Cavalli-Sforza and Cavalli-Sforza 1995). We know that for most of our 5 million years there have been at any one time, and often in the same region, at least two hominin species – and in well-researched periods several more. This all ended between 25,000 years ago as the last Neanderthals in Europe became extinct, and 12,000 years ago when *Homo floresienses* suffered the same fate in Indonesia. Over only the past 60,000 years colonisation in Australia and the Pacific, Siberia and the Americas took place for the first time. Therefore, it took *Homo sapiens* roughly 1 per cent of the total length of hominin evolution to colonise 75 per cent of the Earth – not much more time than the origins of crop agriculture or urban civilisations.

The timing strongly suggests that prime-mover explanations such as population pressure, climatic change or lucky breaks in technology such as inventing boats will not adequately account for such a process. They may contribute to an understanding of how colonisation took place, but they cannot fully explain why it occurred. As Rindos pointed out for agriculture, human innovations facilitated, but did not cause, evolution.

Investigating global colonisation is not a quest for the oldest North American or the first Australian. Rather it uses the timing and the different histories involved in the process to understand humans as colonisers. Therefore, the extent to which intensification, social as well as economic, occurred among colonising societies is very relevant. There would have been no global colonisation without domestication, the deep Pacific shows that. But neither would there have been a start to the process if mobile peoples had not intensified their own production because of revised social demands. The question then becomes one of understanding why society changed at all times and places and how the demands placed on production, distribution and consumption were met. There seems to be some similarity between the processes that put a person on Easter Island and a pyramid at Giza.

For my money, global colonisation, that great prehistoric achievement, was an unintended consequence of processes that also led, as it happened, to agriculture and the urban state. It may have involved purpose among individuals but it was never a goal. By contrast, the historical migrations that had such stated goals all occurred in the context of a full world and state power.

THE PROBLEM WITH ORIGINS RESEARCH

Origins research can be great fun. There is nothing quite like excavating the oldest goat, or the thrill of finding London's first banana, c. AD 1560, dug up in 1999. Origins strikes a chord with the public. And remember, nobody who has found a fossil skull has ever damaged their career prospects – the older the better. But is origins research really a worthwhile archaeological pursuit?

The short answer is: no. I have already referred to the essentialist nature of such research where definitions and checklists (e.g. Box 19) dominate the process. Origins research is like misusing an old-fashioned hearing trumpet. You place the pointed end on the thing you want to hear about – for example language, writing, graphic arts, agriculture – and listen for an explanation at the open end where the noise distortion is greatest. As Alexandra Alexandri (1995: 59) concludes, all this does is to trace the beginning of familiar concepts, echoes of the present in the past.

This is clearly unsatisfactory. We are confusing timing with explanation, cataloguing with understanding. We need to attend to more voices than just that of origins research, where, at its worst, the hunt for the oldest comes to dominate the conversation. Instead, as discussed below, we need to broaden explanation to consider that lifestyles have a 'becoming' (i.e. are constantly originating) rather than an origin in time and space. Such a becoming is a continuous process of creativity, not something that is fixed in time, pinned like a butterfly in a case or lying like a banana skin on the floor.

SCALE AND CHANGES TO THE SYSTEM

While origins research needs to carry a health warning – 'The Chief Archaeologist advises: Too many "firsts" can lead to dialogues with the deaf' – there is no escaping the narrative focus it continues to provide, equivalent in other disciplines to the search for cold fusion, Fermat's last theorem or a cure for the common cold.

I have briefly sketched our current approaches to origins questions because if we lift the lid on such research we find that the more familiar scales of change are addressed underneath. These scales involve all the entities and the temporal and spatial scales discussed in Chapters 3 and 6. Now this was one of the appeals of the systems approach whereby change was traced in the component subsystems of an entire socio-cultural adaptation (Figure 2.2). Hence at the levels of intra-site, site and region a trajectory of change can be plotted for subsistence, trade, settlement, population, craft specialisation, and symbolic and religious subsystems. The extent to which these interlocked is then examined. It is understanding how change arose in these subsystems that has led to the many archaeologies briefly mentioned in Chapters 1 and 2, for example settlement, economic, cognitive, demographic and environmental archaeology.

In the same way, artefact types and their attributes can be examined as they change through time and across space. Explanation is then often sought in terms of new functions or changes in ideology. Hodder's (1982: 73) study of calabashes in East Africa concludes that these important daily objects are integral to the social relations between young men, women and older men. The fluctuating economic and social fortunes of the former have been expressed through changes in design as material symbols are used to disrupt the dominant social order.

BE LOCAL, THINK GLOBAL

Representations of time are important in the process of explanation. Thanks to stratigraphy, archaeology has a vertical vision as well as a linear notion of time. The sections we dig through a cave, a Bronze Age tell or a medieval town demand an explanation, even if nothing seems to change. The vertical dimension strongly emphasises the narrative structure of the way we describe and explain the past. The temporal segments we observe are also of variable length, and obtaining a continuous sequence is rather like building up a tree-ring chronology from many different trees. If change occurs in our trench, then we build explanations for the change in relation to those that occur in other trenches nearby and further afield.

All of this is part of the professional use of our archaeological imagination. The basic point to grasp is that explaining the structure of archaeological archives in time and space will always be a contest between the local and global. For example, you excavate the floor-plan of a seventeenth-century tenement in Southampton. What you are interested in are data that shed light on the rise of mercantile capitalism, but the link may seem tenuous while you empty the contents of a rubbish pit.

As a result it is always tempting to explain the local by the local, but this must be resisted, or at least tested (Wobst 1978). Explaining change in the components of a system or in the segment available in a survey or excavation may seem tempting in terms of immediate conditions. The explanation would sound like this: 'they selected those stone tools because they needed to cut up the rhino whose bones they lie beside', or, 'the shift in the later part of the tell sequence to fully threshed, clean grain rather than the earlier mixed grain and weed assemblage points to local changes in consumption, storage and field management and may correlate with a few larger structures, i.e. elites taking charge, which appear elsewhere on site'.

No doubt in many cases such explanations are basically correct. But archaeology, because it is about objects, simultaneously samples different spatial and temporal scales. Time and again we see how variation is caused by regional as much as local factors.

WHEN CHANGE IS NOT CHANGE BUT VARIATION

Therefore the really big question is: when is it possible to talk of change rather than just document variation? That is another appeal of the big five questions. They deal with qualitative and quantitative differences in organisation, lifestyle, environmental impact, human biology, geographical expansion and inter-connectedness that just can't be ignored.

But there are many smaller changes – a new pot style, a shift from a dispersed to a nucleated settlement pattern, the repositioning of chimneys from the centre to one or both ends of rural cottages – that are of a lesser scale but also need explaining. Most of these are in effect dealing with variation.

To identify change, we need to address two factors. First, and most obviously, there is a chronological element. Second, since all individuals and indeed cultures exhibit variation (see Figure 3.3, polythetic sets) we need to have a view on the limits to variation. Change happens when those limits are exceeded, as I show below for evolutionary landscapes. But change is neither a property nor an essence of the entities we study. Variation and stasis, on the other hand, most certainly are.

I define change as organisation *based on* novel social premises. By contrast variation is the accommodation of novel conditions *within* existing social premises. If the notion of the Neolithic Revolution as one of the hinges in human history has validity, then it is because society moved to new forms of appropriation and not because humans evolved a taste for mutton. Variation always exists. Change requires a new structure.

Now this may seem like splitting hairs. But change and variation are important, owing to the types of explanation involved. Variation, as we have seen, is well catered for by evolutionary approaches – culture history, contextual investigations and processual studies. Those relocated chimneys in the cottages of rural England would, respectively, be explained by cultural transmission, cultural norms, structuring principles of identity and gender or functional requirements following a change in temperature or wind direction. The explanation of variation is based, as we have seen (Chapter 2), on differing views of culture, the nature of variation itself, human agency and the role of scientific method in a causal process. As a result there will always be few real changes to explain in archaeology but a very great deal of variation to account for.

NEO-EVOLUTIONARY ACCOUNTS OF VARIETY AND CHANGE

Sometimes it is simplest to decide on what we don't want in order to find out what we need. Neo-evolutionary schemes are a prime example. They should not be confused with neo-Darwinian approaches.

Neo-evolution was 'new' because it revisited the nineteenth-century schemes of social progress with an anthropological awareness. The ladder of savagery, barbarism and civilisation that Morgan proposed in 1877, and which Childe was still using in 1951, was then replaced by the scheme of band, tribe, chiefdom and state (Service 1962; Sahlins 1963; Fried 1967). This influential framework, outlined in Box 22, has provided archaeologists with ethnographic descriptions to work towards in their studies of function and change. The framework proved very useful as a systems approach to social change.

But the categories are disputed. Chiefdoms, for example, are classed as redistributive societies, although redistribution is found in many other societies on the scale of band to state societies. Ethnographically, Chiefdoms encompass a great range, so much so that the difference between the ranking and stratification of social roles and positions is not always clear. Neither have neo-evolutionists ever been very clear about the division between 'simple' chiefdoms and tribal societies led by charismatic 'big men', a status commonly observed in Papua New Guinea where established political rulers are very rare. The fuzziness is also apparent at the band level where many hunter-gatherer societies exist that are certainly not egalitarian. Hence the further division by some into 'simple' and 'complex' hunters.

Neo-evolution provides an excellent example of a top-down approach (Chapter 4) to the classification and study of society. Band society is an institution created by anthropologists so that they can go about their business of revealing society (Gamble 1999). The individual quickly vanishes, like a government statistic.

BOX 22 A TYPOLOGY OF SOCIETIES FAVOURED BY NEO-EVOLUTIONISTS.

Childe	Service	Sahlins	Fried
Civilisation	State	State	State
Civilisation	Chiefdom	Complex	Stratified society
		Simple	Ranked society
Farmers (barbarism)	Tribe	Big man	
Hunter/gatherers (savagery)	Band	Head man	Egalitarian

(Earle 1994)

COMPLEXITY

While archaeologists no longer talk of progress, either to describe or to explain the changes in society they study, we often view change as a complexification (Chapman 2003).

Something becomes complex when it is made up of ever more parts. It is folded together in more dense and intricate ways. Complexity is another of those terms that results in a trait list for the comparison of simple and complex hunters or tribes with chiefdoms. However, what are needed are measures of complexity, rather than a presence/absence list. Moreover, rather than pick complexity to pieces we need to recognise, as James McGlade and Sander van der Leeuw (1997: 14) point out, that the basic feature of any complex system is that it is more than the sum of its parts. Complexity is irreducible.

The investigation of complexity once seemed well suited to a systems approach where structural differences are dependent upon the organisation and flow of information as the diverse and disparate units, or subsystems, are integrated. Hence for Kent Flannery (1972) complexity is measured via *segregation*, or differentiation, and *centralisation*, the degree of connectedness in the system. Randall McGuire (1983) has examined the components of complexity as variables in cultural evolution. He points out that the concept often includes so much that it becomes a catch-all and explains nothing. His solution is to simplify the concept. He does this by emphasising the vertical and horizontal axes in social structure. In this way measures of complexity can be made for comparative purposes. These involve *inequality*, measured in terms of access to resources, and *heterogeneity*, which refers to the number of social persona in the system. Most importantly, we should not expect these two variables to correlate positively but instead consider them independently in the process of social change.

It is only in the very long term that we can see that change tends towards more complex systems of organisation. That of course is archaeology's unique time perspective. But once again change and complexity do not represent the old-fashioned drive to progress – savagery, barbarism and civilisation. Elsewhere, Shirley Strum and Bruno Latour (1987) reserve the word *complex* to describe primate societies and *complicated* to characterise the simple, repeated actions that structure much of human social life. These habitual actions organise life by making it more routine and hence both more predictable and more variable. The implication is that for social evolution to occur we first had to become more simple, not more complex.

MECHANISMS AND MODELS

I can identify the big questions, although mindful of the health warning, and I can propose what represents change rather than variation. But I still have to discuss the mechanisms and models that account for the overwhelming evidence for stability, the rare moments of change and long-term developments in complexity among the many scales of our archaeological entities.

We fight shy of terms such as 'progress' because that is a legacy, quite rightly, that archaeologists are trying to shed. Instead, biology provides a better set of metaphors to clarify our basic principles simply because biology deals with growth in complexity in organisms, where the egg and sperm race becomes the marathon of multicellular life. Biology also deals with long-term change in the form of speciation. Biology does not explain culture, but it does, as in the case of cultural transmission (Chapter 2), provide a co-evolutionary way of thinking about the problem.

LANGUAGE AND DEVELOPMENT

Terry Deacon (1997) has argued that language, a trait that in anyone's book would ratchet up complexity and signify change, is best explained with such a co-evolutionary perspective. The development of language was not just a brain thing. Neither was it simply due to other biological processes such as the evolution of a suitable voice-box. It did not take place either inside or outside the brain but rather at that critical interface where biology and culture interact.

In Deacon's view the way in which we became a symbolic species, using language without even thinking about it, is best explained as a developmental process. Changes in growth affected components of the biology of hominins, particularly their brains. But these took place in response to selection from the lives they led and the sort of people they were.

The result is a non-linear model of change for what we regard as a fundamental capacity of being human. There was no simple straight line from grunting to singing *Nessun dorma* at the World Cup. There was no single cause or selective pressure for change. Why should spoken language confer advantages in either scoring goals or finding a mate? While chat-up lines have no doubt improved in 5 million years, thanks to language, so too has our ability to head the ball into the back of the net, because at the same time we acquired a forehead.

THE NEOLITHIC REVOLUTION AND THE END OF BIOLOGY?

My point is that much change is an unintended consequence of the complex interaction of biology and culture with which we are all involved. This interaction produces exaptations, whereby traits happen to fit by reason of their pre-existing form, rather than adaptations, where traits become fit by reason of design (Gould and Vrba 1982; Gould 1991). Animal domestication was not an adaptation, the product of deliberate selection to forge a new economic niche. Animals had been part of human economies for hundreds of thousands of years. They were therefore always available for use, either in the same way as hunted resources or in new ways, tethered to the homestead. They were exapted as required, rather than adapted to produce the requirement of more, predictable food.

All too often the Neolithic Revolution is presented as the slackening of biology's grip on the process of cultural change. With the first wheat the biological fetters dropped from our potential for cultural growth and diversity.

To believe this would be to return to the progressive evolution of the nineteenth century. Instead Deacon's co-evolutionary interface still operates. Variation is being adapted and exapted into novel patterns. Individuals and populations are very much constrained by hereditary biology – just think of disease resistance. Change continues to occur neither inside nor outside our biology, neither inside nor outside culture, but as part of the complex interaction between the two.

THE EVOLUTIONARY LANDSCAPE

Many of the issues concerning complexity, stasis and change were illustrated by the biologist C. H. Waddington in his brilliant book *Tools for Thought* (1977). He supplied the metaphor of the evolutionary landscape to describe biological growth as well as the constraints that account for stasis.

His landscape exists in multi-dimensional space and can be conceptualized as a surface with valleys and hills. But rather than the forces of geology shaping such prominent features, in an evolutionary landscape it is natural selection that produces the ridges and furrows. The surface is constantly bending and flexing in response to the selective pushes and pulls of the environment and the organisms it contains. Where once there was a single valley now a fork occurs. Where hills once stood we now find a flat plain. Such a fluid situation nicely captures the complexities of the evolutionary process and the adaptive responses that a complex creature such as a human must make.

The entity under investigation – and Waddington was very interested in the behaviour of complex systems such as globalisation – is integral to this evolutionary landscape. Waddington conceived of the entity, whether an individual hominin or the world's economy, as a ball bearing rolling down the valleys and, with enough momentum, up the sides of the hills. On occasion the momentum would take it over into another valley. Moreover, when it came to a fork, which path it rolled down also contributed to change. It is important to stress how necessary the landscape and the entity are to each other. The one does not exist without the other and the familiar distinction between external and internal forces (see below) is unnecessary.

REGULATING THE SYSTEM AND ORGANISING THE FLOW

One of Waddington's central ideas was *canalisation*. In evolutionary biology canalisation predicts that natural selection will tend to replace flexible adaptive responses to continuing environmental constraints with genetic predispositions. This is how behaviour becomes fixed. Canalisation is what makes systems stable and predictable. As Waddington put it:

> In many systems we come across, some type of stability has been an important property. A natural living system has usually acquired some degree of stability by natural selection (it would have fallen apart and died out if it wasn't stable enough); in artificial systems man commonly designs a series of checks and counter-checks to ensure stability.
>
> (1977: 104)

He then identified two of these checks: *homeostasis*, which preserves a value at a given state, and *homeorhesis*, which preserves a flow. Archaeologists spent a great deal of time talking about the former when the systems model was popular. Hence a homeostatic feature might be an environmental hazard, periodically reducing population to a sustainable level, or a granary presided over by an elite who redistributed the surplus and so avoided civil unrest. Feedback in terms of information flows was considered important for regulation, and stability, to occur. Disruptions to the feedback mechanisms could disrupt homeostatis, and were thus potential explanations for change.

Homeorhesis has been considered less, although a notable application has been in the use of catastrophe theory to analyse the way small variations can lead to unexpectedly dramatic change (Renfrew and Cooke 1979). Potentially homeorhesis is much more interesting than homeostasis, as it leads us back to the complexities of those evolutionary landscapes.

This is the landscape where non-linear modelling of dynamic, that is, changing, systems comes to the fore: as proposed by James McGlade and Sander van der Leeuw (1997: 14), a non-linear approach rejects explanations that describe a linear, progressive unfolding of events. For them a non-linear approach requires a different vision of history and the causes of change. They see the process as a series of unexpected consequences, known as contingency. These arise from the interplay of processes that can be both deterministic and stochastic, or randomly generated. Their bottom line is to encourage the discovery of more and more dimensions of variability in our data rather than to trim them into convenient packages to make plausible narratives.

WHAT MAKES A GOOD EXPLANATION IN ARCHAEOLOGY

Explanation is never easy. It depends upon the paradigm you follow (Chapter 2). For example, Randall McGuire (1992) discusses the advantages that would accrue from aligning archaeological explanation to Marxist theory, and in particular the power of the Hegelian dialectic that this would bring. Stephen Shennan (2002), on the other hand, prefers the explanatory power of natural selection to account for patterns of cultural transmission. Darwinian models of inheritance and mechanisms leading to change such as drift and founder effect depend upon population size and demographic fluctuations. Shennan (2001) argues that the small size of Lower Palaeolithic populations explains the long stasis of Acheulean handaxes since the transmission of this item from one generation to another would be under selection not to change. Finally, processual and interpretive approaches favour, respectively, science and social theory. The preferred option for many, and for culture historians in particular, is to arrange the entities in chronological order and simply describe what happened – to let the explanation emerge by putting their ducks in a row. If there is an explanation, it is that change is somehow inherent in the system. Things will get better, or worse, with enough time. Explanation needs to be taken seriously because simple descriptions of this nature are an insult to the richness of the archaeological record. It is only when we attempt explanation that we begin to understand how the objects of the past actually can assist us in that process of self-knowledge. Description is part of the job, but it remains half finished without an attempt at why and how.

My guidelines for a good explanation in archaeology are as follows:

- Does it abolish the inside – outside, nature – culture dualisms that I have examined in earlier chapters?
- Does it avoid circularity, such as culture explaining culture?
- Does it suggest ways to collect new data to try another draft of the same explanation?
- Does it account for more of the archaeological data than previous explanations?
- Does the narrative avoid turning the past into what we are simply familiar with in the present?
- Does it strike you as plausible, and if so is the plausibility sufficient for the question being asked?
- Does the explanation spin a stronger cable, as advocated in Chapter 4?

TACKING AS THE EXPLANATORY EXERCISE

The last point structures the discussion. In Chapter 4 I compared the exercise of spinning an explanatory cable (Figure 4.4) with that of tacking a sailboat against the wind. This is how we build explanation in archaeology, by tacking between scales of analysis, time, space and entities, and the different resolutions in our data, for example fine- and coarse-grained (Chapter 6). This is how we build up the argument: not as a house of cards but, as Alison Wylie (1993) described, by adding another strand to the cable.

Tacking helps to reunite archaeology by making a virtue of flexibility (Figure 7.2). These are familiar tacks between opposites, but what we have learnt is that it is rarely so simple. The alternative is to keep those oppositions, or dualisms, separate like port from starboard. Then explanation is a matter of coming down firmly on one

Artefact

Attribute

Region

Site

Change

Stasis

Endogenous
change

Exogenous
change

Local innovation

External
diffusion

Figure 7.2 The archaeological strategy of tacking between different levels of data, spatial and temporal scales, and concepts.

side or the other, 'Steady as she goes!', 'Defend your position!', 'Prepare to repel all boarders!', even though you know you are already on the explanatory rocks.

ENDOGENOUS AND EXOGENOUS CHANGE

Many archaeological explanations revolve around the importance of internal (endogenous) or external (exogenous) factors in change. The classic external factors are environmental changes. These can include long-term climatic cycles as well as short-lived events such as the eruption of Santorini, once thought to have destroyed Minoan Crete. The thousand-year cold, dry snap known as the

Younger Dryas, which marks the move from Clovis to Folsom projectile points in North America, may well have contributed to the extinction of that continent's megafauna (Haynes 1993).

However, it is very important to avoid the pitfall of environmental determinism. The archaeological literature is littered with failed explanations of this nature, for example Childe's oasis theory of domestication, which involved climatic deterioration, or Carneiro's geographical circumscription model to account for the origins of the state. Certainly the environment sets limits. Cereal-based agriculture is never going to work in Alaska. Water will always be a limiting factor in Egypt and central Australia irrespective of the scale of society, ranging from hunter-gatherer to pharaonic empire.

But while the environment clearly provides a degree of canalisation, it is the social system that dominates the process. Most of the world's habitats are neither icy nor hot deserts. Rather they present a choice. There is nothing in the oak-mixed forest and grassland habitats of England that says it must be exploited by a mobile foraging lifestyle, settled agriculture or an industrial economy. Social and economic change has proceeded according to the demands set on the environment by the social relations that dominate production and consumption.

Internal, endogenous change can be equally blinkered. For example, the role accorded to elites in social change has been much investigated, particularly in relation to models of how chiefdoms and early states developed. Elites manipulate exchange networks and bring benefits by organising the redistribution of agricultural surplus. The system, not to mention the people, needs them. Apparently the only fee they charge is that large palace on the hill. Contextual explanations generally prefer internal factors. Styles of monument and artefact change to reflect new power relationships structured by age and gender. The tests of plausibility and circularity need to be applied in both examples.

The solution is to reaffirm the mutual relationship between internal and external, to dissolve the difference, as discussed in Chapter 5. The separation of organism and environment is unhelpful because it distracts explanation from considering the whole. Therefore, one way to recognise a good explanation is to test it for that mutual recognition.

DIFFUSION AND MIGRATION: INNOVATION AND AUTONOMY

These mechanisms have, since the beginning, been the stock explanations for change and variation. The diffusion of ideas and the migration of peoples has accounted for the appearance of new pottery types, metal objects, tombs and settlements as well as major changes such as the spread of agriculture into Europe. The concepts take us back to the roots of the subject with the people-culture hypothesis (Chapter 3) and the cultural norms that express ethnicity and identity (Chapter 8).

There is no escaping the fact that both diffusion and migration did occur. Some Saxons did migrate to England. The Romans did invade and conquer, and aspects of Roman-ness diffused ahead of their arrival. What is at issue is the easy option that *any* change is explained as the movement of people or of those people's ideas. First, this reduces the world to producers and consumers. An active centre, as in the *ex oriente lux* models that favour the Near East (Chapter 1), always has all the best ideas and exports them to a grateful periphery. Some years ago Colin Renfrew (1973a) turned this on its head and showed, thanks to calibrated radiocarbon dating, how Bronze Age Wessex developed independently of Mycenaean Greece. Independent invention and autonomous development is as valid a starting position as diffusion and replacement.

Second, the issue of ethnicity has its own problems, as I will examine in the next chapter. Who exactly did the Saxons really think they were? What was involved in Romanisation? New data continues to muddy such explanations. For example, the expansion of agriculture into Europe has been presented as a wave of advance from the Near East into southeastern Europe and then northwards through the fertile basins of central Europe. This process, dated by radiocarbon, took some 4000 years – equivalent to an annual advance of 1 km. While the cereals and some of the animals, cattle, sheep and goats had to disperse from the source area, it is only recently with genetic studies that doubt has been cast on the notion that the covered wagons of the first farmers inched their way into a Europe of hunters and gatherers, brushing them aside as the British colonists did with the Australian Aborigines. Genetic information on today's Europeans shows instead that they have comparatively few genes from the Near East (Richards 2003). Proportionately, the largest set of European genes can be dated to the recolonisation, by small hunting groups, of parts of the continent following the retreat of the ice sheets 14,000 years ago – some 6000 years before the Neolithic package arrives. This is at odds with the hypothesis that the spread of farming from homelands can also be traced by the spread of languages (Bellwood 2005). What is at issue here is when archaeologists believe people like ourselves first appeared (Gamble *et al.* 2005). Many still prefer the first farmers to the last hunters since it apparently presents us with a more flattering origin.

STASIS AND RATES OF CHANGE

Some of these examples raise the issue of rates of change, a return to the scalar problem mentioned at the beginning of this chapter.

In the Lower Palaeolithic, stasis ruled. The biface technology of the Acheulean appears in East Africa one-and-a-half million years ago and remained basically unchanged for more than a million years. During this time it is found in India, western Asia and Europe. Not only was stone technology very similar over this long time frame, but other evidence about lifestyles exhibits a similarly conservative character. Geography makes little difference. The uppermost levels at Olduvai Gorge, on the equator in Tanzania, are a similar age, 600,000–400,000 years old, to the well-preserved Acheulean locales of Boxgrove, Swanscombe and Hoxne in southern England. But these locales, almost 7000 km apart, have the same low-density scatter of bones and stones as well as the same types of artefact. Against such an ecological gradient today we would expect the ethnography of mobile hunters and gatherers to reveal very different campsites and technology, not to mention variation in art and ritual. During the Late Stone Age/Upper Palaeolithic, 15,000 years ago, a similar north–south comparison does indeed reveal a picture of such variation (Gamble and Soffer 1990; Soffer and Gamble 1990).

The Acheulean is a particularly extreme example of stasis. During its span there was significant hominin evolution involving several fossil species, and marked encephalisation. In later periods, not surprisingly, the rate of change speeds up. But nonetheless it is common to find cultures persisting in very recognisable forms for 1000 years. Using a worldwide sample of archaeological cultures,

Robert Foley found that in the period 20,000 to 5,000 years ago their lifespans were on average between 2000 and 5000 years. At a finer scale of analysis, many of the phases within the major traditions of North American prehistory lasted for some 200 to 400 years (Fagan 1991a), or ten to twenty generations.

These lifespans can be compared with the period divisions in the Maya lowlands (Figure 7.3). These are used to discuss the rise, and repeated collapse, of the Maya state and range between 300 and 600 years. Joyce Marcus (1998) has calculated the cyclical changes in the geographical size of the polities within this region. As you can see, there were dramatic shifts in scale within the classic divisions. The constant increase in polity size during the Early Classic period can be compared with the stasis of the Postclassic until the late burst in the fifteenth century. What this figure shows is that archaeological terminology, especially that of periods, can lull you into a feeling that nothing is happening. But once you drill into the database you will find those evolutionary landscapes bending and flexing. Stasis and change are therefore relative terms that need measuring if they are to have any meaning.

Figure 7.3 Political change through time. The cycles of growth and collapse of the Maya State (after Marcus 1998).

GRAPPLING WITH THE BIG QUESTIONS

I have now examined some of the big questions that archaeologists tackle. It is currently through these that we make our major contribution to the wider world of human knowledge. There is great curiosity about our past and our origins. New fossil skulls frequently hit the headlines and the newscasts. However, on the inside pages change and stasis are what archaeologists grapple with in their explanations. The lifespan estimates I have just given above for archaeological entities serve to show that, on a variety of timescales, stasis dominates the picture. Canalisation, as described by Waddington, of both the organisation (homeostasis) and the flow (homeorhesis) helps us to conceptualise how this might occur. Selection for change and selection for stasis are equally powerful mechanisms. However, what these simple lifespan figures mask is the everyday role of individuals in the creation of society within the parameters set by canalisation and selection. Stasis should never be interpreted in the negative sense of stagnation or cultural passivity. Within these periods of 200 or 2 million years, there were vibrant societies based on human creativity. Our task is now to explore such canalisation, where identity emerges as the last basic issue to tackle.

SUMMARY

- There can be an origins of anything you like; but you have to ask if that really tells us anything other than our own desire for an appropriately long ancestry.
- Revolutions seem to drive the process onward, but remember the timescales involved and assess the rhetoric accordingly.
- Things changed slowly for much of the past and in some periods hardly at all. Stasis as much as change needs explaining.
- Explanations can be strengthened by asking some simple questions and seeing how we move between different data at different scales to gain an understanding.
- Never consider explanation to be the done deal. Just when you thought you had a problem wrapped up new information can bite you on the nose.
- Archaeology exists as a scientific study because the data differ. So how do we recognise change rather than variation?

8

IDENTITY AND POWER

What is the identity of the person who was buried in the ship at Sutton Hoo 1400 years ago? We have a name, Raedwald, but as we saw in Chapter 4 that is rather like calling the family pet Frodo. Giving a dog a name does not necessarily establish its identity. The rich grave goods are much more help, especially if you take the view that the power of that identity rests in the trappings of status, in this case kingship. The relative amounts of that power are also expressed by such measures as the craftsmanship of the objects, the distance from which they came, the content of gold and silver, their quantity and the fact that such wealth was ritually disposed of, taken out of circulation, thrown away. The body was not preserved at Sutton Hoo. But the fact that it was apparently dressed in full parade kit – sword, helmet and Sam Browne belt – has led to the automatic assumption that this was a male.

Of course, this is an essentialist view of the social categories of kingship and gender identity. We expect kings to have richer burials. Otherwise they wouldn't obviously be kings. We expect fancy swords and big gold buckles to represent powerful males. In circular fashion we expect their identities to have the properties of power and to be accompanied by objects that share those characteristics. They attract those fine items because they are high status and because they are male. We expect them to be both magnates and magnets.

The alternative that I will explore here is that power is more subtle than that. It is more varied and resides not so much in categories as in overlapping relationships. Power is a network rather than a set of institutions. We all construct our own networks on a daily and lifetime basis. We use objects to do this and, as we saw in Chapter 4, these objects also construct us at the same time. Therefore we, people and objects, all have power by virtue of being caught up in these networks, and not because of some inherent property in the social structure into which we are born. Such network power varies, but it is through that process of construction that our identities emerge.

TWO IDENTITIES

Identity and power therefore have two archaeological aspects. We can investigate them *within* archaeological data, as at Sutton Hoo. The major categories of data concerned are ethnicity, class, gender, sexuality, age and the body. We must also consider the identities that are derived *from* such studies and which often lead to claims of contemporary nationalism and ethnicity based upon the authority of the past. Martin Carver puts this well in his summary of the wider debate over the Sutton Hoo finds. The Sutton Hoo cemetery lasted for less than a hundred years until continental Christianity swept over this part of eastern England and its pagan identity disappeared:

> This episode is seen as the first round in an ideological argument between the benefits of independent enterprise and those of a European union, which has exercised the British ever since.
>
> (Carver 1996: 706)

The basic point about identity, power, ethnicity and nationalism is that the archaeological facts we use to explore these concepts are some of the most theory laden in the whole subject. The reason for this is quite simple: the past is not a neutral subject. It is not something, like trainspotting, that is only of interest to hobbyists in anoraks on station platforms. It cannot be ignored because, as the history of Europe alone has shown over the past 70 years, it will come and drive you from your home, your land and your country.

WHAT WE MEAN BY POWER

I have used the term power throughout this book. It is now time to examine the concept more closely. Power is very often seen as an entity, something that some people have and others do not. Power and position are seen as going together, hand in glove. This view usually stresses the negative aspects of power as force, coercion, imposition. As a result, power becomes a property and an implicit explanation of change, as in 'a shift in power'. One of its properties is asymmetry, for example in a world system (Chapter 6), where centres and peripheries have very different effects upon each other.

Power in these circumstances is often presented as a one-way relationship. Perhaps the most famous expression of this view was set down by the classical historian Thucydides. It takes the form of a lengthy debate between the mainland power of Athens and the small Cycladic island of Melos which, in 416 BC, had refused to join Athens' empire. The Athenians were very upfront about the situation:

> *Athenians:* 'For you know as well as we do, that, when we are talking about relations between human beings, the standard of justice is based on the equality of power to compel and that the strong do what they have the power to do, while the weak accept what they must.'

And the reply:

> *Melians:* '*You* should not destroy the principle of the common good, that is, that all who fall into danger should be treated with fairness and justice . . . And this is the principle which affects you too, since in your own fall you would incur the most terrible vengeance and be an example to the rest of mankind.'

> (Sparkes 1982: 319)

The dialogue changed nobody's position. After a long siege the Melians surrendered and all the men of military age were massacred.

The alternative to such a negative representation is not to deny that massacres happen but instead to see power as a process that flows and changes. It is not inherent in artefacts nor in actions but emerges from the relationships that revolve around the human and material worlds. It is therefore an epiphenomenon, the result of interaction, rather than somehow basic or natural to the system, as implied by the Athenians.

Our old friend scale is once again important here. Much of social theory is concerned with tying together the micro- and macro-levels of interaction and power. To what extent do individuals have power? How do they produce and use it and how far are they constrained by wider social structures?

GENDER AND POWER WITHIN ARCHAEOLOGY

Scale, power and gender studies are closely linked. As we saw in Chapter 2, the rise of an archaeology of gender required an assault on the power structures among archaeologists themselves. Moreover, the demonstration that gender in the past can be studied by archaeologists has begun at the micro-scale. It involves the analysis of individual artefacts, houses and sequences of manufacture rather than the big origins questions I examined in the last chapter. The strategy has been to find gender in the details rather than claim its universal properties (Nelson 1997: 95).

One consequence of these studies of the past is that the route to understanding how we construct our own identities in the present, and the power that goes with it, is now much clearer. Daniel Miller and Christopher Tilley (1984) talk of power *to do* things and power *over* something. In the former a person or network has power to act and influence. This is a consequence of any social relationship or action. We all have power to act. We also invest the institutions of power – the state, the family, the law, the city – with similar power to transform. When power to *do* also involves power *over*, then a relationship of domination exists.

Therefore a feminist archaeology pursuing an archaeology of gender potentially has power to transform the discipline. This is done through the overlapping and very variable actions, interests, commitments and output of those subscribing to that ideology. However, it may not necessarily lead to a change in the way archaeology is done. Other, more powerful paradigms exist, as described in Chapter 2, that have power *over* the discipline and they will defend their turf. However, for some feminist archaeologists (e.g. Nelson 1997) a future goal is to achieve power over an androcentric archaeology.

WHEN ESSENCE IS OK

Let me be clear on one important point here. If power resides in a relationship, then it might be regarded as just another essence like the others I have criticised a good deal in this book. But power is not an essence for a simple reason. If there is good causal connection, as in the statement 'engine-oil reduces friction', then there is no problem in stating that an essential property of engine oil is its ability to stop friction. The problem is that this does not tell us very much beyond the obvious. In evolutionary studies, such a conclusion would be known as the adaptive fallacy, as in 'human feet are adapted for upright walking'. Well they would be wouldn't they? Otherwise they wouldn't be human feet and you would fall over. But the statement that power resides in relationships avoids the 'so-what?' response because this is the starting point for understanding, not the end point for explanation.

BODIES AND SEXUALITY

If gender is a socially constructed category, a vehicle for identity, then so too are our bodies and sexuality. For example, homosexuality was invented as a social category in the late nineteenth century, evidence that the construction of sexuality is a modern project. Lynn Meskell (1999: 97) points out that the ancient Egyptians had no word comparable to our notion of sexuality. We should therefore be wary of imposing our particular interests onto their lifestyles. But 3500 years ago there certainly existed culturally created contexts for the experience and expression of sexual life. However, these did not constitute a series of neat categories but rather, as Meskell argues, reflect the assumption of roles and permutations in different contexts that are revealed to us through tomb paintings and domestic architecture.

IDENTITY, BODIES AND MATERIAL CULTURE

As Jo Sofaer (2006) has argued, the body needs to be rethought as material culture. Put another way, the body is a project that grows and changes with age and it is interpreted in many different ways through its association with artefacts. As discussed in Chapter 6, the body is a source of symbolic force that in a very real sense energises all that it comes into contact with, creating relations not only with other bodies but also with the world of material culture. I also provided examples in Chapter 6 of how containers such as houses and pots blurred the rational view of two separate worlds – one of people and one of objects. As described by John Robb (2004), houses are another example of a project – or as Gell (1998) would describe them, a focus for collective agency. Raising a barn or adding a conservatory to the back of the house expresses in material terms the actions of growing, just as the decline of a house represents another phase in its life. In addition, raising children has even been likened to growing crops and keeping domestic animals (Ingold 2000). Both are material projects that create and confirm identities through the maintenance of relationships that exist because of the material basis of human identity, which dates as far back as the oldest stone tools.

John Chapman (2000) has provided another example of these material projects in his studies of fragmentation. Here a sherd of pottery stands for the whole pot just as an individual stands for the group. The fragmentation of pottery is put to good use by the use of the constituent pieces to enchain people into much larger social wholes. Through such simple acts as breaking and giving gifts, people become distributed across space and time and as a result begin to create identities.

Archaeological examples abound and have been a particular focus in the study of the British Neolithic and early Bronze Age, which saw the first building at Stonehenge. In these periods there was also a new emphasis on the ways bodies and objects were treated and moved around the massive stone-built tombs. Different artefacts were deliberately given fresh meanings by recombining and re-depositing fragmented items such as skulls, pots and stone axes (Jones 2002; Whittle 2003).

But Neolithic identities were also locally determined, as Neolithic bodies experienced the ritual landscapes of southern England, which included burial chambers and monuments such as Stonehenge and Avebury with their processional avenues, ditches and specially constructed sightlines that memorialised the ancestors in stone and wood (Parker-Pearson and Ramilisonina 1998). Here the bodily experience was of a rich cultural landscape with great time-depth. It is these controlled experiences that provide our route to appreciating the construction of local Neolithic identities (Barrett 1999: 258–60; Tilley 1994).

POWER, PRACTICE AND DISCOURSE

The temporal approach to power can also be formalised in terms of scale. Christopher Gosden (1994: 137) links power to the perform-ances that take place in public time and where people come face to face with what seems most natural in their worlds. This includes those rituals and monuments that exist only because they are part of long-term temporal rhythms. Power and knowledge are there-fore very closely linked. If we take the view of the philosopher Michel Foucault, then power resides in discourse, a term he used to refer to all the conditions that are needed for the production of knowledge. Discourse refers to data as well as to concepts, their history and the social conditions within which knowledge is produced and used. This book is part of a discourse about the past and what archaeologists do. So too is a museum exhibit, an archaeological excavation or a visit to ancient ruins. Hence one of Foucault's best-known books is entitled *The Archaeology of Knowledge*. The discourse approach takes a very top-down approach to power: power precedes. Power is a structure, because the many discourses we engage in by dint of being social are also structures. Pushing the metaphor a bit further to make the point more clearly, the discourse approach sees us as 'imprisoned' or 'captured' by these structures. It should come as no surprise to learn that Foucault wrote a great deal about discipline, prison, mental asylums and sexuality as his exam-ples of changing discourses.

Of course, there is an alternative – one that I have already outlined when discussing society in Chapter 4. Gosden contrasts the top-down approach to power with the bottom-up approach. Rather than seeing power and knowledge as residing in discourse, a bottom-up approach considers them as created through practice, as in Pierre Bourdieu's concept of *habitus* (see below) and Gosden's landscape of habit (Chapter 6). I prefer to define practice as routine actions rather than the more commonly encountered 'meaningful actions of knowledgeable agents', which sounds tautologous to me. Power stems from action – I think we could all agree on that.

Therefore the structures and institutions of society that we encounter are all products of daily practice, rituals of creation and renewal (see the papers in Dobres and Robb 2000). The concept of practice therefore gives much greater weight to the actions of individuals at the micro-scale and less to the overarching macro-scale structures. But practice also breaks down this dichotomy between individual and society by treating them as one (Figure 8.1), allowing us to escape from the Cartesian theatre with its many and much-loved oppositions (Chapter 5).

THE IDENTITY WITHIN

At one level we are all concerned with constructing our personal identity, that sense of self. At another we also belong to much larger communities that influence what that self will be and against which it will be tested. Understanding power and using concepts such as *habitus* and landscape of habit can help to clarify the issue of how we become socialised.

As Siân Jones puts it:

the *habitus* is made up of durable dispositions towards certain perceptions and practices (such as those relating to the sexual division of

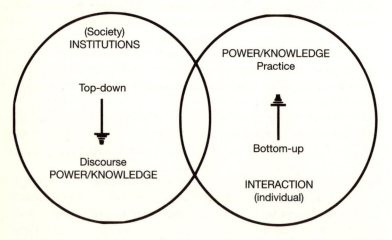

Figure 8.1 The overlapping networks of knowledge about society and the individual that archaeologists have used.

labour, morality, tastes and so on); which become part of an individual's sense of self at an early age, and can be transposed from one context to another.

(1997: 88)

I would only add that for me those durable dispositions she speaks of stem from those routine, oft-repeated actions. As Gilchrist puts it, *habitus* is your 'common-sense knowledge which is socially constructed with reference to the material world' (1993: 16). The *habitus* is a 'collective unconscious' built up from experience rather than consciously mastered. You are what you make yourself to be. Obviously there are constraints: action and interaction are limited by the senses, the physical structure of the body, and the differences between people's bodies based on age, sex and activity. As I have shown (Chapter 4), the networks that result from interaction are not only limited by the resources – emotional, material and symbolic – that define them, but at the same time made possible by them.

It is this dual nature of power, simultaneously offering opportunities as well as imposing constraints, that leads us to an understanding of how canalisation works. In those evolutionary landscapes described by Waddington (Chapter 7), or the landscapes of habit outlined by Gosden (Chapter 6), we routinely dig the canals down which the flow of social life proceeds. They are not dug for us. To be 'stuck in a rut' only suggests that you are capable of digging a new rut. Flex those durable dispositions in your landscape of habit, push the envelope a little, change your routine actions and so nudge Waddington's ball bearing into a new rut. But remember that everyone else is digging their own self-defining rut and so collectively the canal gets deeper. The landscape changes through forces other than yours alone.

BACK TO STYLE

How does all this help the archaeologist? Basically it takes us back to our understanding of similarity and gets us to think again about its significance as that attribute of objects we call style. In Chapter 3 I discussed similarity and the principle of popularity, and showed how archaeologists have generally assumed that the more similar artefacts and cultures are, the more interaction took place between individuals and groups. This approach was refined by Wobst's much tighter definition of style as information exchange. As we saw in Chapter 5, Wiessner then provided a definition of style as 'a means of non-verbal communication to negotiate identity' (1990: 108). Her underpinning idea is that psychologically we derive our identities through comparison. She puts this into an evolutionary context by pointing out that those who create a positive self-image in this manner are also putting themselves at a selective advantage, because the style adopted encourages others to engage in desirable social activity with them.

Wiessner's main point, as we saw earlier, was to distinguish between an *assertive* and an *emblemic* style (1983: 257–58, 1990). She contrasted stylistic variation in material culture that is personally based (assertive) with that which is group based (emblemic). Two types of identity were therefore created. Style manages this without words. At the group level, style works by referring to conscious affiliation; what might be called ethnicity in some contexts. At the personal level, the stylistic references may be ascribed to habit. As Stephen Shennan has pointed out (1989a: 22), because assertive style is neither unique to individuals nor universally prescribed there will be a good deal of variation among individuals within a culture. It is this variation that acts as the seedbed for emblematic uses of style, of which ethnicity (see below) is a particular example.

But before we get too carried away, remember that I also examined in Chapter 5 the notion that the social component of our data resides in style. This depends on a particular way of looking at the world. In particular, it comes from a division of subject and object, material culture and person, style and function (Boast 1997). *Habitus* and the landscape of habit makes such a division unnecessary, and with it goes the analytical power of style. Identity is less a feature coded into designs on pots or the shape of houses than an ongoing process firmly embedded in the practices of daily life. In other words, it is less the product of thought – 'I will colour my hair orange because I think people with orange hair are cool' – than the result of action: 'My hair is orange because that's me. Her hair is brown because that's her. What's your problem?'

SPOTTING THE HABITUS

Style may not be the great ally we once thought it was for investigating social life *or* identity using archaeological data. But how do we conceptualise the *habitus* and these landscapes of habit? Let's face it, the *habitus* is a great idea but it is distinctly fuzzy round the edges for a 'soaked in the data' subject like archaeology. Archaeologists know there is a reality out there which is the past. We trip over it when out fieldwalking to pick up survey data. We can pat a pot appreciatively and tell you its cultural heritage. We can point on our timelines to a style zone. We can map distributions based on similarity in form, shape, attributes and that thing called style. *Habitus*, by comparison, is 'out there' somewhere, like the truth in the X-files.

This criticism returns us to our archaeological imagination and the different archaeologies I outlined in Chapter 2. All of those approaches share common ground in terms of the ways in which they approach the past. Then they part company. Culture historians generally prefer description. Processualists like the rigour of the scientific method. Neo-Darwinists appeal to a higher authority – Darwin – and the power of natural selection. Finally, interpretive archaeologists settle for a self-reflexive, multi-aspectual approach. These approaches sum up the development of the professional archaeological imagination: a move away from the commonsense. However, not all of them are ready to question the significance of contemporary concerns of society about peoples, nations and things for the study of the past, whereas Marxist and feminist approaches are well aware of how an interest in the past is often framed for us.

Ignoring these last developments results in an impoverished imagination. Despite the processualists' demonstration to the contrary 30 years ago, many archaeologists still believe that the subject is terminally limited either by the nature of the data that survives or by the ability of science to produce fresh analytical insights. This is the crunch at the core of Hawkes' onion, which I discussed in Chapter 4. Landscapes of habit will not fit neatly onto distributions of house types or vessel decoration. But how could they, since the visual output of one is not based on the premises of the other? Just as the demonstration of an archaeology of gender had to return to the detail rather than tackle the universals, so the study of identity needs to reformulate and reconceptualise the problem.

The existence, archaeologically, of practice and the *habitus* is nevertheless apparent in the sheer diversity of material culture that archaeologists have discovered. Michelle Hegmon (1998) in rejecting style as the way to understand this diversity, nonetheless focuses on seven aspects that still merit further investigation (Box 23). Some of them are familiar. Number 7, for example, was Wobst's point about target populations and stylistic messaging. Numbers 3 and 4 could be a translation of Wiessner's assertive style.

BOX 23 WHAT THE PATTERNS IN THE DATA SEEM TO TELL US BUT WHICH WE DON'T YET FULLY UNDERSTAND.

1 Complex technologies (for example metallurgy) seem to be heavily loaded symbolically.

2 Decorations that cross-cut a number of media (pots, textiles, metals) are likely to be symbolically meaningful.

3 Very simple decoration may not be particularly significant at a conscious level. It may tell us more about everyday interaction between individuals and the contexts in which objects are made.

4 The objects used in everyday life have an important role in defining who people are socially and are relevant to the concept of *habitus*.

5 Aspects of production that are taught in a relatively formal manner may be useful indicators of learning contexts.

6 Elaboration of non-visible objects (such as medallions or tattoos worn under clothing) are more likely to communicate with yourself and your intimate and effective networks, including your ancestors, than with your extended network partners.

7 Highly visible elaboration is likely to involve communication with your extended network but does not always involve group distinctions but rather your ability to negotiate such far-flung networks in time and space.

(based on Hegmon 1998: 277, with additions)

OVERLAPPING PATTERNS AND MANY NETWORKS

What I have added to Hegmon's patterns (Box 23) is the notion that these regularities can be understood in terms of the networks that we all construct (Chapter 4). Moreover, the elements in these networks, other people and objects, are treated in a similar way because both exist as the result of relationships. Without such relationships there would be no social world, and certainly no distinctively human social world. Our material world of garden gnomes, plates, computers, houses and jumbo jets is therefore replete with cross-cutting distributions of social relationships, linked into a coherent whole by people in motion. The image I have of the landscape of habit with all its many practices being enacted at all sorts of different scales is that of overlapping networks. This is my way of sharpening the fuzzy picture.

Julian Thomas (1996: 178) provides a fully worked-out example for Neolithic southern Britain, arguing that what existed were spatially segregated practices distributed across the landscape. These are recognised as tombs, henges, enclosures, fields, flint mines, pits with animal bones and distinctive pottery. Any identity or social grouping was therefore defined by a series of cross-cutting criteria that worked like this:

> Some activities may have been restricted on the basis of age sets, some according to gender . . . , some by membership of kin groups, some by agnation [relations by marriage], and some by other sodalities such as hunting societies, sorcerer's lodges and so on. In all probability, many of these groupings crossed over the boundaries of any formal social units such as tribes, clans or lineages.
>
> (Thomas 1996: 178–79)

Elsewhere, he describes Neolithic Britain as comprising 'multiple overlapping communities' (1996: 180). It was neither a single society nor a mosaic of tribal groupings. Now, such a model does have an empirical reality in the cross-cutting distributions of styles and decorations on Neolithic objects. We are also propelled towards that bottom-up view of how these intricate, overlapping webs of relationships were constructed. The vocabulary of networks I explored in Chapter 4 helps us to grasp the idea using familiar terms and so broaden our archaeological imaginations to encompass the unfamiliar *habitus* and landscape of habit. It is in the construction of these, rather than in the properties of style, that identity emerges.

A change in emphasis to a vocabulary of *habitus* also helps the archaeologist in considering the key concept of boundaries. We like bounded entities. That is why islands like Orkney, Malta, Iceland and Papua New Guinea are very popular laboratories for the study of social and political systems and their long-term properties of stasis and change. Islands are particularly suitable for measuring inputs and outputs. Goods and peoples flow in and out as archipelagos are fought over and exploited by mainland states. By focusing on islands we can trace the cultural variation of groups as historically diverse as the Vikings and Anglo-Saxons in northwestern Europe and Britain, Mycenaeans and Minoans in the Aegean, and the competitive spread of Muslim and Buddhist religions through the islands of Indonesia.

Islands can also be centres of innovation. As a result, they have been used to model in microcosm the processes of change that are more difficult to grasp on the continents, where defining a particular region is never easy. For example, the archipelagos of the Pacific have been important for the study of social evolution. The independent rise of chiefdoms in Hawaii, Fiji and New Zealand have provided impetus to such studies precisely because they are seen as bounded units to the study of autonomous development.

Islands are an extreme case and in many instances their isolation has been overstated. The vast Pacific Ocean and the cold North Sea in fact acted as highways and *not* as barriers to contact. Islands are significant because they make the job of defining regions that much easier (Chapter 6). But in many cases they are very small regions and hence atypical.

Boundaries on the continents are just as permeable but the job of drawing up regions is much more difficult. Cyril Fox contrasted the highland and lowland zones of Britain and evocatively entitled his essay *The Personality of Britain* (1932). His form of environmental determinism proposed that identity is shaped by climate and landscape as much as by history and culture. Regional building styles in wood or stone reflect a culture of the possible, which only serves to confirm a view that until empires arrived life was local and that innovation came from elsewhere.

Instead, science-based archaeology has repeatedly reinforced the lesson that the local view misrepresents the scale of human action in the past. Radiocarbon dating freed Europe from *ex oriente lux* diffusion, where before the arrival of American know-how the answer to the question 'What's new?' always came from the Near East (Chapter 1). Independent dating opened up for archaeologists the possibility of autonomous economic and social development, as demonstrated by Colin Renfrew's snappy title 'Wessex Without Mycenae' (1968), which heralded a new prehistoric world order. Characterisation studies of ceramics, metals and stones such as obsidian revealed that even mundane items such as cooking pots, wherever they are found and whether they date to the prehistoric, classical and historic worlds, were often transported over many kilometres from the source of the raw material. And now genetic studies are reversing the patterns of simple diffusion hypothesised to result from the supposed economic superiority of the first farmers (Chapter 7). Natural boundaries have never looked more unnatural.

BOUNDARIES: CULTURAL

Boundaries must also be considered at the scales of human interaction, from the macro to the micro.

At the grand scale, boundary markers such as the Limes that the Romans built to fence-off barbarian Germany are very popular objects for archaeologists to study. Hadrian's Wall in England, which did the same job against the Scots, is probably the most studied archaeological monument in the country and a World Heritage Site to boot. Boundaries are also chronological, as in the Norman invasion of 1066 and 1492, which marks the end of pre-Colombian America.

When it comes to boundaries around social groups we find ourselves back among those text versus non-text arguments (Andrén 1998) that I explored in Chapter 1. Often the aim seems to be to produce a tribal ethnography linking style zones to named geographical groupings. This applies to prehistoric Australia as well as to Iron Age societies in Africa and Europe and the states of the ancient Near East and Mesoamerica. The basic point is that a boundary represents an interruption in similarity. This could be a cessation of interaction or a change in the type of interaction from, say, exchange to warfare.

Boundaries can be gendered. Such boundaries exist because they have been culturally constructed. Martin Hall (1997: 227) has shown how, in the layout of Cape Town, South Africa, gender structured not only the colonial city but also the surrounding countryside. He argues that the gridded streets and symmetrical manor houses imply the stamp of a gendered social order. Contemporary accounts reveal the freedom of males in public display as they moved through the streets, while their women were kept indoors. Much remains to be done, as Hall readily admits, to go beyond these implications and uncover through the study of household contents how gender relations were articulated in everyday life. The probate record of one early settler in 1827 is a masculine document recording the owner's possessions, including his African servants. By contrast, the items excavated from the well in his backyard provide not only an individual portrait of the owner – gout-suffering, shortsighted and military-minded – but also evidence for the European women in the household – shoes, dolls, jewellery, thimbles.

Male–female boundaries may seem clear cut in this example. However, our interest must reside less in the dichotomy and more in the process of domination and resistance to it, much of which would have been worked out in the material realm. It is through the fine detail that the micro-scales of gender relations will be reconciled with the macro-framework of power.

At the micro-scale, boundaries exist around settlements and houses, graves and persons. Ditches, walls, pits and clothing are all examples of the cultural divisions that divide the indivisible and from which categories emerge. These may be easy to identify archaeologically but difficult to interpret. For example, to Western perceptions the precision with which a new city such as Canberra, the capital of Australia, is laid out contains many boundaries and an ordered appreciation of space. However, to an Australian Aborigine, Frank Gurrmanamana, the geometry of Canberra appears as primordial chaos instead of an orderly arrangement (Jones 1985). The straight roads, property boundaries, mowed lawns and zoned activity that we see when driving around Canberra's artificial Lake Burley-Griffin is to Gurrmanamana an unnamed, 'natural' landscape with no significance, since the people who inhabit it have forgotten the rights that the land demands. By contrast, the savannahs of northern Australia where Gurrmanamana lives, a 'wilderness' to our perception, have been transformed in both the physical and metaphorical sense as a result of continuous human action.

But all is not doom and gloom for those periods of archaeology that do not have eye-witness accounts. Boundaries exist within houses, and Matthew Johnson (1993: 341) shows how space came to be demarcated in different ways (Figure 4.1) between the late-medieval and post-medieval periods. Class interests were eventually served as segregation between people within the same space turned into the occupation of separate rooms which now contained their status and their private lives within a capitalistic structure of social relations. Just as the ancient Egyptians had no word for sexuality (see above), so late-medieval texts are largely mute on the identities being expressed by the architecture of the time. As Johnson argues:

> Identities were negotiated through movement through space, placement of actions, and visual and iconic images such as heraldry; not in the first instance through writing things down.
>
> (1999b: 77)

This eloquently summarises the power of material culture to access areas of the human past once thought to be the sole prerogative of the text. There will always be disagreement over the identification of boundaries and the attribution of significance to them. Consequently it is better to investigate the process of boundary maintenance, which leads us directly to the size of networks.

CONSUMING IDENTITY AND CUTTING THE NETWORK

Identity is not something that is given. Even though your status might be ascribed by the fact of your birth, as in hereditary kingship, you will still create your identity within that role. Identity, like power, is both enabling and constraining.

Identity, as we have seen, is best conceptualised as a set of overlapping fields: different practices which add up to a *habitus* or, as I prefer, an archaeological landscape of habit. This view stresses the individual and the web of networks we all create. The temporal and spatial scales of these networks vary and the resources we use to negotiate them are likewise varied (Chapter 4). The creation of identity is therefore dependent on a wide range of different selective pressures. We are canalised, though often this is habitual rather than consciously deliberate. The important point to grasp, as emphasised by anthropologist Johnathan Friedman, is that what people do is not merely representative of who or what they are but basically constitutive of it (1994: 107). Friedman uses the example of Western fashion in urban Zaire, where designer labels do not just declare your allegiance to a group. Their consumption is the means by which you possess any identity at all by relating to others. In his study of consumption in contemporary society Daniel Miller reaches a similar conclusion:

> The consumer society exists when, as in industrial societies today, most people have a minimal relationship to production and distribution such that consumption provides the only arena left to us through which we might potentially forge a relationship with the world.
>
> (1995: 17)

Archaeologists can investigate the same relatedness through their myriad material cultures and extend it to their general model of culture as repetitious patterning in time and space. The difference is that besides the activity of consumption, people in the past were more directly involved in forging links with the world through production and distribution. This difference lies at the heart of two rather different theories of exchange.

As Miller states, when objects are commodities, as in our own society, relationships are created through collective ownership, distribution and consumption. Importantly, objects are regarded as having symbolic and material significance, just as they have been seen by archaeologists to have passive and active styles (Chapter 5).

The alternative is a situation where social relations rather than commodities shape the significance of objects and hence how we deal with one another. Here, as Marilyn Strathern points out (1988: 172), social relations can only be turned into other social relations. So when objects are exchanged they become other social relationships. The material and the symbolic are therefore fused rather than analytically separate. Moreover, the objects have identities. When a transaction involving feathers, shells or salt takes place you also give a bit of yourself or receive a bit of someone else. Those pots and rare stones are integral to the system of relatedness.

But networks and relatedness cannot go on forever. I outlined in Chapter 4 how three kinds of network – intimate, effective and extended – have expected sizes that depend on the resources – emotional, material and symbolic – that are used to create them. These limits, however, form rather weak boundaries as the resources cut across one another. For example, symbolic resources such as a statue of the Virgin Mary on the mantelpiece can be part of your intimate network. It is also possible to get emotional with strangers.

The basic point for archaeologists is how networks are cut. An individual maintaining those three ideal networks is at the same time engaged in the practice of boundary maintenance. We should expect this because of what I said in Chapter 6 about the difference between relational and modernist approaches to society and identity. From a modernist perspective networks are cut when the resources can no longer be negotiated into a relationship through transactions. 'Not fade away' may be the desire, but in practice there are only so many network partners an individual can maintain. The refrain is much more often 'Get off of my cloud!'

If you prefer to stress the importance of relatedness in studying how people interact (Bird-David 1999) then the loss of immediacy can sever the principle. But once again it is the break in social transactions that leads to a boundary. The significance for archaeology is that we should not be looking for hard and fast boundaries: rather, the interruptions in the social world are the result of complex, interleaved practices. Many of these boundaries are permeable in terms of items, resources and individuals which flow through time and space.

Neither should we be misled by style, in terms of the shape and distribution of artefacts, which at first glance might seem to help. I could show you many maps with crisp changes in space, as well as time, between objects that stylistically are chalk and cheese. These encourage us in our belief that we are studying something real, and yes, of course there is a pattern there. However, I hope I have now said enough to make it clear why understanding that pattern is not just a simple matter of equating distribution with identity, as many archaeologists still maintain. Trying to be precise about boundaries will always be hazardous and is well illustrated by the next major topic: ethnicity.

IDENTITIES FROM THE PAST

The notion of ethnicity forms a boundary between the investigation of identity *within* the past and the uses of the past to create an identity from. I have intentionally left discussion of this key concept in archaeology until now, because so much of what we know about the past comes from its application rather than from what is so often assumed to be the inherent nature of cultural data. Three different political contexts define the use of archaeological evidence to create identities (Box 24).

BOX 24 THE POLITICAL IDENTITIES OF ARCHAEOLOGY.

Nationalist: Monuments and artefacts were frequently used to forge the identity of the new nation states of Europe. These emerged during the process of industrialisation and particularly in the nineteenth century. To understand the history of archaeology and the aspirations of archaeologists you definitely need to appreciate the force of nationalism (Díaz-Andreu and Champion 1996). The trend continues: the state of Israel, for example, places great emphasis on monuments, such as the fortress of Masada, sacked by the Romans in AD 73, as symbols of resistance and sacrifice en route to nationhood in 1948. The significance and interpretation of such monuments are often contested, as indeed are the boundaries and existence of many modern countries.

Colonialist: The European colonial powers, particularly Great Britain, investigated the archaeology of their dependent territories in Africa, India and Australia. Interpretations were often highly coloured by a colonial viewpoint that liked to see all change and improvement as coming from outside. The explanations for the ruins of Great Zimbabwe in what was Rhodesia are a good example. Until recently the notion that such developments in the archaeological record might have African origins was usually discounted from the start. The spectacular city was put down to the influence of either European or Arab traders even though no evidence existed to support such claims. On independence, colonial archaeology becomes nationalist, as in the case of Rhodesia again: Zimbabwe became the symbol and the name of the country in 1980.

Imperialist: The three great empires of the modern world – those of Great Britain, the United States and the former Soviet Union – all developed a form of world archaeology. A world archaeology is a universal way of looking at the past, usually from a single view point. Soviet archaeologists followed a Marxist stance on the construction of history (McGuire 1992: 56–62). The British model was comparative, seeking to establish a league table of achievement by period, region and continent. Hence Grahame Clark's description of technology in prehistoric Australia as 'crude and rather colourless' (1968: 21). Unsurprisingly, given its super-power status after World War II, the United States model has been the most widely followed. Trigger regards the 'new' archaeology of the 1960s (see Chapter 2) as an example of this imperialist approach. More widely known as processual archaeology, it champions a scientific approach, in both methods and explanation, to the study of the past.

(after Trigger 1989)

WHO ARE YOU?

Let me illustrate just how laden with concepts of ethnicity the archaeological facts are by asking: Who do you think you are? How do you classify yourself? By your bodily phenotype, how you see yourself – skin colour, hair type, stature, sex – or your inner genotype – the history of your genes? Would you instead stress the importance of the culture you live in, with all its weird and wonderful ways of greeting people, behaving at table, and body language in different social situations – not to mention the conventions surrounding what you wear, how you cook ('you are what you eat'), and so on? Are the various identities attributable to your body, class, sexuality, age and gender sufficient to draw a boundary around your ethnic status?

   Answering such questions in any multicultural society would produce a very complex array of traits. Be reflexive about it. Ask yourself why you use some categories and not others to classify yourself and other people. Do those categories and the significance you attach to them differ between your effective and extended network and the company of complete strangers whom you see every day? I think you will find very quickly that most of your categories are very polythetic (Chapter 3). Do we see groupings because, like one of those archaeological detectives (Chapter 4), we are great classifiers? Categories work well when the traits are kept minimal. As you expand the number of traits to reflect the complexity of the situation, you will find the boundaries dissolving.

Yes, you might counter, but living in Southampton, Denver or La Plata is very different to living in a rural community in Africa, India or China, where the opportunity for cultural and biological diversity is much smaller. There the boundaries are less permeable simply because the range of variation is much less. That argument does not stand up for long. Just because we expect rural communities to be conservative does not mean that people are not actively creating their roles. Richard Lee discovered that the !Kung San bushmen at their waterhole in the Kalahari desert of southern Africa were quick to change their affiliations as the economic climate of the region shifted. Traditional hunters and gatherers could soon become wage-labourers in the region's cattle industry, thus exchanging a key trait of their ethnicity – foraging – for ranching.

Ian Hodder (1982: 18–21) also found that individuals moved between ethnic groups in East Africa. His study of material culture indicated sharp boundaries because individuals change their dress at the 'frontier'. The boundaries might indicate a form of ethnicity but have little to say about the pattern of mobility, which contradicts the view that ethnicity is historically fixed to a place. Ethnicity is therefore malleable and contingent, and there is no reason to suppose that it was not the same in the past. These examples make it difficult to sort out some of the claims archaeologists make.

ETHNICITY

Perhaps a definition will help:

> Ethnicity must be distinguished from mere spatial variation and should refer to self-conscious identification with a particular social group at least partly based on a specific locality or origin.
>
> (Shennan 1989a: 14)

Self-conscious identification is the basic point. For example, there are many white Australian Aborigines who totally confound the racial and ethnic stereotype. But they self-consciously identify with the general ethnic category Australian Aborigine for reasons of descent, history, residence and oppression.

How can archaeologists cope with self-conscious identification? The recently discovered child burial from Laghar Velho in Portugal poses the problem (Darte *et al.* 1999). It is dated to 24,500 years ago, and after careful measurement and study it appears to its discoverers to be a hybrid between Neanderthals (*Homo neanderthalensis*) and modern humans (*Homo sapiens*). Since these categories are regarded as separate species, we could also reasonably claim an ethnic distinction. The mixture of anatomical features does not help us in determining what this child thought about his/her identity. However, the one pierced shell found with the body could point to a self-conscious affiliation with *Homo sapiens* rather than with Neanderthals, as such objects are commonly found with individuals of the former rather than the latter species. Alternatively he/she could have slipped the simple necklace on and off any time he/she passed across the 'frontier'.

But what assumptions, what theory-laden facts, are really on display in this extreme example? Judgements about affiliation could bring us very close to the disreputable history of archaeology and anthropology that judged people, morally and practically, by how they looked. At its worst this led to the programme of eugenics, where deliberate intervention to change the human blueprint was proposed. Ethnic cleansing and holocausts attest to the practical application of such obnoxious beliefs.

In hindsight such statements can seem innocuous. For example, in his hugely popular *Human Origins*, published in 1895, Samuel Laing conveys the racism of the times based on an effortless sense of European superiority:

> The form of the chin seems to be wonderfully correlated with the general character and energy of the race. It is hard to say why, but as a matter of fact a weak chin generally denotes a weak, and a strong chin a strong, race or individual.
>
> (1895: 395)

But spotting such 'chinless wonders' is a deadly serious and very dangerous matter, especially when science underpins social policy

(Gould 1984). Neither does it diminish when applied to ancient skulls, precisely because archaeology was once used to authorise the uncritical application of such bogus approaches to the living. 'Styles' of heads and bodies were, and for some observers continue to be, indicative of intelligence, industriousness and the capacity for progress.

Neither does a hundred years seem to make much difference in the application of prejudice based on a reading of anatomy. Nelson Mandela, when practising law in Johannesburg in the 1950s, came across an instance where the classification of people under apartheid legislation led to similar judgements:

> I once handled the case of a Coloured man who was inadvertently clas-sified as an African ... The magistrate seemed uninterested in both my evidence and the prosecutor's demural. He stared at my client and gruffly asked him to turn round so that his back faced the bench. After scrutinising my client's shoulders, which sloped down sharply, he nodded to the other officials and upheld the appeal. In the view of the white authorities in those days, sloping shoulders were one stereotype of the Coloured physique. And so it came that the course of this man's life was decided purely on a magistrate's opinion about the structure of his shoulders.
>
> (1995: 175)

Definitions are not always helpful.

THE ETHNIC IMPERATIVES

The basis of ethnicity, and the significant role archaeology has played in its current form, has been dissected by Siân Jones (1997). She traces the idea of a people as being represented by but not constitutive of their material culture back into the nineteenth century. Subsequent to this, we have merely elaborated on two central ideas. The first she refers to as the *primordial imperative* where ethnicity is best summed up as being 'in the blood'. According to this imperative, ethnicity is a form of sociobiology. We inherit it as part of the biological makeup that conditions our social life. I am English not just because I carry an umbrella on the sunniest of summer days but because I was born English. This is a convenient doctrine for many who use ethnicity as a political slogan, since apparently we cannot do anything about it. To renounce this form of ethnicity would be like cutting off your right arm.

The second key idea is the *essentialist imperative*. Here culture, whether defined by anthropologists or archaeologists, is directly equated with ethnicity. Jonathan Friedman (1994) has argued that culture, and by implication ethnicity, is a typical outcome of modernist thinking in western countries that turns cultural difference into ideal types. It is a very simple equation, and one followed by archaeologists. The different cultural practices in the world therefore become the essence of ethnic identities. End of analysis. Let your society do your thinking for you.

THE ETHNIC TRINITY

The essence of the notion of ethnicity – that a bowler hat and a beret really do distinguish the English from the French – merges with the idea of the primordial inheritance flowing in our veins. These imperatives are founded on three expectations that stem from the idea of culture that I have examined, and criticised, time and again throughout this book: boundedness, similarity and continuity (Jones 1997: 136). These properties underpin much archaeological methodology, and are the reasons we can recognise patterns in our data. Archaeologists have supplied their patterns with meaning by interpreting their significance as ethnic markers by reference to the two imperatives.

NATIONAL IDENTITIES

But what does it matter? Archaeology, you might say, only deals with dead things and has no influence on the present. Nothing could be further from the truth. Remember, the past is not a neutral subject. It is a source of authority for action in the present. It shapes political ideologies. Let me give you two examples from politicians who have led the fight for independence and freedom in their countries.

In 1961, just before his long imprisonment for leading the struggle against apartheid, Nelson Mandela visited Egypt:

> I spent the whole morning of my first day in Cairo at the museum, looking at art, examining artefacts, making notes, learning about the type of men who founded the ancient civilisation of the Nile valley. This was not amateur archaeological interest; it is important for African nationalists to be armed with evidence to refute the fictitious claims of whites that Africans are without a civilised past that compares with that of the West. In a single morning, I discovered that Egyptians were creating great works of art and architecture when whites were still living in caves.
>
> (1995: 353)

India's first Prime Minister, Pandit Nehru, wrote *The Discovery of India* from his prison cell in 1944. He also looked to the monuments and relics of the past to chart the future road to independence:

> These journeys and visits of mine, with the background of my reading, gave me an insight into the past. To a somewhat bare intellectual understanding was added an emotional appreciation, and gradually a sense of reality began to creep into my mental picture of India, and the land of my forefathers became peopled with living beings, who laughed and wept, loved and suffered; and among them were men who seemed to know life and understand it, and out of their wisdom they had built a structure which gave India a cultural stability which lasted for thousands of years.
>
> (1946: 51–52)

The readings of the past by these two leaders provided alternatives to imperial power and state oppression.

NATIONALISM AND THE NAZIS

However, not all claims on the past have been made in such just causes. While patriotism has been described as the last refuge of the scoundrel, so too might nationalism be termed the first haven of the archaeologist. As Marguerita Díaz-Andreu and Timothy Champion discuss (1996: 3–8), the wave of nationalism that swept Europe at the end of the eighteenth century converted the production of history into a patriotic duty. The existence of nations had to be buttressed by a past, and thus archaeology was both created by nationalism and helped create the nation states we now take for granted.

In 1849, as the independent Danish state was being forged, the archaeologist J. J. A. Worsaae called his countrymen to arms:

> The remains of antiquity thus bind us more firmly to our native land; hills and vales, fields and meadows, become connected with us, in a more intimate degree; for by the barrows [prehistoric burial mounds], which rise on their surface, and the antiquities, which they have preserved for centuries in their bosom, they constantly recall to our recollection, that our forefathers lived in this country, from time immemorial, a free and independent people, and so call on us to defend our territories with energy, that no foreigner may ever rule over that soil, which contains the bones of our ancestors, and with which our most sacred and reverential recollections are associated.
>
> (1849: 149–50)

Antiquities, as we saw in Chapter 1 with the work of C. J. Thomsen, were very important in Denmark. They were tangible products unearthed as the country industrialised and as the middle classes rose to political ascendancy, not only here but across the Western world. Institutions such as national museums which expressed the new order sprang up in all the countries of Europe.

Denmark's struggle was to regain the independence it had once apparently enjoyed in Viking and prehistoric times. By contrast, and using the same notions of culture and peoples, the German archaeological tradition began to support reasons to expand. One major difference lay in the different histories of these states. Denmark had historical claims to being a nation state. Germany did not. It was only unified in 1871, a year after Italy. Before that there had not been *a* Germany and only *an* Italy in the Roman period. These very unhistorical nations used the past to underpin their nationalist agendas, but while Germany stressed prehistory, Italy looked back to the glories of the Roman imperial past.

The ultra-nationalist German archaeologist Gustav Kossinna extended the nineteenth-century agenda. In 1911 he delivered a lecture on *German Prehistory, An Eminently National Discipline*, and in 1926, a few years before Childe's famous formulation of the notion of an archaeological culture, Kossinna set down his core principle linking people to archaeological provinces (see page 00).

But as Heinrich Harke points out (1992: 204–5) in his discussion of this archaeological bogeyman, such innocent-sounding statements rested on ethnocentric notions of racial supremacy. There was an underlying belief in a Nordic, Aryan race that was superior to other races in both physical and intellectual qualities.

Kossinna was very much against the notion of *ex oriente lux* that Gordon Childe would later champion using similar concepts of culture but combined with a very different political philosophy (Chapter 3). Kossinna's heartland lay to the north, not the east. The repeated movements south of the Nordic races was for him the dynamic in both European and world history (Harke 1992: 205).

Kossinna died in 1931, two years before the founding of the Third Reich. His interpretations and methods were influential on Nazi ideology, which sought reasons to invade and annex neighbouring countries which they saw as having formerly been part of the Aryan homeland. The SS commander Heinrich Himmler founded the *Deutsches Ahnenerbe*, an organisation whose task was to create a scientific theory of German dominance, and archaeology was a leading discipline in this enterprise. Research was politicised and had to be ideologically useful to the Third Reich. Combined with the worst sort of physical anthropology, the categorisation of peoples and cultures and the development of an ultimate solution to the apparent threat to Aryan ethnic purity were visited upon Europe. Among many atrocities underpinned by a bogus theory of the past was the invasion of Denmark and the suppression of Worsaae's free and independent people.

ALTERNATIVE POWER: WHO OWNS THE PAST?

I have dealt with identities from archaeology on the large scale: ethnicity and nationalism. The final question to ask is if there are alternatives to the equation of culture with people? Jones for one thinks there is, so long as we change the very notion of how ethnic identity is constructed (1997: 140). It is necessary to get out of the mindset that sees the past as fixed, with the only changes coming from re-interpretation following new discoveries. According to this approach, artefacts and monuments, ancient cities and landscapes are static because they belong to the past; the older they are, the more rooted to the spot they become. In this mindset it is therefore a short step to plucking the objects out of the past to use them in the present. It is easy to insist on boundedness, similarity and continuity in the patterns we draw up on our plans and distribution maps. The past, and all the identities it contains and can support, is like a freeze-frame on the video. The flow of creativity is stopped and the past can be owned just like any other commodity.

A good example of this paradigm is provided by legislation about monuments. Most countries have laws that protect and bring into the safekeeping of the state either all or a selected range of antiquities. The World Heritage Convention sponsored through UNESCO does something similar with its list of World Heritage Sites, which have to be nominated. Once approved it is the responsibility of the country in which they are found to manage them and hold them in trust for all the peoples of the world.

But such legislation, while clarifying rights and obligations to the material remains of the past, raises issues of who owns them. Local concerns can differ significantly from national interests. First Nations such as those of the Australian Aborigines or Native North Americans have a very different view of the relics to which they claim affinity. Moreover, the keeping of many objects in the museums of the world rather than where they were originally deposited raises issues of ownership. A famous case such as the return of the Parthenon [Elgin] Marbles from the British Museum, requested by the Greek Government, highlights the issues that elsewhere may involve the return of simple stone tools. The respective artistic merits or even the historic importance of an object or set of objects is conflated with the issues of universality, the control of cultural 'centres' and their relationship with the identities of the periphery.

THE FUTURE OF ARCHAEOLOGY

'We hope that, by shedding light on the past, the cycle of pain can be broken and slavery's continuing wounds might finally be tended.' So writes anthropologist Michael Blakey (1998) about the African Burial Ground project in New York. During a period of over one hundred years, ending in 1796, between ten and twenty thousand slaves were buried outside the walls of the colonial city. Then the cemetery was built on and in 1991 the United States General Services Administration, although aware of the significance of the site, began digging foundations for a Federal Office tower. In little more than a year over 400 graves were recovered by archaeologists. The excavations rapidly became a focus for resistance among African Americans in New York. They mobilised public opinion and insisted that the laws relating to historic preservation and the treatment of human remains be observed. In its day the cemetery had provided, in Blakey's words 'a rare setting in which the enslaved could assert their humanity and respect their own culture'. Two hundred years later it formed another site for the assertion of identity and rights among the African-descended community of New York that in the intervening period had acquired not only emancipation but political rights and power. Finally the African Burial Ground became a National Monument by Presidential proclamation in February 2006 and a major memorial will be erected there (http://www.africanburialground.gov/ABG_Main.htm).

As Blakey explains, the scientific research on the people buried there has a definite purpose:

> Our job is to see that the memorial on the site will not be dedicated to 'unknown Africans' by a people of unknown ancestry. We seek to restore knowledge of the African-American origins and identities that were deliberately obscured in the effort to dehumanize Africans as 'slaves'.
>
> (1998)

The African Burial Ground has challenged teaching about African-American origins by pursuing a better understanding of the ties this community has to Africa and the rest of the world. The project's home page carries the headline 'Return to the past to build the future'.

The power and potential of archaeology to provide the material for resistance and understanding is well illustrated by this project. Material remains matter. They matter because of the relationships they build. They link the humanity and identity of a mistreated community to the local conditions of existence and the global context of shifting economic and political power. They reveal that resistance can lead to change and, as Blakey says, that reconciliation can occur through recognition.

While these ancestral remains from New York provide a window on another world, the view is also one of the future of a subject only now coming of age. I therefore end almost as I began. Archaeology is basically about three things: objects, landscapes and what we make of them, now and for the future. Archaeology is quite simply the study of the past through material remains and with that activity comes responsibilities.

REFERENCES

Aiello, L. and R. Dunbar (1993) 'Neocortex size, group size and the evolution of language'. *Current Anthropology* 34: 184–93.

Aiello, L. and E. Wheeler (1995) 'The expensive-tissue hypothesis: the brain and the digestive system in human and primate evolution'. *Current Anthropology* 36: 199–221.

Aitken, M. (1990) *Science based dating in archaeology*. London: Longman.

Alexandri, A. (1995) 'The origins of meaning'. In I. Hodder, M. Shanks, A. Alexandri, V. Buchli, J. Carman, J. Last and G. Lucas (eds) *Interpreting Archaeology; Finding Meaning in the Past*, pp. 57–67. London: Routledge.

Andrén, A. (1998) *Between Artifacts and Texts: Historical archaeology in global perspective*. New York: Plenum.

Andrews, G. and R. Thomas (1995) 'The management of archaeological projects: theory and practice in the UK'. In M. A. Cooper, A. Firth, J. Carman and D. Wheatley (eds) *Managing Archaeology*, pp. 189–207. London: Routledge.

Arnold, D. E. (1985) *Ceramic Theory and Cultural Process*. Cambridge: Cambridge University Press.

Ascher, R. (1961) 'Analogy in archaeological interpretation'. *Southwestern Journal of Anthropology* 17: 317–25.

Bailey, G. N. (1983) 'Concepts of time in quaternary prehistory'. *Annual Review of Anthropology* 12: 165–92.

Baillie, M. G. L. (1995) *A Slice Through Time: Dendrochronology and precision dating.* London: Batsford.

Baines, J. and N. Yoffee (1998) 'Order, legitimacy and wealth in Ancient Egypt and Mesopotamia'. In G. M. Feinman and J. Marcus (eds) *Archaic States*, pp. 199–260. Santa Fe: School of American Research.

Balter, M. (2005) *The Goddess and the Bull. Çatalhöyük: an archaeological journey to the dawn of civilization.* New York: Free Press.

Bar-Yosef, O. (1998) 'On the nature of transitions: the Middle to Upper Palaeolithic and the Neolithic revolution'. *Cambridge Archaeological Journal* 8: 141–63.

Barker, P. (1982) *Techniques of Archaeological Excavation* (second edition). London: Batsford.

Barrett, J. (1999) 'The mythical landscapes of the British Iron Age'. In W. Ashmore and B. Knapp (eds) *Archaeologies of Landscape*, pp. 253–65. Oxford: Blackwell Publishers.

Bellwood, P. (1978) *Man's Conquest of the Pacific.* Auckland: Collins.

Bellwood, P. (2005) *First Farmers: The origins of agricultural societies.* Oxford: Blackwell.

Bender, B. (1978) 'Gatherer-hunter to farmer: a social perspective'. *World Archaeology* 10: 204–22.

Bettinger, R. (1991) *Hunter-Gatherers: Archaeological and evolutionary theory.* New York: Plenum.

Binford, L. R. (1962) 'Archaeology as anthropology'. *American Antiquity* 28: 217–25.

——(1964) 'A consideration of archaeological research design'. *American Antiquity* 29: 425–41.

——(1972a) *An Archaeological Perspective.* New York: Academic Press.

——(1972b) 'The new archaeology – an American archaeologist gives his own opinion'. *The Listener* 87: 174–76.

——(1973) 'Interassemblage variability – the Mousterian and the "functional" argument'. In C. Renfrew (ed.) *The Explanation of Culture Change*, pp. 227–54. London: Duckworth.

——(1978a) *Nunamiut Ethnoarchaeology.* New York: Academic Press.

——(1978b) 'Dimensional analysis of behaviour and site structure: learning from an Eskimo hunting stand'. *American Antiquity* 43: 330–61.

——(1980) 'Willow smoke and dogs tails: hunter-gatherer settlement systems and archaeological site formation'. *American Antiquity* 45: 4–20.

——(1981a) *Bones: Ancient men and modern myths.* New York: Academic Press.

——(1981b) 'Behavioral archaeology and the Pompeii premise'. *Journal of Anthropological Research* 37: 195–208.

——(1983) *In Pursuit of the Past.* London: Thames and Hudson.

——(2001) *Constructing Frames of Reference: An analytical method for archaeological theory building using ethnographic and environmental datasets.* Berkeley: University of California Press.

Binford, L. R. and S. R. Binford (1966) 'A preliminary analysis of functional variability in the Mousterian of Levallois facies'. *American Anthropologist* 68: 238–95.

Binford, S. R. and L. R. Binford (eds) (1968) *New Perspectives in Archaeology.* Chicago: Aldine.

Binford, S. R. and L. R. Binford (1969) 'Stone tools and human behaviour'. *Scientific American* 220: 70–84.

Bird-David, N. (1994) 'Sociality and immediacy: or, past and present conversations on bands'. *Man* 29: 583–603.

——(1999) '"Animism" revisited: personhood, environment, and relational epistemology'. *Current Anthropology* 40: 67–91.

Blakey, M. L. (1998) 'The New York African Burial Ground: an examination of enslaved lives, a construction of ancestral ties'. http://www.huarchivesnet. howard.edu/0008huarnet/blakey5. htm.

Boast, R. (1997) 'A small company of actors: a critique of style'. *Journal of Material Culture* 2: 173–98.

Bordes, F. (1950) 'L'evolution buissonnante des industries en Europe occidentale. Considerations theoretiques sur le paléolithique ancien et moyen'. *L'Anthropologie* 54: 393–420.

——(1972) *A Tale of Two Caves.* New York: Harper and Row.

——(1973) 'On the chronology and contemporaneity of different Palaeolithic cultures in France'. In C. Renfrew (ed.) *The Explanation of Cultural Change: Models in Prehistory,* pp. 217–26. London: Duckworth.

Bordes, F. and D. de Sonneville-Bordes (1970) 'The significance of variability in palaeolithic assemblages'. *World Archaeology* 2: 61–73.

Bowden, M. (1991) *Pitt Rivers: The life and archaeological work of Lieutenant-General Augustus Henry Lane Fox Pitt Rivers, DCL; FRS, FSA.* Cambridge: Cambridge University Press.

Boyd, R. and P. J. Richerson (2005) *The Origin and Evolution of Cultures.* Oxford: Oxford University Press.

Bradley, R. (1997) *Rock Art and the Prehistory of Atlantic Europe.* London: Routledge.

Brain, C. K. (1981) *The Hunters or the Hunted?* Chicago: University of Chicago Press.

Brooks, A. and B. Wood (1990) 'The Chinese side of the story'. *Nature* 344: 288–89.

Brothwell, D. R. and A. M. Pollard (2005) *Handbook of Archaeological Sciences.* New York: Wiley.

Brumann, C. (1999) 'Writing for culture: why a successful concept should not be discarded'. *Current Anthropology* 40: 1–27.

Bryson, B. (1995) *Notes from a Small Island.* London: Black Swan.

Carrithers, M. (1990) 'Why humans have cultures', *Man* 25: 189–206.

Carsten, J. and S. Hugh-Jones (eds) (1995) *About the House: Lévi-Strauss and beyond.* Cambridge: Cambridge University Press.

Carver, M. (1996) 'Sutton Hoo'. In B. Fagan (ed.) *The Oxford Companion to Archaeology,* pp. 705–6. Oxford: Oxford University Press.

——(1998) *Sutton Hoo: Burial ground of kings?* London: British Museum Press.

Cavalli-Sforza, L. L. and F. Cavalli-Sforza (1995) *The Great Human Diasporas: The history of diversity and evolution.* Reading, Mass.: Perseus Books.

Champion, T. C. (ed.) (1989) *Centre and Periphery: Comparative studies in archaeology.* London: Unwin Hyman.

Chapman, J. (2000) *Fragmentation in Archaeology: People, places and broken objects in the prehistory of south-eastern Europe.* London: Routledge.

Chapman, R. W. (2003) *Archaeologies of Complexity.* London: Routledge.

Childe, V. G. (1925) *The Dawn of European Civilisation.* London: Cape.

——(1929) *The Danube in Prehistory.* Oxford: Oxford University Press.

——(1935) 'Changing methods and aims in prehistory'. *Proceedings of the Prehistoric Society* 1: 1–15.

——(1936) *Man Makes Himself.* London: Watts.

——(1942) *What Happened in History.* Harmondsworth: Penguin.

——(1947) *Archaeology as a Social Science.* University of London, Institute of Archaeology, Third Annual Report, pp. 49–60.

——(1951) *Social Evolution.* London: Watts.

——(1956a) *Society and Knowledge.* New York: Harper.

——(1956b) *Piecing Together the Past: The interpretation of archaeological data.* Harmondsworth: Penguin.

Chorley, R. J. and E. Haggett (eds) (1967) *Models in Geography.* London: Methuen.

Clark, J. G. D. (1952) *Prehistoric Europe. The economic basis.* London: Methuen.

——(1957) *Archaeology and Society* (third edition). London: Methuen.

——(1968) 'Australian stone age'. In K. Jazdzewski (ed.) *Liber Iosopho Kostrzewski octogenaria a veneratoribus dicatus*, pp. 17–28. Warsaw: Ossolineum, Polish Academy of Sciences.

Clark, J. D. and J. Walton (1962) 'A late stone age site in the Erongo mountains, South West Africa'. *Proceedings of the Prehistoric Society* 28: 1–16.

Clarke, D. L. (1968) *Analytical Archaeology.* London: Methuen.

——(ed.) (1972a) *Models in Archaeology.* London: Methuen.

——(1972b) 'A provisional model of an Iron Age society and its settlement system'. In D. L. Clarke (ed.) *Models in Archaeology*, pp. 801–69. London: Methuen.

——(1977) 'Spatial information in archaeology'. In D. L. Clarke (ed.) *Spatial Archaeology*, pp. 1–32. London: Academic Press.

——(1979) *Analytical Archaeologist.* London: Academic Press.

Conkey, M. and J. Spector (1984) 'Archaeology and the study of gender'. *Advances in Archaeological Method and Theory* 7: 1–38.

Cooper, M. A., A. Firth, J. Carman and D. Wheatley (eds) (1995) *Managing Archaeology.* London: Routledge.

Courbin, P (1988) *What is Archaeology?* Chicago: University of Chicago Press.

Coward, F. (2005a) 'Transitions, change and prehistory: an ecosystemic approach to change in the archaeological record'. In H. Cobb, F. Coward, L. Grimshaw and S. Price (eds) *Investigating Prehistoric Hunter-Gatherer Identities: Case studies from Palaeolithic and Mesolithic Europe.* BAR International Series 1411. Oxford: British Archaeological Reports.

——(2005b) *Transitions, Change and Identity: The Middle and Upper Palaeolithic of Vasco-Cantabrian Spain.* Unpublished PhD Thesis, University of Southampton.

Darte, C., J. Mauricio, E. Pettitt, P. Souto, E. Trinkaus, H. van der Plicht and J. Zilhao (1999) 'The early Upper Palaeolithic human skeleton from the Abrigo do Lagar Velho (Portugal) and modern human emergence in Iberia'. *Proceedings of the National Academy of Science* [USA] 96: 7604–09.

Darvill, T. and A. K. Fulton (1998) *MARS: The Monuments at Risk Survey of England.* Poole: School of Conservation Sciences, Bournemouth University.

David, N. and C. Kramer (2001) *Ethnoarchaeology in Action.* Cambridge: Cambridge University Press.

Dawkins, R. (1976) *The Selfish Gene.* Oxford: Oxford University Press.

d'Errico, F. (2003) 'The invisible frontier: a multiple species model for the origin of behavioural modernity'. *Evolutionary Anthropology* 12: 188–202.

d'Errico, F., C. S. Henshilwood, G. Lawson, M. Vanhaeren, A.-M. Tillier, M. Soressi, F. Bresson, B. Maureille, A. Nowell, J. Lakarra, L. Backwell and M. Julien (2003) 'Archaeological evidence for the emergence of language, symbolism, and music: an alternative multidisciplinary perspective'. *Journal of World Prehistory* 17: 1–70.

de Laet, S. (ed.) (1994) *History of Humanity. Volume 1, Prehistory.* London: UNESCO and Routledge.

de Lumley, H. (ed.) (1976) *La Prehistory Française.* Paris: CNRS.

Deacon, T. (1997) *The Symbolic Species: The co-evolution of language and the human brain.* Harmondsworth: Penguin.

Deetz, J. (1977) *In Small Things Forgotten: The archaeology of early American life.* New York: Anchor Books.

Dennett, D. (1991) *Consciousness Explained*. Harmondsworth: Penguin.

Diaz-Andreu, M. and T. Champion (1996) 'Nationalism and archaeology in Europe: an introduction'. In M. Diaz-Andreu and T. Champion (eds) *Nationalism and Archaeology in Europe*, pp. 1–23. London: University College London Press.

Dietler, M. and I. Herbich (1998) 'Habitus, techniques, style: an integrated approach to the social understanding of material culture and boundaries'. In M. T. Stark (ed.) *The Archaeology of Social Bound-aries*, pp. 232–63. Washington, DC: Smithsonian Institution Press.

Dobres, M.-A. (2000) *Technology and Social Agency*. Oxford: Blackwell Publishers.

Dobres, M.-A. and J. Robb (eds) (2000) *Agency in Archaeology*. London: Routledge.

Doran, J. and R. Hodson (1975) *Mathematics and Computers in Archaeology*. Edinburgh: Edinburgh University Press.

Douglas, M. and B. Isherwood (1978) *The World of Goods: Towards an anthropology of consumption*. London: Allen Lane.

Dunbar, R. I. M. (1996) *Grooming, Gossip and the Evolution of Language*. London: Faber and Faber.

Dunnell, R. C. (1978) 'Style and function: a fundamental dichtomy'. *American Antiquity* 43: 192–202.

Earle, T. (1994) 'Political domination and social evolution'. In T. Ingold (ed.) *Companion Encyclopedia of Anthropology*, pp. 940–61. London: Routledge.

Fagan, B. M. (1991a) *Ancient North America: The archaeology of a continent*. London: Thames and Hudson.

——(1991b) *Archaeology: A brief introduction* (fourth edition). New York: Harper Collins.

——(1992) *People of the Earth: An introduction to world prehistory*. New York: Harper Collins.

——(1997) *In the Beginning: An introduction to archaeology* (ninth edition). New York: Addison Wesley Longman.

——(1999) *Archaeology: A brief introduction* (seventh edition). New York: Harper Collins.

——(2001) *The Seventy Great Mysteries of the Ancient World*. London: Thames and Hudson.

Fagan, B. M. (ed.) (1996). *The Oxford Companion to Archaeology*. Oxford: Oxford University Press.

——(2004) *The Seventy Great Inventions of the Ancient World*. London: Thames and Hudson.

Feder, K. L. (2004) *Linking to the Past: A brief introduction to archaeology*. Oxford: Oxford University Press.

Feinman, G. M. and J. Marcus (eds) (1998) *Archaic States*. Santa Fe: School of American Research.

Flannery, K. V. (1967) 'Culture history versus cultural process: a debate in American archaeology'. *Scientific American* 217: 119–22.

——(1972) 'The cultural evolution of civilizations'. *Annual Review of Ecology and Systematics* 3: 399–426.

——(1973) 'Archaeology with a capital S'. In C. Redman (ed.) *Research and Theory in Current Archaeology*, pp. 47–53. New York: Wiley.

Flannery, K. V. (ed.) (1976) *The Early Mesoamerican Pillage*. New York: Academic Press.

Fowler, C. (2004) *An Archaeology of Personhood: An anthropological approach*. London: Routledge.

Fox, C. (1932) *The Personality of Britain*. Cardiff: Cardiff National Museum and University of Wales.

Frank, A. G. (1993) 'Bronze Age world system cycles'. *Current Anthropology* 34: 383–429.

Fried, M. H. (1967) *The Evolution of Political Society: An essay in political anthropology*. New York: Random House.

Friedman, J. (1994) *Cultural Identity and Global Process*. London: Sage.

Gamble, C. S. (1986) *The Palaeolithic Settlement of Europe*. Cambridge: Cambridge University Press.

——(1987) 'Archaeology, geography and time'. *Progress in Human Geography* 11: 227–46.

——(1993) *Timewalkers: The prehistory of global colonization*. Stroud: Alan Sutton.

——(1998) 'Palaeolithic society and the release from proximity: a network approach to intimate relations'. *World Archaeology* 29: 426–49.

——(1999) *The Palaeolithic Societies of Europe*. Cambridge: Cambridge University Press.

——(2007) *Origins and Revolutions: Human identity in earliest prehistory*. New York: Cambridge University Press.

Gamble, C. S., S. W. G. Davies, M. Richards, P. Pettitt and L. Hazelwood (2005) 'Archaeological and genetic foundations of the European population during the Lateglacial: implications for "agricultural thinking"'. *Cambridge Archaeological Journal* 15: 55–85.

Gamble, C. S. and O. Soffer (eds) (1990) *The World at 18000 BP, Volume 2: Low Latitudes*. London: Unwin Hyman.

Gamble, C. S. and M. Porr (eds) (2005) *The Individual Hominid in Context: Archaeological investigations of Lower and Middle Palaeolithic landscapes, locales and artefacts*. London: Routledge.

Gebauer, A. B. and T. D. Price (eds) (1992) *Transitions to Agriculture in Prehistory*. Madison: Prehistory Press.

Geertz, C. (1975) *The Interpretation of Cultures*. London: Hutchinson.

Gell, A. (1992) *The Anthropology of Time*. Oxford: Berg.

——(1998) *Art and Agency: Towards a new anthropological theory*. Oxford: Clarendon Press.

Geneste, J.-M. (1988) 'Systemes d'approvisionnement en matières premières au paléolithique moyen et au paléolithique supérieur en Aquitaine'. *L'Homme de Néandertal* 8: 61–70.

Gero, G. and M. Conkey (eds) (1991) *Engendering Archaeology: Women and prehistory*. Oxford: Blackwell Publishers.

Giddens, A. (1984) *The Constitution of Society*. Berkeley: University of California Press.

Gifford, D. P. (1981) 'Taphonomy and paleoecology: a critical review of archaeology's sister disciplines'. *Advances in Archaeological Method and Theory* 4: 365–438.

Gifford-Gonzalez, D. (1993) 'You can hide, but you can't run: representation of women's work in illustrations of Palaeolithic life'. *Visual Anthropology Review* 9: 23–41.

Gilchrist, R. (1993) *Gender and Material Culture: The archaeology of religious women*. London: Routledge.

Gimbutas, M. (2001) *The Language of the Goddess*. London: Thames and Hudson.

Glassie, H. (1975) *Folk Housing in Middle Virginia*. Knoxville: University of Tennessee Press.

Goodall, J. (1986) *The Chimpanzees of Gombe: Patterns of behavior.* Cambridge, Mass.: Belknap Press.

Gosden, C. (1994) *Social Being and Time.* Oxford: Blackwell Publishers.

——(1999) *Anthropology and Archaeology: A changing relationship.* London: Routledge.

——(2003) *Prehistory: A very short introduction.* Oxford: Oxford University Press.

Gould, R. A. (1980) *Living Archaeology.* Cambridge: Cambridge University Press.

Gould, S. J. (1984) *The Mismeasure of Man.* Harmondsworth: Penguin.

——(1991) 'Exaptation: a crucial tool for an evolutionary psychology'. *Journal of Social Issues* 47: 43–65.

Gould, S. J. and E. S. Vrba (1982) 'Exaptation – a missing term in the science of form'. *Palaeobiology* 8: 4–15.

Gowlett, J. A. J. (2005) 'Seeking the Palaeolithic individual in East Africa and Europe during the Lower-Middle Palaeolithic'. In C. Gamble and M. Porr (eds) *The Individual Hominid in Context: Archaeological investigations of Lower and Middle Palaeolithic landscapes, locales and artefacts,* pp. 50–67. London: Routledge.

Greene, K. (1999) 'V. Gordon Childe and the vocabulary of revolutionary change'. *Antiquity* 73: 97–109.

——(2002) *Archaeology: An introduction. The history, principles and methods of modern archaeology* (fourth edition). London: Routledge.

Haggett, P. (1965) *Locational Analysis in Human Geography.* London: Edward Arnold.

Hall, M. (1997) 'Patriarchal facades: the ambivalence of gender in the archaeology of colonialism'. In L. Wadley (ed.) *Our Gendered Past: Archaeological studies of gender in southern Africa,* pp. 221–36. Johannesburg: Witwatersrand University Press.

Hamilakis, Y., M. Pluciennik and S. Tarlow (eds) (2002) *Thinking through the Body: Archaeologies of corporeality.* New York: Kluwer Academic/Plenum.

Harke, H. (1992) 'All quiet on the western front? Paradigms, methods and approaches in West German archaeology'. In I. Hodder (ed.) *Archaeological Theory in Europe. The last three decades,* pp. 187–222. London: Routledge.

Harris, E. C. (1989) *Principles of Archaeological Stratigraphy* (second edition). New York: Academic Press.

Harris, D. R. (ed.) (1996) *The Origins and Spread of Agriculture and Pastoralism in Eurasia*. London: University College London Press.

Hawkes, C. (1954) 'Archaeological theory and method: some suggestions from the old world'. *American Anthropologist* 56: 155–68.

Haynes, C. V. (1993) 'Clovis-Folsom geochronology and climatic change'. In O. Soffer and N. D. Praslov (eds) *From Kostenki to Clovis: Upper Palaolithic-Paleo-Indian adaptations*, pp. 219–36. New York: Plenum.

Hearne, C. M. and M. J. Heaton (1994) 'Excavations at a Late Bronze Age settlement in the Upper Thames Valley at Shorncote Quarry near Cirencester, 1992'. *Transactions of the Bristol and Gloucestershire Archaeological Society* CXII: 17–57.

Hegmon, M. (1998) 'Technology, style and social practices: archaeological approaches'. In M. T. Stark (ed.) *The Archaeology of Social Boundaries*, pp. 264–79. Washington, DC: Smithsonian Institution Press.

Hodder, I. (1982) *Symbols in Action*. Cambridge: Cambridge University Press.

——(1990a) *The Domestication of Europe: Structure and contingency in Neolithic societies*. Oxford: Blackwell.

——(1990b) 'Style as historical quality'. In M. W. Conkey and C. A. Hastorf (eds) *The Uses of Style in Archaeology*, pp. 44–51. Cambridge: Cambridge University Press.

——(1991) *Reading the Past* (second edition). Cambridge: Cambridge University Press.

——(1999) *The Archaeological Process: An introduction*. Oxford: Blackwell Publishers.

——(2000) 'Developing a reflexive method in archaeology'. In I. Hodder (ed.) *Towards Reflexive Method in Archaeology: The example of Çatalhöyük, by members of the Çatalhöyük teams*. Cambridge: McDonald Institute, British Institute of Archaeology at Ankara Monograph no. 28.

——(2006) *Çatalhöyük: The Leopard's Tale, revealing the mysteries of Turkey's ancient 'town'*. London: Thames and Hudson.

Hodder, I. and C. Orton (1976) *Spatial Analysis in Archaeology*. Cambridge: Cambridge University Press.

Hosfield, R. (1999) *The Palaeolithic of the Hampshire Basin: A regional model of hominid behaviour during the Middle Pleistocene.* Oxford: British Archaeological Reports, British Series 286.

Ingold, T. (1993) 'The temporality of the landscape'. *World Archaeology* 25: 152–73.

——(1994) 'Introduction to culture'. In T. Ingold (ed.) *Companion Encyclopedia of Anthropology*, pp. 329–49. London: Routledge.

——(2000) *The Perception of the Environment: Essays in livelihood, dwelling and skill.* London: Routledge.

Isaac, G. (1978) 'The food sharing behaviour of proto-human hominids'. *Scientific American* 238: 90–108.

Johnson, A. W. and T. Earle (1987) *The Evolution of Human Societies.* Stanford: Stanford University Press.

Johnson, M. (1993) 'Notes towards an archaeology of capitalism'. In C. Tilley (ed.) *Interpretative Archaeology*, pp. 327–56. London: Berg.

——(1999a) *Archaeological Theory: An introduction.* Oxford: Blackwell Publishers.

——(1999b) 'Reconstructing castles and refashioning identities in Renaissance England'. In S. Tarlow and S. West (eds) *The Familiar Past?*, pp. 69–86. London: Routledge.

Jones, A. (2002) *Archaeological Theory and Scientific Practice.* Cambridge: Cambridge University Press.

Jones, R. (1985) 'Ordering the landscape'. In I. Donaldson and T. Donaldson (eds) *Seeing the First Australians*, pp. 181–209. Sydney: George Allen and Unwin.

Jones, S. (1997) *The Archaeology of Ethnicity: Constructing identities in the past and present.* London: Routledge.

Keay, S., M. Millett, L. Paroli and K. Strutt (2006) *Portus: An archaeological survey of the port of Imperial Rome*: Archaeological Monographs of the British School at Rome 15, British School at Rome.

Keeley, L. H. (1988) 'Hunter-gatherer economic complexity and "population pressure": a cross-cultural analysis'. *Journal of Anthropological Archaeology* 7: 373–411.

Kelly, R. (1995) *The Foraging Spectrum: Diversity in hunter-gatherer lifeways.* Washington, DC: Smithsonian Institution Press.

Kessing, R. M. (1981) *Cultural Anthropology: A contemporary perspective.* Fort Worth: Holt, Rinehart and Winston.

Kidder, A. V. (1924) *An Introduction to the Study of Southwestern Archaeology.* New Haven: Papers of the Southwestern Expedition, Phillips Academy, no. 1.

Kirch, P. V. (1984) *The Evolution of the Polynesian Chiefdoms.* Cambridge: Cambridge University Press.

Knappett, C. (2005) *Thinking through Material Culture: An interdisciplinary perspective.* Pittsburgh: University of Pennsylvania Press.

Kristiansen, K. (1998) *Europe Before History: The European world system in the second millennium BC.* Cambridge: Cambridge University Press.

Kristiansen, K, and M. Rowlands (1998) *Social Transformations in Archaeology: Global and local perspectives.* London: Routledge.

Kuper, A. (1999) *Culture: The anthropologist's account.* Cambridge, Mass.: Harvard University Press.

Laing, S. (1895) *Human Origins.* London: Chapman and Hall.

Lakoff, G. and M. Johnson. (1980) *Metaphors We Live By.* Chicago: University of Chicago Press.

Leech, R. (1999) 'The processional city: some issues for historical archaeology'. In S. Tarlow and S. West (eds) *The Familiar Past?*, pp. 19–34. London: Routledge.

Leone, M. E. (ed.) (1972) *Contemporary Archaeology. A guide to theory and contributions.* Carbondale: Southern Illinois University Press.

Leroi-Gourhan, A. (1993) *Gesture and Speech.* Cambridge, Mass.: MIT Press.

LiPuma, E. (1998) 'Modernity and forms of personhood in Melanesia'. In M. Lambek and A. Strathern (eds) *Bodies and Persons: Comparative perspectives from Africa and Melanesia*, pp. 53–79. Cambridge: Cambridge University Press.

Lourandos, H. (1997) *Continent of Hunter-gatherers: New perspectives in Australian prehistory.* Cambridge: Cambridge University Press.

Lubbock, J. (1865) *Pre-Historic Times, as Illustrated by Ancient Remains and the Manners and Customs of Modern Savages.* London: Williams and Norgate.

Lyman, R. L. (1994) *Vertebrate Taphonomy.* Cambridge: Cambridge University Press.

Lyman, R. L., M. J. O'Brien and R. C. Dunnell (1997) *The Rise and Fall of Culture History.* New York: Plenum.

Mandela, N. (1995) *Long Walk to Freedom.* London: Abacus.

Marcus, J. (1988) 'The peaks and valleys of ancient states: an extension of the dynamic model'. In G.M. Feinman and J. Marcus (eds) *Archaic States,* pp. 59–94. Santa Fe: School of American Research.

McBrearty, S. and A. S. Brooks (2000) 'The revolution that wasn't: a new interpretation of the origin of modern humans'. *Journal of Human Evolution* 39: 453–563.

McGlade, J. and S. van der Leeuw (1997) 'Introduction: archaeology and non-linear dynamics – new approaches to long-term change'. In S. van der Leeuw and J. McGlade (eds) *Time, Process and Structured Transformation in Archaeology,* pp. 1–31. London: Routledge.

McGuire, R. (1983) 'Breaking down cultural complexity: inequality and heterogeneity'. In M. B. Schiffer (ed.) *Advances in Archaeological Method and Theory,* vol. 6, pp. 91–142. New York: Academic Press.

——(1992) *A Marxist Archaeology.* San Diego: Academic Press.

McIntosh, J. (1999) *The Practical Archaeologist.* London: Thames and Hudson.

McNairn, B. (1980) *Method and Theory of V. Gordon Childe.* Edinburgh: Edinburgh University Press.

Mellaart, J. 1967. *Çatal Hüyük: a Neolithic town in Anatolia.* London: Thames and Hudson.

Mellars, P. A. (1970) 'Some comments on the notion of "functional variability" in stone tool assemblages'. *World Archaeology* 2: 74–89.

Mellars, P. A. and C. Stringer (eds) (1989) *The Human Revolution: Behavioural and biological perspectives on the origins of modern humans.* Edinburgh: Edinburgh University Press.

Meskell, L. (1999) *Archaeologies of Social Life.* Oxford: Blackwell Publishers.

Miller, D. (1994) 'Artefacts and the meaning of things'. In T. Ingold (ed.) *Companion Encyclopedia of Anthropology: Humanity, culture and social life,* pp. 396–419. London: Routledge.

——(1995) 'Consumption as the vanguard of history: a polemic by way of an introduction'. In D. Miller (ed.) *Acknowledging Consumption: A review of new studies,* pp. 1–57. London: Routledge.

Miller, D. and C. Tilley (eds) (1984) *Ideology, Power and Prehistory.* Cambridge: Cambridge University Press.

Miller, D., M. Rowlands and C. Tilley (eds) (1989) *Domination and Resistance.* London: Unwin Hyman.

Mintz, S. W. (1985) *Sweetness and Power: The place of sugar in modern history.* New York: Viking.

Mithen, S. (1993) 'Individuals, groups and the Palaeolithic record: a reply to Clark'. *Proceedings of the Prehistoric Society* 59: 393–98.

Morgan, L. H. (1877) *Ancient Society.* New York: World Publishing.

Moser, S. (1998) *Ancestral Images: The iconography of human origins.* Stroud: Alan Sutton.

Nehru, J. (1946) *The Discovery of India.* New Dehli: Jawaharlal Nehru Memorial Fund.

Nelson, S. M. (1997) *Gender in Archaeology: Analyzing power and prestige.* Walnut Creek, Calif.: Altamira Press.

O'Brien, M. (ed.) (1996) *Evolutionary Archaeology: Theory and application.* Salt Lake City: University of Utah Press.

Orser, C. (1999) 'Negotiating our "familiar" pasts'. In S. Tarlow and S. West (eds) *The Familiar Past?*, pp. 273–85. London: Routledge.

Orton, C. (2000) *Sampling in Archaeology.* Cambridge: Cambridge University Press.

Paddayya, K. (1995) 'Theoretical perspectives in Indian archaeology: an historical review'. In E. J. Ucko (ed.) *Theory in Archaeology: A world perspective*, pp. 110–49. London: Routledge.

Parker-Pearson, M. and Ramilisonina (1998) 'Stonehenge for the ancestors: the stones pass on the message'. *Antiquity* 72: 308–26.

Patrik, L. E. (1985) 'Is there an archaeological record?'. In M. B. Schiffer (ed.) *Advances in Archaeological Method and Theory*, vol. 8, pp. 27–62. New York: Academic Press.

Peacock, D. E. S. (1968) 'A petrological study of certain Iron Age pottery from Western England'. *Proceedings of the Prehistoric Society* 34: 414–27.

Piggott, S. (1965) *Ancient Europe.* Edinburgh: Edinburgh University Press.

Pitt-Rivers, A. H. L. (1887) *Excavations in Cranborne Chase*, vol 1. Privately published.

Preucel, R. and I. Hodder (eds) (1996) *Contemporary Archaeology in Theory: A reader*. Oxford: Blackwell Publishers.

Prown, J. D. (1993) 'The truth of material culture: history or fiction?'. In S. Lubar and W. D. Kingery (eds) *History from Things: Essays on material culture*, pp. 1–19. Washington, DC: Smithsonian Institution Press.

Rathje, W. (1992) *Rubbish!: The archaeology of garbage*. New York: Harper Collins.

Redman, C. L. (1978) *The Rise of Civilization: From early farmers to urban society in the Ancient Near East*. San Francisco: W. H. Freeman.

Renfrew, C. (1968) 'Wessex without Mycenae'. *Annual of the British School of Archaeology at Athens* 63: 277–85.

——(1972) *The Emergence of Civilisation: The Cyclades and the Aegean in the third millennium BC*. London: Methuen.

——(1973a) *Before Civilization*. London: Jonathan Cape.

——(1973b) *Social Archaeology*. Southampton: University of Southampton Press.

——(1977) 'Space, time and polity'. In J. Friedman and M. Rowlands (eds) *The Evolution of Social Systems*, pp. 89–112. London: Duckworth.

——(1982) 'Explanation revisited'. In C. Renfrew, M. J. Rowlands and B. A. Segraves (eds) *Theory and Explanation in Archaeology: The Southampton conference*, pp. 5–23. New York: Academic Press.

Renfrew, C. and K. L. Cooke (eds) (1979) *Transformations: Mathematical approaches to culture change*. New York: Academic Press.

Renfrew, C. and S. J. Shennan (eds) (1982) *Ranking, Resource and Exchange*. Cambridge: Cambridge University Press.

Renfrew, C. and J. M. Wagstaff (eds) (1982) *An Island Polity: The archaeology of exploitation in Melos*. Cambridge: Cambridge University Press.

Renfrew, C. and P. Bahn (1991) *Archaeology*. London: Thames and Hudson.

Renfrew, C. and P. Bahn (eds) (2005). *Archaeology: The key concepts*. London: Routledge.

Richards, M. B. (2003) 'The Neolithic invasion of Europe'. *Annual Review of Anthropology* 32: 135–62.

Richerson, P. J. and R. Boyd (2005) *Not By Genes Alone: How culture transformed human evolution*. Chicago: University of Chicago Press.

Rindos, D. (1985) *The Origins of Agriculture: An evolutionary perspective.* New York: Academic Press.

——(1989) 'Darwinism and its role in the explanation of domestication'. In D. R. Harris and G. C. Hillman (eds) *Foraging and Farming: The evolution of plant exploitation*, pp. 27–41. London: Unwin Hyman.

Robb, J. (2004) 'The extended artefact and the monumental economy: a methodology for material agency'. In E. DeMarrais, C. Gosden and C. Renfrew (eds) *Rethinking Materiality: The engagement of mind with the material world*, pp. 131–40. Cambridge: McDonald Institute of Archaeological Research.

Ruggles, C., F. Prendergast and T. Ray (eds) (2001) *Astronomy, Cosmology and Landscape.* London: Ocarina Books.

Sackett, J. R. (1982) 'Approaches to style in lithic archaeology'. *Journal of Anthropological Archaeology* 1: 59–112.

——(1990) 'Style and ethnicity in archaeology: the case for isochrestism'. In M. W. Conkey and C. A. Hastorf (eds) *The Uses of Style in Archaeology*, p. 32–43. Cambridge: Cambridge University Press.

Sahlins, M. (1963) 'Poor man, rich man, big man, chief: political types in Melanesia and Polynesia'. *Comparative Studies in Society and History* 5: 285–303.

Schiffer, M. B. (1976) *Behavioral Archaeology.* New York: Academic Press.

Service, E. R. (1962) *Primitive Social Organization: An evolutionary perspective* (second edition). New York: Random House.

——(1966) *The Hunters.* Englewood Cliffs, N.J.: Prentice-Hall.

Shanks, M. and C. Tilley (1987a) *Reconstructing Archaeology: Theory and practice.* Cambridge: Cambridge University Press.

——(1987b) *Social Theory and Archaeology.* London: Polity.

Shennan, S. (1989a) 'Introduction: archaeological approaches to cultural identity'. In S. J. Shennan (ed.) *Archaeological Approaches to Cultural Identity*, pp. 1–32. London: Unwin Hyman.

——(1989b) 'Cultural transmission and culture change'. In S. E. van der Leuuw and R. Torrence (eds) *What's New? A closer look at the process of innovation*, pp. 330–46. London: Unwin Hyman.

——(1993) 'After social evolution: a new archaeological agenda?'. In N. Yoffee and A. Sherratt (eds) *Archaeological Theory: Who sets the agenda?*, pp. 53–59. Cambridge: Cambridge University Press.

——(2001) 'Demography and cultural innovation: a model and its implications for the emergence of modern human culture'. *Cambridge Archaeological Journal* 11: 5–16.

——(2002) *Genes, Memes and Human History: Darwinian archaeology and cultural evolution*. London: Thames and Hudson.

Sherratt, A. (1997) *Economy and Society in Prehistoric Europe: Changing perspectives*. Edinburgh: Edinburgh University Press.

Skibo, J. M., W. H. Walker and A. E. Nielsen (eds) (1995) *Expanding Archaeology*. Salt Lake City: University of Utah Press.

Sofaer, J. (2006) *The Body as Material Culture*. Cambridge: Cambridge University Press.

Soffer, O. and C. S. Gamble (eds) (1990) *The World at 18000 BP, Volume 1: High Latitudes*. London: Unwin Hyman.

Sollas, W. J. (1911) *Ancient Hunters and Their Modern Representatives*. London: Macmillan.

Sparkes, B. A. (1982) 'The melian dialogue of Thucydides *Historiae V* 84–116'. In C. Renfrew and J. M. Wagstaff (eds) *An Island Polity: The archaeology of exploitation in Melos*, pp. 319–22. Cambridge: Cambridge University Press.

Spector, J. (1993) *What this Awl Means: Feminist archaeology at a Wahpeton Dakota Village*. St Paul: Minnesota Historical Society Press.

Spencer, H. (1876–96) *The Principles of Sociology*. London: Williams and Norgate.

Sperber, D. (1996) *Explaining Culture: A naturalistic approach*. Oxford: Blackwell Publishers.

Spriggs, M. (ed.) (1984) *Marxist Perspectives in Archaeology*. Cambridge: Cambridge University Press.

Sterner, J. (1989) 'Who is signalling whom? Ceramic style, ethnicity and taphonomy among the Sirak Bulahay'. *Antiquity* 63: 451–59.

Stiner, M. C. (1994) *Honor Among Thieves: A zooarchaeological study of Neandertal ecology*. Princeton: Princeton University Press.

Strathern, M. (1988) *The Gender of the Gift: Problems with women and problems with society in Melanesia*. Berkeley: University of California Press.

——(1996) 'Cutting the network'. *Journal of the Royal Anthropological Institute* 2: 517–35.

Stringer, C. and C. Gamble (1993) *In Search of the Neanderthals: Solving the puzzle of human origins.* London: Thames and Hudson.

Strum, S. S. and B. Latour (1987) 'Redefining the social link: from baboons to humans'. *Social Science Information* 26: 783–802.

Tarlow, S. (1999) 'Strangely familiar'. In S. Tarlow and S. West (eds) *The Familiar Past?*, pp. 263–72. London: Routledge.

Taylor, W. W. (1948) *A Study of Archaeology.* Menasha, Wis.: Memoirs of the American Anthropological Association 69.

Thomas, D. H. (1998) *Archaeology* (third edition). Fort Worth: Harcourt Brace.

Thomas, J. (1995) 'Where are we now?: archaeological theory in the 1990s'. In P. J. Ucko (ed.) *Theory in Archaeology: A world perspective*, pp. 343–62. London: Routledge.

——(1996) *Time, Culture and Identity: An interpretive archaeology.* London: Routledge.

——(2004) *Archaeology and Modernity.* London: Routledge.

Tilley, C. (1993) 'Introduction: interpretation and a poetics of the past'. In C. Tilley (ed.) *Interpretative Archaeology*, pp. 1–27. London: Berg.

——(1994) *A Phenomenology of Landscape: Places, paths and monuments.* Oxford: Berg.

——(1996) *An Ethnography of the Neolithic.* Cambridge: Cambridge University Press.

——(1999) *Metaphor and Material Culture.* Oxford: Blackwell.

Trigger, B. G. (1989) *A History of Archaeological Thought.* Cambridge: Cambridge University Press.

Tylor, E. B. (1865) *Researches into the Early History of Mankind and the Development of Civilization.* London: John Murray.

——(1871) *Primitive Culture.* London: John Murray.

Ucko, E. J. and G. Dimbleby (eds) (1969) *The Domestication and Exploitation of Plants and Animals.* London: Duckworth.

Ucko, E. J., R. Tringham and G. W. Dimbleby (eds) (1972) *Man, Settlement and Urbanism.* London: Duckworth.

Veit, U. (1989) 'Ethnic concepts in German prehistory: a case study on the relationship between cultural identity and archaeological objectivity'. In S.

J. Shennan (ed.) *Archaeological Approaches to Cultural Identity*, pp. 35–56. London: Unwin Hyman.

Vita-Finzi, C. and E. S. Higgs (1970) 'Prehistoric economy in the Mount Carmel area of Palestine, site catchment analysis'. *Proceedings of the Prehistoric Society* 36: 1–37.

Vonnegut, K. (1987) *Galapagos*. London: Grafton Books.

Waal, F. D. (1982) *Chimpanzee Politics*. London: Jonathan Cape.

Waddington, C. H. (1977) *Tools for Thought*. London: Paladin.

Wadley, L. (ed.) (1997) *Our Tendered Past: Archaeological studies of gender in southern Africa*. Johannesburg: Witwatersrand University Press.

Wainwright, G. J. (1989) 'Saving the Rose'. *Antiquity* 63: 430–35.

Wallerstein, I. (1974) *The Modern World System: Capitalist agriculture and the origins of the European world economy in the nineteenth century*, vol. 1. New York: Academic Press.

——(1980) *The Modern World System*, vol. 2. London: Academic Press.

Wenke, R. J. (1990) *Patterns in Prehistory: Humankind's first three million years*. New York: Oxford University Press.

West, S. (1999) 'Social space and the English country house'. In S. Tarlow and S. West (eds) *The Familiar Past?*, pp. 103–22. London: Routledge.

Wheatley, D. and M. Gillings (2002) *Spatial Technology and Archaeology*. London: Routledge.

Wheeler, R. E. M. (1954) *Archaeology from the Earth*. Harmond-sworth: Penguin.

White, L. A. (1959) *The Evolution of Culture: The development of civilization to the fall of Rome*. New York: McGraw-Hill.

Whittle, A. (1996) *Europe in the Neolithic: The creation of new worlds*. Cambridge: Cambridge University Press.

——(2003) *The Archaeology of People: Dimensions of Neolithic life*. London: Routledge.

Wiessner, P. (1983) 'Style and social information in Kalahari San projectile points'. *American Antiquity* 48: 253–76.

——(1990) 'Is there a unity to style?'. In M. W. Conkey and C. A. Hastorf (eds) *The Uses of Style in Archaeology*, pp. 105–12. Cambridge: Cambridge University Press.

Willey, G. R. (1966) *An Introduction to American Archaeology, Volume 1: North and Middle America.* Englewood Cliffs, N.J.: Prentice-Hall.

Wilson, D. (1862) *Prehistoric Man.* London: Macmillan.

Wilson, E. O. (1975) *Sociobiology: The new synthesis.* Cambridge, Mass.: Bellknap.

Wobst, H. M. (1977) 'Stylistic behaviour and information exchange'. In C. E. Cleland (ed.) *Papers for the Director: Research essays in honor of James B. Griffin,* vol. 61, *Anthropological Papers,* pp. 317–42. Museum of Anthropology, University of Michigan.

——(1978) 'The archaeo-ethnology of hunter gatherers or the tyranny of the ethnographic record in archaeology'. *American Antiquity* 43: 303–9.

Woodburn, J. (1991) 'African hunter-gatherer social organization: is it best understood as a product of encapsulation?'. In T. Ingold, D. Riches and J. Woodburn (eds) *Hunters and Gatherers 1: History, evolution and social change,* pp. 31–64. New York: Berg.

Worsaae, J. J. A. (1849) *The Primeval Antiquities of Denmark.* London: Parker.

Wylie, A. (1985) 'The reaction against analogy'. *Advances in Archaeological Method and Theory* 8: 63–111.

——(1991) 'Gender theory and the archaeological record: why is there no archaeology of gender?'. In J. M. Gero and M. W. Conkey (eds) *Engendering Archaeology: Women and prehistory,* pp. 31–54. Oxford: Blackwell Publishers.

——(1993) 'A proliferation of new archaeologies: "beyond objectivism and relativism"'. In N. Yoffee and A. Sherratt (eds) *Archaeological Theory: Who sets the agenda?,* pp. 20–26. Cambridge: Cambridge University Press.

——(1995) 'An expanded behavioral archaeology: transformation and redefinition'. In J. M. Skibo, W. H. Walker and A. E. Nielsen (eds) *Expanding Archaeology,* pp. 198–209. Salt Lake City: University of Utah Press.

——(2002) *Thinking from Things: Essays in the philosophy of archaeology.* Berkeley: University of California Press.

Yoffee, N. (2005) *Myths of the Archaic State: Evolution of the earliest cities, states, and civilizations.* Cambridge: Cambridge University Press.

Zeder, M., E. Emshwiller, B. D. Smith and D. G. Bradley (2006) 'Documenting domestication: the intersection of genetics and archaeology'. *Trends in Genetics* 22: 139–55.

INDEX